Remember My Name
In Sheboygan
◆
Sheboygan Revisited

Remember My Name
In Sheboygan

◆

Sheboygan Revisited

More Stories About
Growing Up In Sheboygan

Glenn W. Martin

iUniverse, Inc.
Bloomington

Remember My Name In Sheboygan - Sheboygan Revisited
More Stories About Growing Up In Sheboygan

iUniverse books may be ordered through booksellers or by contacting:

iUniverse
1663 Liberty Drive
Bloomington, IN 47403
www.iuniverse.com
1-800-Authors (1-800-288-4677)

ISBN: 978-1-4759-3546-2 (sc)
ISBN: 978-1-4759-3545-5 (e)

Library of Congress Control Number: 2012912062

Printed in the United States of America

iUniverse rev. date: 7/10/2012

Other Books
by Glenn W. Martin

Christmas Stories My Grandpa Wrote For Me (2000)

Christmas Stories For Children of All Ages (2001)

*Remember My Name In Sheboygan: Recollections of Another
Time and Another Place – People and Places (2002)*

Christmas Memories and Merry Moments (2003)

*Some of the Funniest Things Happen In the Most
Unlikely and Unexpected Places (2005)*

Things I Learned Along The Way (2005)

Dedication

This book is for my daughter and partner, Carol. She wanted to know more about Sheboygan and my life as a boy there. She said that of all of the books we have published together, our first book about Sheboygan is her favorite.

She knew that after we did that one, I had lots of stories about Sheboygan left over that she had not heard yet. And she still had some pictures in her files that we were not able to use in our first book. It would be a shame to see those go to waste.

Though I had been dragging my feet and resisting writing and publishing another book, Carol is not only very persuasive, but she also deserves it. She has worked so hard on our other books, that I owe her a book of her own.

So when you read this book, I hope you will enjoy it.

But this book is for Carol. She has earned it!

Acknowledgments

Though this book is mostly about a town, the places in it, and the events that took place there, I could not have written it without the help of many people who lived there with me when I was a boy. Some of them might still be living, but most of them have passed away. They will never know how much they influenced me and helped me along the way.

Of course there were the members of my family, the teachers, leaders, and mentors, some whose names I no longer remember.

And then there were my classmates; like Warren Dittes, Wesley Jerving, Joe Bifano, Jane Stroo, Betty, Donny, Andy, Ginny, and many, many others. We started out together and we grew up together.

I was also helped by the memories of some of my cousins, like Ron and Doug Huebner, and Mary Jo Ploetz.

And, I can never write a book about Sheboygan without the use of the genealogical material supplied to me by my brother-in-law, Jim Pool.

There were others, people in Sheboygan who sent me letters and e-mails, made phone calls or talked to me in person after I wrote my first Sheboygan book, sharing with me what they recalled about their growing up years in Sheboygan.

And, last but certainly not least, I owe a special word of gratitude to the late Rev. T. Perry Jones, who was not only my Minister all of those early years, but also my role model, mentor, and very good friend as both of us grew older.

Contents

Sheboygan Revisited

In June of 2002, my wife, Margaret, and I took a trip to Sheboygan, Wisconsin to attend my 60th Central High School Class Reunion. I graduated from that school on June 11, 1942. I still have the fancy black, red, and gold diploma to prove it. It says that I had "completed the required units of work prescribed by the Board of Education." It was signed by three men, whose signatures I cannot read. I still remember that day because it rained all day and the graduation ceremony had to be moved to the new Armory instead of being held outside at Vollrath Park, where graduations usually took place at that time. We were very disappointed, but it was all very official and final. Sixty years later, it didn't make any difference.

Those of us who were still alive gathered at the Elks Club for a grand dinner and program, where we recalled how special our class was. We were the first class that went away, or worked on the home front, during World War II. We were the last class to have lived in Sheboygan as it used to be.

During those few hours, we remembered fondly the days when we were young and carefree, mourned those who were no longer with us, and sang our school song one more time. It was worth the miles many of us had driven to get there, because my classmates and I knew that this would be our last reunion. We savored every precious moment and lingered long, reluctant to part when it was finally time to go. Most of us would never see each other again and most of the travelers headed back home the next morning.

But, since we were making such a long trip, my wife and I decided to stay over a few more days to do some other personal things; like a little book business, including a short visit to the Sheboygan County Historical Research Center to find some things I needed for my books. I also wanted to see and a cousin and my last living aunt.

My cousin was a gracious hostess and we enjoyed a couple of delightful days at her house, but my aunt did not recognize me and we were not able to have much of a visit. A few months later she died. I was glad I had been able to see her one last time. But as I said good-bye to her I realized that now I was the last living person of those generations, on both sides of my family, that was still alive.

One day, I took my camera and rode around town by myself, reliving experiences and taking pictures of things that reminded me of my life in Sheboygan when I was a child. That's why this book is entitled, "Sheboygan Revisited." That is exactly what I did that day. I saw my beloved town once more, both physically and emotionally.

In this book, like in my first Sheboygan book, I will try to capture the flavor of what my hometown was like back in the 20s and 30s, but I will not concentrate on the people I knew, like my first book did, but on the places and activities I still vividly and fondly remember.

I want to tell you about our churches and our schools, our parks and playgrounds; the places where people worked and where they did their shopping.

I want to tell you about the places where we went to have fun and the activities we participated in.

I want to tell you about what it was like to skate and slide in winter and swim in summer, and how much fun it was to play kick the can or tag every night until it got dark.

I want to tell you about the bands I played in, the parades I marched in, and the picnics that went on all over town all summer.

I want to tell you about the things we kids did in our free time, how we spent our money, and how much things cost at that time.

I will try to keep these stories short so there can be more of them, and I want to choose the ones that will may help you to remember what it was like when you were a kid growing up somewhere in a town like mine.

A Lasting Legacy

As I drove around town that day in 2002, taking pictures and revisiting places that used to be very important in my life, I was keenly aware of the changes that have taken place since I was a boy living there. I shouldn't have been surprised. That was long, long time ago. But it was a bit distressing. I found myself frequently getting disoriented. Some of the places that were once so important to me were no longer there or had significantly changed. There were whole new neighborhoods that did not even exist when I lived there, and some of the old ones had been displaced and moved to new locations.

The big, new mall, out on the way to Kohler, has replaced the downtown as the main shopping center. Not much is left downtown that used to be there. Much of the space that was once filled with thriving businesses has been turned into large parking lots. It looks like a different town. I wondered as I roamed the main street if anyone comes downtown anymore. I got the feeling that only visitors and tourists do. The local folks are all out at the mall.

Many old landmarks are either gone completely or have moved to different locations. The old library used to be next to the Sheboygan Press building; the new library, now called the Mead Library, is now blocks away, right on 8th street across from where the Pranges Department Store used to be. The old stone and brick library building is still standing where it was, but it now houses the offices of the County Human Services. This is where my Aunt Harriet worked until she retired.

The former building that was once the Welfare Department is still down on 8th Street where the old Longfellow School used to be, but must be used for other purposes. It may be a museum. It sure looks like one.

There is a new and fancy harbor area now, dedicated to fishing, boating, and tourism, not the delivery and stacking of coal for the manufacturing plants in Sheboygan and Kohler.

There are lots of motels and restaurants where the C. Reiss Coal Company coal yards used to be. I think the company still has an office there, but I didn't see any coal piles. The building where my Grandpa Wisch had his barbershop, and the tavern next to it, are gone. I don't remember what is there now. I think it is some kind of traffic turnaround leading to and from the 8th Street bridge.

The 8th Street drawbridge over the channel is still there, but it looks different. It still connects the South and North ends of town as it always did. You can't get from here to there without it, unless you want to jump in the water and swim across.

Most of the old schools have been replaced by new ones, though a few of them look the same as they always did....old and dirty. There isn't any Central High School anymore (though the building is still there and is used for some educational purposes). Central was replaced by a South High School many years ago. My mother once worked in the lunchroom there. I think North High School is still much the same.

The whole lakeshore along Lake Michigan has been re-designed and improved. The Armory, Court House, Yacht Club, and Coast Guard Station nearby are in the same locations and look much the same as they always did. I don't remember seeing the old YMCA, which used to be in that area.

All over town there are stores with different names that I did not recognize, and lots of new restaurants, filling stations, and factories where others used to be. I don't know if the old baseball park, right in back of the Vollrath Company where my dad used to work, is still there. I looked for it, but couldn't find it. If it got torn down it is a shame. We used to spend many happy hours there. My mom and dad were avid baseball fans.

The hospitals are still in the same places, improved and enlarged, but the clinic, which used to be on 8th Street across the street from Fountain Park and the Rex Theater (where Uncle Gilbert worked) now houses the various offices for County services. There is a huge new clinic out near the mall. I think most everyone in Sheboygan goes there.

I think all of the theaters that were downtown are gone. The building that housed the Sheboygan Theater may still be there, but I don't think they show movies there anymore. There is a big movie complex across the highway from the mall.

All of the houses I once lived in are still in the same locations, but they all looked smaller to me than I remembered them. All of the vacant lots I used to love to play in are filled in or have houses on them. Now the kids have to go to the public playgrounds for their pick-up games, if they still do that.

The public parks are in the same locations but do not look the same. The same is true of the playgrounds I used to enjoy so much. The cemetery has not changed at all. But all of our family plots are filled.

The whole Southside, where I lived most of my young life, is now a new suburb, with fine houses, new schools, and shopping areas. My mother and my Aunt Myrtle lived in a nursing home in that area at the end of their lives, and so did my Aunt Harriet.

I think that as the city expanded, it moved mainly south and west. The city now extends far out into what used to be country or farm land. The Big Apple, where we used to play on Saturday nights with my band, is still there, but it is no longer on the edge of town as it used to be. You hardly notice it as you drive by.

Sheboygan is kind of a mega city now, with housing areas going right out into Kohler, Sheboygan Falls, and almost to Plymouth. There are many more motels and restaurants than there used to be. And Terry's, our favorite place to get brats, is gone. It finally closed and was torn down to make room for a new highway.

The other surprise I had that day was exactly the opposite. As I traveled around the city, I also noticed there were many things had not changed since I graduated from high school.

Most of the churches that I remember from my boyhood are still there and in the same locations. And they look pretty much the same as they did when I was a boy. Some showed signs of age, but most have been well kept and well maintained. There were additions to the buildings, larger parking lots behind and around them, and new and bolder identification signs on the lawns. But I had the feeling that people, like me, who had been gone for more than 50 years would still recognize them and remember them as they were when they were growing up.

The morning I attended the Sunday morning service at First Methodist Church (now called St. Luke's), it was very much like the services I attended years ago. The lovely sanctuary has not changed a bit, at least not that I could see. There is still the same dark wooden pulpit and lectern and Communion table, with the carvings done by the German woodcarvers. There are the same beautiful stained glass windows. There is still the Baptismal Font where I was baptized and the

Communion railings where I knelt when I joined the church. The choir sits in the same place and there is still the balcony where we kids used to sit when we were teenagers. I could almost see myself marching up the main aisle when I sang in the Boys' Choir. Everything looked and felt the same. It was like coming home.

When I think of the theme of the first part of this book, Churches, Children, Chairs, and Cheese, (the things Sheboygan was once best known for), I see the glaring contrast.

The chair factories are mostly gone and there are not many cheese factories anymore either, at least not in Sheboygan. And the children I knew are all grown up, gone away, or dead.

But the churches are still there, still standing strong and tall and proud.

Maybe there is a message in that!

Part 1

Churches, Children, Chairs, and Cheese

When I was a boy,
Sheboygan was known for four things,
Churches, Children, Chairs, and Cheese.
We had plenty of all of them!

Churches

A Child Of The Church

From almost the time I was born, I have been a child of the church.

My life-long association with the Methodist Church started very early in my life with my baptism, which was on April 20, 1924. My parents brought me to the First Methodist Church that day and I was baptized by a Rev. John Perry. This was not the Rev. T. Perry Jones, who was to become my beloved pastor later. I never got to know Rev. John.

It was probably my mother's idea. She was brought up in a strict Lutheran Church, where they believed, like the Catholics, that children should be baptized as soon as possible after they were born. Parents were worried that if something should happen and their baby should die without being baptized, he or she could not get to Heaven, but would have to spend eternity in Limbo. Methodists didn't believe that, but mother apparently still did and wasn't taking any chances. I was there, of course, but I was not aware of anything that was happening to me that important day. Not only was I becoming a precious child of God; I was also becoming a beloved child of the church.

After going to Sunday School for many years I became an official member of the church at the end of my sixth grade year. The Methodist Church did not call it Confirmation at the time, though the Lutherans and the Catholics did. We just called it "joining the church," but we took it just as seriously as the Lutherans and Catholics did. I know that I was very proud to become a member of my church, and I had earned the honor.

For one whole year, we sixth graders had to come to instructions every Saturday morning. The class was taught by Rev. Jones, whom we all admired and respected. He was an excellent teacher. This was before the time of audio-visuals and learning by discussion and projects. He lectured and we listened and learned. We had to memorize a lot of doctrine and Bible passages. And he gave us hard tests that we had to pass. It was interesting, but I must admit that there were times when we would rather have been out playing ball than learning about John Wesley and what the Methodists believed. But it was only one year. Our Lutheran friends had to go longer and were required to learn the whole Catechism by heart. We got off easy.

At the end of the year, there was a special service for us. We got all dressed up, were presented to the congregation, said our parts, and took the vows. We confessed that Jesus Christ was our Lord and Savior and it was impressed upon us that we were now full members of the church and were expected to support it with our "attendance, prayers, gifts, and service." Then we were promoted to the youth class and program. In the spring every year, these special services were going on in churches all over town and most of my friends were becoming members of their churches at the same time I was. We all did it with little thought or protest. In Sheboygan, we were all raised to be children of our churches.

I was hardly old enough to know what all that meant. I only knew that I belonged to that church, had friends there, and had a good time when I was there. Until I got into high school, I attended Sunday School and the church services every Sunday and enjoyed being an official Methodist. As the adults often said, I was given "a solid foundation." It was expected to last a lifetime. And, for me, it did. I still go to church every Sunday, and it is almost always to a Methodist Church.

In Sheboygan, having a church, attending a church, and being a member of a church, was the thing to do. And we all did it!

Churches, Churches.…Everywhere

When I was growing up, Sheboygan was full of churches. There seemed to be one on almost every corner. I never bothered to count them, but I would be willing to bet that there were almost as many churches in Sheboygan as taverns.…and there were a lot of those. That made it handy for everybody.

You didn't have to be very religious or even a firm believer, but you almost had to belong to some church. It would be one of the first things people would ask you when they first met you. They would ask, "What church do you belong to?" And you better have the name of one ready.

The church you belonged to was part of your identity, just like your nationality was. If you wanted to brag a little you might say, "I am a German Lutheran" or "I am a member of Holy Mary's." If you said that, they would not only know that you were a Roman Catholic, but also an Italian. And, if you professed to be a member of some church, you were expected to be active and supporting. People wanted to know who you were and whose you were. If you met someone at a tavern or ballroom on a Saturday night they might ask, "What service are you going to attend tomorrow morning?" (If you said you were a Catholic, they might ask what Mass you were going to and if you went to Confession on Friday night and couldn't eat meat.)

Being a member of a church was not a requirement. But it was a good idea. It saved a lot of embarrassment. And it defined a lot of things, like if you were a marriage prospect or not. I would guess that at that time almost 98% of the people in Sheboygan belonged to some church, and there were a lot of them to choose from.

Most religious groups in Sheboygan were Christian, so they were identified by their historic names. The most and biggest churches were either Roman Catholic or Lutheran because most of the people in Sheboygan came from European countries where those churches were predominant.

7

But, there were also a lot of Reformed churches (many of them Dutch), and I know that there was a Congregational Church across the street from our Methodist church and an Episcopalian Church down the street. I am sure you could find a Presbyterian Church somewhere in town. There were a lot of Greek people in Sheboygan so there must have been a Greek Orthodox Church and maybe a Ukrainian and Russian Orthodox one, as well. I don't know if there was a Unitarian Church in Sheboygan or a Friends Society, but I knew where the Christian Science building was. They also had a library, but I never saw anyone go in there to read any books.

There was also a small Synagogue in the Jewish neighborhood on the North Side. It was a small plain white building with a large Star of David on the front near the top. I think that was made of stained glass, but I am not sure. We always wondered what it looked like inside but never had the nerve to go in and look. We didn't know much about Jews, but people said that Jews were kind of strange because they had their services on Friday nights and Saturday instead of Sunday.

Then there was the Gospel Tabernacle where my Aunt Aimee used to preach, but some people did not consider that a church. It was more like a meeting house for people who called themselves Evangelicals or Pentecostals. They said Aimee was not really a minister, but that she was an evangelist.

The churches were scattered all over town, though I don't think there were many churches on Indiana Avenue, where most of the taverns were, or downtown, where the stores and movie houses were. There were lots of churches out in the country. There seemed to be churches everywhere, usually on some corner.

So, it was easy to be religious in Sheboygan. You could find, chose, and join a church any time you wanted to, or you were born into one, like most of us were. And you could also change churches if you wanted to. I started out being a Lutheran and ended up being a Methodist. That was not my choice, however, that was my parent's choice. I am glad they did. I would not have been happy being a Lutheran or a Roman Catholic. They were much too strict!

The point is, that religion was very important in Sheboygan. You would have had a hard time finding someone in Sheboygan who would admit that they did not belong to any church. If they didn't, they would either not admit it or they would feel that they had to come up with a very good reason why. In our town, going to church was not just a good and interesting thing to do, but part of the normal and necessary weekly ritual. You went to work every day, usually Monday through Friday, or sometimes even on Saturday. You started at the same time and came home for supper at the same time, unless you were on the night shift.

Then, on Friday night, you would go out for a fish fry at some tavern or go downtown to do some shopping. You might go back to that same tavern or one of the service clubs for supper and some dancing on Saturday night.

On Sunday, everything was closed (remember the blue laws?) Everyone went to church on Sunday morning. You didn't feel right if you didn't. You might go on a picnic or to a ball game in the summer in the afternoon or, if your church allowed it, you might go to a movie or bowling. And then, at night, if your church allowed it, you might be found on the dance floor at one of the ballrooms. Some people went back to their church on Sunday night for Bible Study, an evening service, or some activity like a hymn sing or a colored slide presentation by some Missionary home on furlough.

It made for a nice pleasant weekend.

Some churches offered regular mid-week services on Wednesday nights. Devout Catholics went to mass every day, and Confession on Friday afternoons or evenings. We Methodists used to go the church on Wednesday nights for a potluck supper, a program or classes, and a short worship service. We kids loved to go there because sometimes it was the best meal we had all week.

I don't think that just because there were so many churches in Sheboygan meant that the people in Sheboygan were any more religious or better or more moral than people anywhere else. It just meant that they had discovered that the church was a good place to go to for many things that were important in their lives. If you lived in Sheboygan, church was just a good place to go. When you did, you would find your best friends there, too.

The First Methodist Church

There were two Methodist churches in Sheboygan when I was a boy. The bigger one, the First Methodist Church, was on the North Side, one block east of the Sheboygan Hotel, the Fox Theater, and Fountain Park. The smaller church was on the South Side, right off of 8th Street and only a few blocks from the grade school I attended.

Most of the time our family attended and was active in the First Methodist Church, but for a couple of years, when I was in Elementary School, for some reason I attended the Sunday School at the South Side church. We did live on he South Side and it might have been more convenient walk there. We must have returned to First Methodist when I started my membership training (that was in the sixth grade) and attended there from then on until I left the city. My mother and father continued their membership at that church for the rest of their lives.

I can't reconstruct the sequence of time or events or put things in their proper order, but I do remember fondly a few things about my relationship with those churches and the people I knew there and the programs I took part in. Being a South Side kid going to a North Side church caused some logistical problems, which we apparently got figured out.

For us kids, church meant going to Sunday School. We liked going to Sunday School because our friends were there and we had excellent teachers, who prepared well for their classes and liked kids. In most churches we moved from class to class with the same kids and in some cases our teachers moved with us. We developed very strong bonds of loyalty and affection. I enthusiastically attended Sunday School regularly until I got into high school and had perfect attendance pins to prove it.

At the smaller church on the South Side, I was the class secretary/ treasurer. I took attendance, passed out papers and messages to take home, took the collection, and counted the offerings. I took my job very seriously and was proud to be an "officer." I know I always gave a nickel or a dime, a good sum at the time.

At First Methodist Church they did a neat thing. Instead of having children's' sermons during the morning service like most churches do now, we were all marched into the church and sat in the front rows for the opening part of the service. That lasted about 15 minutes.

Then we were dismissed to go to the beautiful small Chapel, where a layperson showed us colored slides of Bible places and stories. I was fascinated by that. When the service was over upstairs we went to find our parents. And then we all went home together. It was a nice arrangement for everybody.

On Special Sundays and for special services we were allowed to stay in the service for the whole hour. That's when I began to enjoy and appreciate the fine sermons Rev. Jones gave, not knowing that some day I would be the one giving them.

Generally speaking, we kids were well behaved in church and Sunday School. And we learned a lot. I am sure those associations with the church influenced my decision to go into the ministry later on.

Though First Methodist Church sponsored a Boy Scout troop, I did not belong to it. I joined a troop on the South side instead, which was much more convenient since we lived on that side of town.

But I did join the fine Boy's Choir at First Methodist Church. The Boy's Choir was something special, patterned after the famous Boy's Choirs in English. Girls were not allowed. It was for boys only. We had to pass auditions to get in. It was a privilege to be a member of this fine choir. I learned not only how to sing great music, but the importance of discipline and performance skills which I used the rest of my life as a musician, actor, and speaker. We rehearsed once a week and those practices were intense. We had to pay attention, behave, and learn difficult music. We had to memorize it all, because we never used any printed music in any performance. Our leader impressed upon us the importance of sounding good and looking good.

We didn't do concerts or put on programs. We were trained and used to be part of the worship life of the church. We only sang for worship services. Once a month (and for some special services) we sang in the Sunday morning church service. We had fancy outfits to wear; bright red robes, with a white surplice and big white flowing bow ties. We really looked classy. Some of the boys, who could not pass the auditions, laughed at us, but we didn't care. To this day I can remember all of the words to the song that we always marched up the aisle to in the Processional, "When Morning Guilds the Skies.....May Jesus Christ Be Praised." The days we sang we got to sit in the choir loft and pews until we had done our special Anthem and then we were dismissed. We felt very important doing that. It was one of my first tastes of the joy that comes with performing good music.

The churches at that time were not only places of worship but also important social centers. The socializing that was not done in taverns or in private homes was done at church. Your church was the place to go to meet and enjoy activities with your friends. Also, personal things w usually held at church, things like weddings, funerals, anniversaries, and family reunions and parties. The women of the church were great cooks and put out great meals and refreshments. This was during the depression when we had to provide our own entertainment for low or no cost. By sharing responsibility people could do things cheaply.

There was always something going on at the church, lots of things that had nothing at all to do with religion. At times there was more eating going on in church than praying. In Sheboygan the most popular events were picnics in the summer and potluck suppers in the fall, winter, and spring. Almost every activity at church started or ended with a meal. We kids loved them, because we got lots of food and great desserts. I don't think my mom and I ever missed a Wednesday night potluck supper at First Methodist Church. Too bad my dad had to miss them, but he had to work nights and was not available on weekdays. I think part of the success of these events was the friendly competition of the women. Everyone wanted to bring their favorite best dish, salad, or dessert to impress everyone else. I don't know how it got organized but there was always great variety and was served in simple but elegant style. The tables were heaped with food, and like the feeding of the five thousand story in the Bible there was always some left to take home. If you liked to eat, church was the place to come on Wednesday nights.

After the meal there might be a simple devotional service and sometimes entertainment. Then there were programs or classes according to age. There was childcare for the little ones, age groups for the kids and youth, and choices of activities for the adults. I always liked the talks given by returned missionaries from all parts of the world. They usually showed colored slides of life in the countries where they were serving, and told about their work in those lands. We usually took a special offering to support their work. We learned that Christians were people who healed, and taught, and cared about other people all over the world.

And, of course, everyone went to church to celebrate the Christian holidays, starting with Advent leading up to Christmas Eve and Christmas Day, and then later on Ash Wednesday to start the season of Lent leading up to Maundy Thursday, Good Friday, and Easter. All of the those holidays started in church with services featuring special music and messages about what Christ did when he was here on earth. Some churches no longer celebrate those seasons of the Church Year. I am glad I lived in Sheboygan when all of the churches did.

I loved that First Methodist Church (now named St. Luke's) and I had a very personal reason for liking Sundays especially. It was one of the few days of the week that I got to see and be with my dad.

The Rev. Dr. T. Perry Jones

When I was a boy, I often wondered why the Christians in town made such a big deal about Martin Luther, John Calvin, John Wesley, or the Pope.

We had someone much better.

We had The Rev. Dr. T. Perry Jones.

I suppose, next to my father and my Boy Scout leader, he was the most important man, model, and influence in my life. He probably was the one who is largely responsible for my decision later to become a minister myself.

The Rev. Dr. T. Perry Jones was an amazing man.

He grew up in a small mining town in Wales. He knew poverty, ignorance and the hard life, and was determined to do better than his ancestors had. He knew that meant getting an education. I don't know how or where he was trained, but he must have had fine teachers. He had a brilliant and restless mind and would have made a great teacher at any of the many fine colleges or universities in Britain. Or he could have gone into any other profession and been successful. Had he stayed in Britain, he might have become a member of Parliament or even the Prime Minister. But Rev. Jones was not interested in politics; he was interested in service.

Dr. Jones was a natural leader, teacher, and orator. But he did not stay in Wales. He came to America, where he became a Methodist! Early in his career, his Bishop assigned him to our church in Sheboygan, one of the largest and most prominent churches in Wisconsin. We were lucky to get him and be able to hold him.

After he earned his degrees and was ordained, he chose to be a preacher, and he was a fine one.....perhaps the best one in Sheboygan and maybe one of the best in our whole Methodist denomination. He prepared his sermons well and spoke them with that charming accent that he never quite lost. He was a popular speaker in and out of the church. He was always giving a talk or a speech somewhere.

He could have been a successful politician, but he chose not to be. He had the mind of a Theologian and the heart of a Saint. And he was committed to being a disciple of Jesus, a servant of the church, and a witness to the Christian faith.

He was also a fine writer. I still read his sermons and talks, which were often published. They are as fresh and relevant now as they were then. He also spoke on the radio every Sunday and those sermons were published and distributed widely.

Why or how he became a Methodist Minister I don't know, but he was one of the best of the best. Unlike other Methodist clergy in America who like to move around and change their appointments frequently, he was happy and content to stay in one place.

Once Rev. T. Perry Jones got to Sheboygan, he stayed there and lived there for the rest of his life. When he became the Pastor of the First Methodist Church, he had no desire to go anywhere else. The church congregation was always happy to have him stay and asked the Bishop year after year to re-assign him to Sheboygan. He served the First Methodist Church until he retired.

The people of that church were richly blessed by his long and fruitful ministry, and he was my minister and mentor from the time I was little until I left to go to the Army. After that, he was my friend for life. He was also a dear friend of my mother and father and helped them in many ways. He presided at my sister's wedding and my father's funeral, but he died before my mother did.

His last big project was to build a fine nursing home on the block the church was on. It was his crowning glory and legacy. He always wanted my mother to live there, but she never did.

I can not say enough about him, so I will say just a little bit more, because his life illustrates what clergy were expected to be and do at that time.

Rev. T. Perry Jones was not only a fine preacher, but also an able administrator, builder, educator, and pastor. He was also a community leader. The stories are legend about how he spoke out for justice, demanded equal treatment for the poor, the outcast, and the oppressed, and for his secret and silent acts of charity. No one will ever know, nor will he ever get the credit due him, for how things changed in Sheboygan after he came on the scene.

He made a good salary but he never had any money, probably because he gave most of it away, usually to the poor and needy. He never sought reward or praise. His ministry went well beyond the bounds of his own church. He was a champion for the mission of the church and raised money for our many missions overseas. He also was involved in political activity and community improvement when called upon or felt compelled to do so. When he spoke, people listened. But he was never interested in running for public office. He preferred to work behind the scenes. He knew all the movers and shakers in town and frequently made them move and shake.

He took the words of Jesus seriously and was always getting someone out of jail, bringing food baskets to the elderly or the widowed, sobering up a drunk, or trying to reconcile a quarrel and save a marriage. He had a hard time saying no to anyone in need. He lost all sense of time when he was doing a good deed, sometimes neglecting his own health and family responsibilities. He must have been a hard man to live with at times, because his work and his mission often ran counter to common sense or family duties and responsibilities.

I appreciated and loved him. He was not only a generous, but a kind man. He never forgot a face or a name, and when anyone was in trouble, or sick, or needed something, he was there to give comfort and aid before it was asked for.

He was especially kind to me when I was growing up and needed encouragement. When I was ordained, he gave me one of his robes, which I wore for many years. He was very helpful to my father when he was ill and unable to work, and to my mother when she was a widow and needed to be cared for. After my father died, he saw to it that my mother was never in want.

He gave his professional and personal life to Sheboygan and will be fondly remembered there.

The Catholic Church has its Saints.

We Methodists in Sheboygan had The Rev. Dr. T. Perry Jones.

I think we got the best of the deal!

What Catholics Confess On Friday Night

What is it about human nature that makes us so curious about what other people, who are different than we are, do? What business is it of ours, anyhow? Do we really have an honest interest and concern in them or are we just being nosey?

When I was a boy in Sheboygan, we kids were just naturally curious about things. We hardly knew anything about our own church's beliefs and practices, but we were almost obsessed to know what our Catholic friends did and why....things like, why Catholics had to eat fish and not meat on Fridays, why Catholics had to stop eating and drinking after midnight on Saturdays, why Catholics called their service a Mass, why Catholics prayed to the Virgin Mary instead of God or Jesus, why Catholics used those funny necklaces to say their prayers, and why Catholics thought Protestants were so bad and thought we were all going to go to Hell.

Sometimes we used to sneak into their churches (we knew we were not supposed to be there), just to look at the statues and smell the incense. They were always so big and so quiet, and felt so cold. We sometimes hid in the pews and watched people light those little candles under the cross with Jesus on it or by the Virgin Mary holding her baby. We wondered why they did that. Sometimes someone would tell us they were lighting a candle to get a family member out of Purgatory. We wondered where that was, and how they got there, and how lighting candles got them out.

It was all kind of spooky, mysterious, and secret. We wanted to know those secrets, but our Catholic friends would not tell us. They told us that they were not supposed to talk to Protestants about their faith and their church. That only made us more nosey and a little angry. There must be some things going on there that were not right if they wouldn't talk about them. Only people who have things to hide keep secrets.

At that time, Protestants were not allowed in Catholic churches and Catholics were instructed that it was a deadly sin for Catholics to attend

Protestant services. We might be together at school, on the playground or in our neighborhoods, but not in church. That was a whole different world, and we Protestants were not welcome there.

So, of course, we were curious. Most of all we were dying to know what our Catholic friends said to the Priest when they went to see him on Fridays. They called it "going to Confession." We knew what Confession was, sort of. It meant that you admitted things that you did that were wrong (sinful). We wondered what wrong things our friends were doing.

Of course, we Protestants were glad we didn't have to go to Confession. We didn't want our ministers to know what we were doing. If we told them they might tell our parents. And then we would get it.

But our Catholic friends did it all of the time. They were always going to Confession on Fridays. That must mean that they did a lot of bad things every week And there were all kinds of rumors of what happened in those mysterious places called the Confessionals. Hopefully they were not true. But who would know? It was all so secret!

Once my Italian friend described the Confessional to me. He said that it was like a small closet, dark and private, and kind of scary. The Priest was on one side of a screen and you were on the other; he could see you but you couldn't see him. That didn't seem fair. My friend said that you better tell the truth, the whole truth, and nothing but the truth or you would really get punished bad!

So, they told the Priest everything. All the bad things. In detail! Then the Priest told them they were forgiven, never to do those things again, and gave them their penance, which meant punishment. It didn't amount to much. They were sent to a pew to do something with those little string of beads Catholics carry around. He called it a rosary. My friend never told me how it worked, only that it had something to do with praying special prayers to the Virgin. That didn't make a whole lot of sense when you were just a kid.

No wonder we thought Catholics were strange. We didn't understand what they were doing. And we were suspicious that there were things going on in those churches that shouldn't be going on; like girls and boys telling older men about their sexual thoughts and sins. My goodness! We Protestants would never tell our ministers things like that, or even our parents. We didn't even always tell our friends everything! It all seemed very silly.

It wasn't until I was an adult, and became a Catholic myself for a time, that I learned and came to understand what went on in the Confessional.

Frankly, I was disappointed.

It wasn't mysterious or exciting at all. I just told the Priest the bad things I had done during the past week, he advised me not to do them again, and then said that I was forgiven, and instructed me to sit out in a pew and say a certain number of Hail Marys and Our Fathers. It only took a few minutes and I was out of there. I was free from guilt and punishment......until next Friday.

No big deal!

If we had known what happened in Confession when we were kids, we could have spent our time wondering and learning about more important things, and we wouldn't have asked our Catholic friends all of those silly questions.

Mixed Marriages

When we get caught in our prejudices and are confronted and have to defend them, we often resort to an old trick, asking that ultimate question which we assume will settle things once and for all, "Well, that's all well and good, but would you want your daughter to marry one?"

"One" meaning, of course, any person representing someone who is of a different nationality, race, or ethnic group that you do not like and don't want to have anything to do with.

In Sheboygan, if you asked that question, everyone knew that you did not mean a Negro, an Asian, a Latino, or an Indian. There weren't any or many of those around at that time. The people Sheboyganites didn't want their daughters to marry were persons of other religions. When people used that "marry your daughter" line in Sheboygan, they were being very specific. They were talking about mixed marriages, which were taboo at the time.

In Sheboygan, when I was a boy, when you came of age, you would never even consider getting involved in a mixed marriage. If you fell in love with someone of another religion, you knew that you better get over it in a hurry or you were in for a whole lot of trouble. Everybody knew that mixed marriages didn't work and were not allowed! The rules were clear, strict, observed, and final. Those who defied them soon left town.

Protestants were not supposed to marry Catholics and vice versa. Jews were not supposed to marry Gentiles. Protestants could marry other Protestants, but they had to decide on whose church to join and attend, and where their kids were going to be baptized, go to Sunday School, and be confirmed. And you certainly would not want to get involved with or marry a non-believer. At the time, this was a major issue.

Of course, there might have been other reasons why parents might object to the marriage choices of their children. Some rich people did

20

not want their daughters marrying beneath them, and some parents did not want their daughters to marry at all. Or the parents might just not like the boy or girl that had been chosen.

If there was an early or unwanted pregnancy involved (this happened more often than anyone dared to admit), things got even more complicated and that was a whole different issue and problem that had little to do with religion. If that did happen, and one of the parties was a Catholic, there were lots of promises to make and papers to sign.

Mixed marriages were not impossible, but no one was happy about them. When couples followed their hearts and defied their parents, everybody got very upset. There were some severe punishments for such behavior. Parents refused to come to weddings, children were asked to leave or were disowned, and families broke up over the issue and were never reconciled. Lots of children (the products of such marriages) suffered for something that was not their fault.

Religion can be a good thing, but at that time, not much good could be expected to come out of a mixed marriage. Religion, love, and sex did not always mix very well in Sheboygan. That's why, when we reached puberty, we were constantly warned against mixed marriages. It had nothing to do with love; it had a lot to do with society's expectations.

However, love often has its own ways and its own set of rules. Sometimes it is messy and sometimes it is even tragic. Young people in Sheboygan were no different from young people anywhere else. Some of them defied the community and broke the rules. And they paid the price.

But, by the time we graduated from high school, more and more of my young friends fell in love with someone of an opposite faith. And they insisted on getting married regardless of the consequences or the costs.

Things had changed. Regardless of the feelings of parents and the rigid policies of the churches, some acceptable compromises were agreed upon, for the sake of church order and family solidarity.

Now mixed marriages were allowed under these conditions:

1) A Catholic could marry a Protestant if the Protestant party would sign an agreement that said that he/she would not interfere with the practice of the faith by the Catholic party, and that the children of the union would be baptized and confirmed and brought up and raised in the Catholic faith.

2) The Protestant party could convert or vice versa so they could both share the same faith. Then, technically, there would not be a mixed marriage. Sometimes that was done and worked well. But it was usually the Protestant party who converted and became a Catholic. Now and then, a Protestant or a Catholic would convert to the Jewish faith, but not very often.

Now and then, either of these two compromises worked. Most often they did not. The hurt feelings, resentments, and broken promises often led to divorce. Accommodations and compromises play by their own set of rules. Usually, one of the parties just dropped out of religion entirely, gave up going to church, and the other person continued in his/her faith alone. The children often gave up going to church or being religious as soon as they came of age or were confirmed and were able to make up their own minds.

Then, after World War II was over, no one seemed to care anymore.

Fortunately, none of what I described above applied to me. I must admit that I was attracted to a few pretty Lutheran girls, went steady with a Presbyterian girl once, and liked to dance with girls of any and all faiths. I went so far as getting engaged to a Catholic girl when I was in college and fully intended to marry her. I even became a Catholic for a few years. As it turned out, however, she found another Catholic guy she liked better than me and that ended that. None of these relationships ended in a mixed marriage.

In the end, I married another Methodist and we raised all of our children to be the same. If my wife's father said anything when he heard that Margaret and I had become engaged and planned to get married, it may have been, "Isabel, do we want our daughter to marry.......a musician?"

Children

A Curious Kid

I was always a curious kid, or should I say, a kid full of curiosity.

I had a good mind and a vivid imagination, was a keen observer, and was an eager and fast learner. I absorbed knowledge like a sponge. I would read anything I could get my hands on, listened carefully to what my teachers and other adults told me, and asked lots of questions. And I retained what I learned very well. I also learned from watching the people around me, from every experience I had, and even from the mistakes I frequently made.

When I got to school and was tested, it was discovered that I had a high I.Q. When they did it again in the Army, I was told that my I.Q. was "much higher than average." When I got to college, I did very well, and by the time I got to Seminary and had the privilege of enjoying a post-graduate education, I was a straight A student and graduated Cum Laud (which simply means with honors.) All through my life and through the various stages of my formal education, I was usually one of the better students in my classes.

I am not telling you this to brag or boost my own ego. And this is not my judgment. It is a matter of record. The point is, I was a good student because of my insatiable curiosity.

Though I would like to claim that my intellectual achievements were due to hard work, long hours, good discipline, and determination and grit, I cannot take much credit for my academic accomplishments. I couldn't help it. I didn't consciously plan to be a good student and was not interested in setting any records or getting any rewards. I was just doing, what for me, came naturally. Chalk it up to my genes, or better still, to my highly active, extraordinary, and lively CURIOSITY!

I am grateful for it. It is a great gift to have!

But, I will take a little credit for what I have learned and how I have applied those lessons to the decisions I have made. I paid my dues. I was an excellent student because, unlike some of my friends, I went to all my classes, studied all my lessons, did all my assignments, and handed them in on time. As I result, I usually passed my tests with higher marks than my friends who did not take school seriously and wasted their time doing fun but unproductive things. But I didn't do it for the grades. It was fun to learn and it satisfied my curiosity. I was one of those pupils that teachers love to have in their classes. But I was not a teacher's pet and I didn't bring apples to my teachers in order to get some advantage.

Quite the contrary.

I didn't know I was a good student. I always thought of myself as just an ordinary normal kid, trying to learn what life was all about and how things worked, and how to make it successfully in the world I was going to live in.

I loved school and wasn't afraid to admit it. Unlike some of the other boys in my classes, I looked forward to going to school every day. I was not one who complained when vacations were over and we had to return to classes. I was eager to get back. I thought it was foolish not to take advantage of this great resource....an education....that we were being given as a gift. Our parents and grandparents were not so lucky.

I also loved to learn things in other places, like in Sunday School, at my church, in Boy Scouts, or just listening to adults tell about their experiences. I didn't know then that I was headed for college and graduate school from the day I was born. I never in my wildest dreams ever thought I would do that. I was the first and only person in my family who ever went to college and got a degree. My mother and father were never even able to go to high school. I would have been a fool not to take the opportunities that were given to me.

So my curiosity served me well and I probably ought to thank the Lord for that. He gave me the gift of what is sometimes called, "a thirst for knowledge." As it turned out, my thirst was quenched and I was very wonderfully filled.

From the start, I have been a natural and lifelong student, and later, a trained teacher and reporter. I not only loved to learn, but I loved to share what I discovered with others. I grew up wanting to know everything there was to know and how everything worked. I also wanted to know why. I hung out in libraries, and still do. And I still go to classes and sometimes teach them to this day. I will be curious until the day I die. Curiosity is part of my being.

This may sound like a lot of bragging, and you may think I am egotistical and that this piece is self-serving. But that is not true.

I am telling you these things so you will know why this section of the book about Children, is longer than all the rest. It is a collection of stories and essays about how and where I learned the things I did and who the persons were who taught me. If you are anywhere near my age, some of these things will sound very familiar to you.

By telling you my story, about what happened to me in Sheboygan, perhaps your curiosity will be peaked and you may be more interested in learning more about yourself and what happened to you as you were growing up, wherever you came from.

Maybe you, too, were a curious kid. I sure hope so!

The Houses I Lived In

On the day I took my tour to re-visit the places that were important to me when I lived in Sheboygan, I started out to find the houses I had lived in during those first 18 years of my life, just to see if they were still there and how they looked now.

Since I don't know exactly where I was born and lived the first couple years of my life, I couldn't find that place. My mother used to talk about "the flat" and "climbing all those stairs." But I don't ever remember seeing such a place. I knew it was somewhere downtown, in back of the Sheboygan Theater, but that whole area had been redeveloped and hardly anything that was there exists anymore. I assume that the upstairs flat, my first home, disappeared when that house was torn down a long time ago.

I did find the house on Swift Avenue where I spent some of the best years of my life. I saw that the house number was still 1007 and it looked much the same as I remembered it, with that long front porch and the little hill up to it and the long narrow backyard in the back. I wandered back there to see if the old shed and garage were still there. The shed is gone and has been replaced by a new and better garage. The house is still painted white.

I had a strange sensation when I looked at the house that we lived in on 14th Street. I had always remembered it as a very big house, but now it looks very small. It also is painted a different color. I think it was brown when we lived there and now it is white. It did not look at all like the house I remembered all these years, except for that nice, big front porch. Of course, I have been remembering it through the eyes of a young boy, not an adult.

The house on Kentucky Avenue still looks the same in every way. We lived in the upstairs flat there, so I got a better view of the house from the back than from the front. I remember those long back stairs going up to our flat and how I used to carry the oil container for our oil heater every day in the winter. I also remembered the old icebox outside the door at the top of the stairs. That was later replaced by our first refrigerator, which was right in our kitchen. I don't remember if the old barn that was in the back is there anymore. I forgot to look for that. I should have, because we had lots of good times in that old barn.

While I was looking at houses, I also went over to 13th Street to see the house that my Aunt Myrtle, Uncle Gilbert, and cousin, Dick, lived in. I spent lots of time there when I was a kid. I was surprised to see that it had not changed a bit, except that there is a lady living there now who got all excited when she saw me and started to yell at me when I put my camera to my eye to take a picture. When I told her who I was and why I was there, she cooled off, apologized for her anxiety, and kindly let me take my picture.

I was very disappointed when I saw the house at 1643 N. 3rd Street where my Grandma and Grandpa Huber and Aunt Gladys lived (and later Aunt Evie and Uncle Carl). It had been totally redecorated, and I wouldn't have recognized it if it had not been in the same spot that I remembered, right across the street from Cole Park. I was smart enough this time to seek permission from the owners to take a picture of their house before I took out my camera.

The people who live there now were very nice. Not only did they let me take a picture of their house, but they invited me to come in for a cup of coffee. I lingered a bit, telling them about the members of my family who had once lived there. They showed me the changes they had made on the inside of the house, as well as those on the outside. But, it just wasn't the same. I liked the house better the way it was when I was a kid.

And that was it. Five stops and five houses. It was interesting to see those houses again, but I discovered that I had no longer had any strong emotional feelings about them. At one time, those houses served us well and were at the core and center of our lives. But not anymore. As Margaret Mead once said, "Houses are not homes, they are just houses. Homes are where the people you love live." All of my Sheboygan houses are now occupied by total strangers. And that is okay...the way it should be. Lives move on! Only the houses remain behind.

As much as I enjoyed my revisiting journey, I was glad, a few days later, to get back to my own home in Minneapolis, knowing that that is where I now belong.

Critters

In my first book about Sheboygan, I told the story about my beloved dog, Trixie, and his untimely death.

After Trixie, my next pet was not a dog. It was a rabbit. Yes, a rabbit! It was not my idea. It was something my Aunt Gladys thought up. She was always doing things like that, which drove everyone in the family crazy.

One year (I must have been in the first or second grade then), just before Easter, Gladys either heard on the radio or read in the newspaper that one of the merchants was advertising as an "Easter Special," the "ideal gift for your child." That ideal gift was either a live baby chicken or a live baby rabbit. It sounded harmless and fun, at least to Gladys, and a bit different from the usual chocolate candy and jelly beans that we ended up playing with until they were too dirty to eat. This would be her surprise that Easter. She was very excited about this, and it was hard to keep it secret, but for once in her life she did. It might have been better if she had talked it over with the mothers first.

When we came to her house that Easter to find our baskets, we found these live little surprises in them. Nellie Mae and Luverne each got a chicken. One was dyed blue and one was dyed pink. I got a cute little baby rabbit. He was white with pink eyes and a black nose.

We kids were delighted, but my mother was not. She had a fit! We didn't understand what she was so upset about. We thought it was a great idea….but Mom was really mad at Gladys for a long time after that. However, instead of taking her anger out on Gladys, like she should have, she started to take it out on me, which was very unlike her. After all these years, I can remember the exact words she said to me that day, "What are we ever going to do with a RABBIT?"

I didn't know how to answer that question. I had never ever thought about having a rabbit. I had no idea what one did with a rabbit or how one took care of a rabbit or even why anyone would want to have rabbit for a pet.

My mom must have been thinking the same things I was when she said, more to herself than to me, "Where do you think we are we going to put it and who is going to take care of it?" I knew the answer. I was! And I did!

Fortunately, my mom let me keep the rabbit and I had a lot of fun taking care of it, even though at times it was hard and messy work. My dad helped me, but my mom did want to have anything to do with this pet. Not only did I take care of my rabbit, but also I learned a lot of things from him.

All rabbits seem to be interested in is eating, pooping, and reproducing. We were lucky that we only had one rabbit and that he was always kept in a cage. At first, he was just cute, like all baby animals seem to be, all fluffy like a little ball of cotton. But, as is often said about babies, "They don't stay little long." My rabbit quickly grew until soon he was about the size of a large cat or a small dog. If you have ever tried to raise rabbits, you will know it is a very different from raising a dog or a cat. They are not good companions.

First of all, they don't seem to understand anything. They don't even respond when you call them by name. I don't know if I ever gave my rabbit a name. The only rabbit names I knew then were Cottontail or Peter and I didn't want to name him either of those. I don't remember calling him anything or calling him at all. We soon discovered that rabbits never listen to us humans or respond to anything we say. They do only what they want to do and can get away with. Rabbits seem to be totally self-centered.

I could never figure out Mom's hostile attitude toward my rabbit. It was not like her. She usually liked animals and she almost treated them like one of her own children. But there was something about this rabbit that ticked her off. I never found out what it was.

My dad was more understanding. He helped me to build a small pen at one end of the shed, with a little door opening up into an outdoor..... whatever it was....a cage or a fenced-in playpen? Anyhow, my rabbit had the best of two worlds, inside and outside, and he seemed to enjoy both. As long as he had enough to eat and was able to sit in the sun, he seemed happy. The only trouble I had with him was trying to keep him out of mom's garden, which started right where his cage ended. The rabbit was determined to get into it and often found ways to do it. He didn't have to. He was well fed and didn't need any more to eat, but the stuff must have tasted better when he stole it. Rabbits just can't seem to resist a garden!

We thought we had built an escape-proof pen. My dad had used a very fine chicken wire reinforced with wood and metal stakes, with a completely closed top and high sides. But when vegetables began to disappear from mom's garden, we discovered holes where the rabbit had dug and tunneled under the fencing and escaped. It was not enough to fill up the holes. My dad had to put a thick layer of chicken wire under the dirt floor and hook it up tightly to the walls of wire. For a time that worked. But now and then, things were still missing from the garden. We never found out how.

I must admit that my rabbit was no replacement for Trixie but I did get fond of him, and I was very sad when he met the same fate that Trixie had.

Everything was fine when we were living on Swift Avenue, but this adventure with my rabbit quickly came to an end when we moved to 14th Street and had to make a new and not as secure cage for my rabbit there. Shortly after we moved there, I went through a similar experience with my rabbit that I had gone through with Trixie.

One morning, I went out to feed my rabbit, only to find him dead. It was an unpleasant sight. Unlike Trixie, who was stiff and cold, the rabbit was all torn apart and bloody. My dad thought that a weasel got him, but it could have been a cat or dog. It was my second pet death experience, but this one did not affect me as badly as the first one did. I was getting kind of sick of taking care of the rabbit and cleaning up his messes. And I can't honestly say I missed him after he was gone. I was a little older and had become fascinated with pigeons, which caused a whole set of new problems (.....my mom did not like pigeons either). This time she won; I never got to raise my own pigeons.

But later on, when we moved again, I experienced the next best thing.

When we moved to the upper flat on 17th Street, with that large old red barn in the backyard, guess what? The boy downstairs raised pigeons! The upstairs of that old barn was full of his pigeons. The whole loft on the second story of the barn was filled with little cages for them. There was a lot of straw, little cups with water, and other receptacles for seeds....pigeons eat a lot! He was forever filling them. I don't remember the count, but he had lots of pigeons, of all different colors and markings.

Some of them had won prizes. I was awed by them. They were beautiful birds, if you didn't have to clean up after them.

My mother was right, they were messy and dirty and smelly. It took some of the charm and glamour out of the idea of raising pigeons. To tell you the truth, I soon became glad that they were not mine.

As I look back, I have come to realize that my mother was right and that it would have turned out to be a horrible experience if I had ever seriously tried to raise pigeons. I am glad I ended up having the best of both worlds. I could enjoy my friend's lovely birds, but I didn't have to feed them or clean their cages. Thanks, Mom!

This brings me to the last part of my stories about critters, at least for this part of the book. All of what I will tell you here was going on at the same time I was taking care of my dog and rabbit, and watching those pigeons.

I never had much fondness for cats, and still don't. But I did like other critters of all kinds.

In another world and another time I might have been a biologist or a zoologist, or any of the "ologists" who observe and describe natural growing things. I was blessed not only with a good mind for learning, but a keen eye for observing, an imagination for seeing what was going on with the things I was not seeing, and a way of capturing, collating, and cataloging information in a way that made sense. My first great laboratory was my own backyard, where there were endless wonders and unlimited numbers of critters to watch and enjoy. I have spent enough time on the mammals, so let me move on to the birds.

Our backyards in Sheboygan must have been bird heaven. They were natural bird sanctuaries. Our yards were full of birds because the food supply was so great. There were worms for the Robins, and lots to eat for Blue Jays, Cardinals, Finches, and Sparrows. There were seeds early on, then berries and fruit, and when winter came they would fly south. I don't remember people having bird feeders like we have at our house now. We didn't need them to attract the birds. There was plenty for the birds to eat already. In return, they rewarded us with their lovely colors and beautiful songs. Some of them honored us by making our yard their home.

Our trees were ideal places for their nests and, as the spring and summer progressed, we would observe the eggs turn into little wiggly things. We could watch the mothers feed their young ones and watch them push them out of the nest when they were ready to fly. The next year, the cycle would be played out all over again. We learned about the rhythms of life by watching the birds. It was awesome to observe and enjoy them.

Then there were the worms, bugs and beetles. I used to spend hours watching them, busy about their work of survival and multiplication. There were so many of them and so many varieties and kinds. I tried to figure out what they ate and where they made their homes and how they cared for their young.

Of all of the smaller creatures, I loved the ants the most. I once wrote a sermon about what I learned from the ants, which was a great deal. Just recently, I revised that parable for one of my books.

Now and then, there was great excitement when one of the kids would find, and possibly catch, a grass snake. But that experience was rare, making it even more exciting. There are not many snakes in Sheboygan. They were all small and harmless. But they were fun for kids to chase, catch, and hold in their hands.

We never kept any of these critters long and we were never cruel to them and never destroyed them. Without knowing it, I was developing what would become my creed when I was a camp director and spent a lot of time with children in wilderness areas. It was a strict and punishable rule that one must "let living things live." You could catch, hold, observe, and enjoy. But then you had to put back and let go. You could not kill a living thing, unless it was a fly or a mosquito, and then you had to do it with respect, like the Indians have for all living things. We also had lots and lots of those flying wonders and pests right in our own back yards in Sheboygan. We didn't have to travel long distances to see these things in wilderness areas.

But my very favorite critters were the caterpillars and the butterflies, not knowing at first that they were one and the same thing. If there is any symbol of life and resurrection, it is these creatures. At first, caterpillars look ugly. They are kind of like an accordion, crawl on their bellies, and have all of those dot marks and hairs. Not in the wildest imagination can you see them becoming a beautiful butterfly until you actually watch them and see the transformation, and realize what a miracle has happened....one that happens over and over again.

You can also learn patience by watching them, because it takes such a long time to go through their whole process of changing from one thing into another; the larvae into the caterpillar, into the cocoon, into that lovely and colorful flying machine...the butterfly. What a process! Just recently, I have discovered the theological significance of this process. Only a mind much greater than ours could have thought this up.

Now my favorite Easter symbol is no longer a lily, or an egg, or a rabbit, and even an empty tomb. It is a BUTTERFLY! I have butterflies in many forms all over my house to remind me of God's presence in our transformations.

As I wrote that last paragraph I had this startling thought.

What if Trixie had been a caterpillar instead of a dog? Then when he died, he could have become a beautiful white butterfly, and we wouldn't have had to bury him under my favorite cherry tree in our backyard.

He could have just flown away!

Mud, Tar, And Other Dirty Things

Kids love to get dirty. They also like to get wet. They like to mix dirt and water and make mud. And they like sand and tar. Kids are pretty basic. They play with anything that is at hand. Find a kid, and you will usually find some dirt and water nearby. And the kid will be in it! In Sheboygan, when I was a boy, we were lucky. We had all of the necessary ingredients right in our own yards.

Fortunately, our mothers were not too fussy about cleanliness and sterility. They let us get dirty. In the summer, they would just clean us off with a hose; in the winter they would plunk us into the bathtub. They must have done a lot of laundry!

Tar was another matter. That stuff was almost impossible to get off.

We loved tar for two reasons: when it got hot and melted, we would chew it like gum. And if we got it before it got hard, we could mold it into shapes like clay. The only problem was that when it got really hot and you tried to get across the street, you would burn your bare feet. That hurt! Ouch! And when we tramped it into the house, our mothers were not happy at all.

They loved to watch us play with and in dirty things, as long as we didn't bring it home and into their clean houses. Maybe that is why we went barefoot most of the time in summer. The mothers had learned that it was much easier to get stuff (even tar) off our feet, than it was to get it off our shoes.

Sand and soil, mud and tar. How we loved it! And there was always plenty of water around to wash it off when we got too dirty. And then there was soap and those nice thick towels.

Oh, the joys of being a kid!

What Boys Did In Their Rooms

When I was a boy growing up in Sheboygan, a boy's room was almost a sacred place, his own personal sanctuary from the outside world. It was one of the places he could go when he wanted complete privacy.

No one was supposed to bother you when you were in there and your door was closed, and people were supposed to knock if they wanted to talk to you or come in and visit with you. A boy's room was the place where he slept, dressed, played, rested, and pondered the mysteries of life. It was the place where he could get away from it all. When he was in his room, a boy was not supposed to be bothered. It was no one else's business what he was doing or thinking when he was in his room.

But for some reason, that always seemed to make his parents, particularly his mother, nervous. It sort of violated a cardinal principle in Sheboygan at that time...that parents had a right to know at all times, where you were, what you were doing, and with whom.

Let me be clear right from the start. I don't know what other boys in Sheboygan did when they went to their rooms, closed their doors, and no one was looking. I only know what I did. And I can tell you that I never did anything close to being forbidden, sinful, or immoral. When you read this, you might even be disappointed. The things that your imagination will tell you might have happened, never happened there.

I can understand why my Mother felt the way she did and why she, at times, might be suspicious when I closed my door. She was a mother, and mothers are supposed to worry about their children. But she needn't have been concerned about me at all. When I was in my room, I was always perfectly safe. Just because I was quiet didn't mean that I was doing something I was not supposed to do. If she wanted to worry about me, she should have checked me out when I was on the playground, or in the shed, or in some back alley. At that time, those were the places where the real action was.

When I went to my room and closed the door, I was not smoking or taking drugs or experimenting with alcohol. And I was not looking at any of those dirty books the older boys used to show us in the alley or behind the garage. If I ever looked at those books, I would never be stupid enough to bring them home. And I didn't start carrying a condom in my wallet until I was in the Army.

The older boys may have been the pushers of the day, but they never tried to sell us any pot, if there was such a thing then. All they asked us to do was to experiment with a Camel or Lucky Strike cigarette, to see which one we liked the best. It was taken for granted that we were going to experiment with smoking. Everybody did. But never in our rooms. That would have been stupid. When we smoked, we did it in the shed. For most guys who got hooked on smoking, it happened when they were in the Army or some other branch of the service, but not in their rooms.

And where would I have hidden a bottle of alcohol? In my underwear?

Poor Mother. If she had seen what I was doing in my room, she wouldn't have wasted a minute's time worrying about me. I never did any of the things that adults those days thought the kids must be doing when they were not around. I am not sure that would be true today. Now we have the internet coming into those rooms, and lots of little pills around that look harmless but can kill you if you take the wrong kind and too many. And I am told that boys sometimes sneak girls into their rooms after school, while their parents are working.

Everything I did in my room when I was all alone was either perfectly harmless or highly creative. I even hesitate to write about these things because they seem so uninteresting, if not terribly boring. But I liked to do them, and they kept me busy and out of trouble. If you had been a boy at that time you would probably have done the same things.

I always liked to read so I did a lot of reading in my room. I always had a book or two going, like the Big Little Books about Tarzan, Flash Gordon, or the Lone Ranger. Or, it might have been one of the Hardy Boys series. I read them all. Sometimes it was to read something in my Boy Scout Manual, getting ready for my next merit badge. When I was in Confirmation Training, I had to read the Bible, though I never understood most of what our minister assigned us to read for class.

I also collected things and would spend hours sorting out the assortments we bought in big bags for a cheap price, selecting, and posting new stamps in my stamp collection books. Most of them were duplicates and got thrown away, but in every bag there were a few that we didn't have and were looking for. I often wonder what ever happened to my stamp collection.

I also collected pins and buttons with slogans and pictures on them. I pinned them on banners that were hung on my wall. I had hundreds of them, some of which would be antiques now and quite valuable, especially the political ones from former elections.

For a time, I was into jigsaw puzzles, probably inspired by my Uncle Gilbert and Aunt Myrtle, who did them all the time. You could buy them cheaply or rent them. My Mother sometimes joined me and helped me put them together. I let her come into my room to do that when she came to make my bed or pick up dirty clothes on wash day.

I spent a lot of time listening to records and the radio, mainly big band and jazz music. I had quite a collection of records and knew them all by heart, as well as the names of all of the members of the bands that had made them. I often heard the late night broadcasts of the Big Bands from across the countries and frequently went to sleep with my radio on. I always owned my own record player and small radio.

Of course I slept in my room, had my clothes there, and had all of my precious things neatly arranged. I was lucky to have a room of my own. Not only did I not have to share it with a brother (I never had one), but I could arrange it in any way I wanted. My Mother used to complain that it was hard to dust around my things, but I always told her she didn't have to dust everything as much as she did.

At one period of my life, when I was in grade school, I spent a lot of time building model airplanes. That was a very popular hobby for boys at that time. They were scale models of real planes. I did it the hard way, not doing those solid ones you just had to put together and paint, but the ones that were made out of small pieces of balsam wood that you glued together according to a printed plan. You then glued paper over the frame and added symbols, wheels, propellers, and sometimes small motors. They were very fragile and they also burned easily. Usually, I hung them up around my room from the ceiling. The ones I tried to fly usually cracked up on the first try. Those were quickly burned. I had quite a collection and, at one point, buying new kits took most of my spending money.

I never did homework in my room. I always did it in the library at school (which is also the place where I looked at those neat pictures of the girls in Africa in the National Geographic Magazines, the ones I never took home for my mother to find in my room).

And then there were those precious moments when I would just sit and think. Teenagers have a lot of things to think about. Adults do not have a corner on the world's problems. And all creativity starts with random thought and crazy ideas. I never minded being alone, and I did a lot of thinking about a lot of important things. How do you think I got to be so smart?

So you see, my parents had no cause to worry about me when I went to my room and closed the door. I was just getting out of the way and claiming my privacy….and learning a whole lot that would prove valuable later in life.

They Only Called A Doctor
If You Were Going To Die

Though doctors made house calls when I was a kid, you wouldn't call one unless it was a dire emergency. They used to call it "a matter of life or death." There wasn't anything like Medicare or health insurance, and even though some doctors didn't send bills or took whatever was offered, no one called a doctor unless they had to. For routine and ordinary things, you might go to his office. Most things were taken care of by our mothers or grandmothers, who were not trained nurses, but were more like shamans or witch doctors in other cultures. When we got sick or injured, they knew how to make us well.

It was all kind of mysterious how they did it. We endured lots of goose grease on our necks and chests, ate a lot of chicken soup, and used up a lot of iodine or salves. We also had to drink a lot of that horrible Rocky Mountain Tea.

But there were times when it was necessary to quickly call the doctor. Today, we would consider those "life threatening" situations and we call 911. When they did call the doctor, he dropped everything he was doing and came as fast as he could get there. There were times when he got there too late. There were some untimely deaths. But he usually got there in time and knew what to do when he got there. I can remember one of those times very vividly.

One day, I was playing with my erector set and I stuck a screw up my nose! That was a dumb thing to do, but kids sometimes do dumb things. The blood came spurting out and went all over the place. My mother did the right thing. She called the doctor. It didn't take him long to get there.

He opened his bag and took out a lot of scary looking tools. He probed around in my nose and the blood continued to flow. At first, he wasn't able to stop it. My mother stood next to him and caught the blood in a dishpan.

But he couldn't find the screw. He kept trying until he was convinced that there was nothing more he could do. He said it had gone in too far and that all he could do was try to stop my nose from bleeding, which he did.

After he got the bleeding to stop, he told my mother not to worry, that "some day it will just come out....you know....in the normal way." I don't think she was relieved.

For days we kept looking for that screw. But we never found it.

Of course, I never did that again. I had learned by lesson.

Neighborhood Kids

I was raised as an only child.

I didn't have any brothers or sisters to fight with or play with until my only sister was born when I was 16 years old, which by then was too late. Soon after she was born, I left to go into the Army. We did not grow up together.

Being an only child had its advantages and disadvantages.

The upside was that I never had to deal with sibling rivalry, never had to wear hand-me-downs, and didn't have to share my toys with anyone. I got all the attention from my parents and always had a room of my own.

The downside was that when I needed and sought companionship, other kids to talk to, or kids to play a game with, I would have to go find the neighborhood kids. I was lucky we lived in a neighborhood where there were plenty of them and many my own age.

As someone wisely said, "the work of a child is play." And, because this was a different time and during the depression, most of that play we had to make up and provide for ourselves. We didn't have money to buy our entertainment and we couldn't always wait for adults to provide our recreation for us, make up the rules, and supervise our play. That meant we needed to develop good imaginations and learn to use the things at hand to our advantage...like trees, backyards, alleys, streets, vacant lots, and playgrounds (....later in this book I will tell you about all of these.) But we did not feel deprived and we seemed to always find things to do.

I have already told about the things boys did in their rooms when they were alone. Now I will tell about some of the things we did when we could round up a friend or get all the neighborhood kids together.

Whenever we could, we played outside, but when the weather was nasty or there weren't enough kids around to get up a good group game, a friend and I would get together at one of our houses and play checkers, chess, or listen to records or the radio. Sometimes we would just talk or hang out. But if we wanted to play some board game, like Parcheesi, Monopoly, or Poker (when our parents were not around), we had to round up a few more players. Sometimes we would play Monopoly for weeks on end, letting the board stay up, and playing it when we had time. If we played Poker (which was not often), we didn't gamble. We used chips or matchsticks instead of money. Putting puzzles together was also very popular and doing them with others enhanced the fun. Some outside games required lots of players, so we would have to round up lots of boys and girls of all ages to play. We played most of them at night after supper. These games had to be played either in the street, an alley, or on a vacant lot. We usually didn't go to a park or playground. We liked to stay closer to home, where our parents could easily call us for meals or when it was time to come home and go to bed.

All kids learn very early to play simple games, like some form of Tag, Hide and Seek, or Dodgeball. We didn't need anyone to teach these to us or supervise or referee us, and we just made up our own rules as we went along. One of our very favorite games was Kick the Can. There were times we would get up a game and play it every night for weeks on end. If you have never played Kick the Can, it was simple. A tin can was placed in the middle of the street or alley and someone volunteered to be "it." That person would close his/her eyes and count to ten while the rest of the players would scatter and hide. The game continued until all of the players were found and then the player that was found first would be "it" for the next game. But, if at any point, anyone could get to the can and kick it, everyone would scatter and hide again. We played this game until it got too dark to see the can.

Some of the games were too rough for the girls. They might involve pushing and pulling, hitting and punching, or even wrestling. At that time, girls weren't into things like that. The girls might join us for a game of Red Rover, but they usually sat out and watched when we guys got to playing a rough game of King of the Hill. They would cheer us on, like they did later when they became cheerleaders at school.

One of the team games that I liked the best could not be played in our neighborhood. It required a lot more space. It was called Capture the Flag and we boys usually played it with our Boy Scout Troop when we were on a hike or an overnight out at the Sand Dunes in Terry André Park. Later, I taught it to the kids at my camps when I was a Counselor and Director.

In case this game is new to you, this is how we played it. Two guys choose up teams and become Captains of them. Then two flags were put up on long poles where they could be easily seen from a distance. The name of the game reveals how it was played. Like other games, such as soccer or hockey, some of the players on your team tried to guard the flag and the rest went out to capture the flag of the other team. If you got caught and tagged, you became a prisoner. If that happened to you, you were guarded until one of your teammates came to tag and release you, or the game ended. The point of this game was to capture the flag of your opponents, which was much easier said than done. There was a lot of strategy and teamwork involved, and sometimes a game would last for hours. It was great fun.

So you can see, when I was a kid, we seldom got bored, because we didn't sit around complaining that there wasn't anything to do. We just used our imaginations, made up our own games, and entertained ourselves. In Sheboygan, at that time, kids ALWAYS found something to do. The problem we had was that we didn't always have enough time to do everything we wanted to do.

When our games had to get called off because of rain, or it got too dark to see what we were doing, or we just got tired, we would quit, say good night, and go off to our own homes and go to bed.

Tomorrow would be another day to play again.

Things We Did In
Our Own Backyards

One of the benefits of living in Sheboygan was the way the neighborhoods were laid out and the houses were built. Everything was square or oblong, not like the places in our modern suburbs with those curved streets and cul-du-sacs that look like big horseshoes. All of our houses were in straight lines. But they did not all look alike as some of the developments in our suburbs do now. Each was individually designed and built, often by the owners themselves. The houses were almost always built on large oblong lots, narrow in width and close together, but with long yards in the back going out to an alley. They must have been at least 100 to 150 feet in length, or more.

A good share of the space in those yards was reserved for the large gardens that the women planted and tended. In our yard on Swift Avenue, my mother's garden took up at least half our yard. Much of our food came from those gardens, either fresh in summer or canned and eaten in the winter. The rest of the yard was a big grassy area that my father always kept neatly cut and trimmed. On that part of the plot, there were two big cherry trees, an apple tree, and lots of blooming bushes and flowerbeds. That was also the area where my parents put some lawn chairs and our outdoor fryer. There were also poles with clotheslines where my mother hung our clothes out to dry (...this was before the days of washers and dryers where everything is done inside). Then there were flowers planted on the sides of the house and a grassy hill, steps, and sidewalks in the front, leading out to the street.

Some of the people would put up low fences to mark their property lines or keep their pets and small children contained, but in most cases, there weren't any markers. People knew where the property lines were and they were respected by their neighbors.

In the middle of the long lot, there was usually a narrow sidewalk going out to the shed, the garage, and the alley. It took a lot of shoveling to keep that open at all times in the winter.

In the back of the yard there might be cans for garbage and trash, and maybe a place to pile lumber and junk that would later be taken to the dump. Most yards were well kept. People in Sheboygan liked to have everything neat, clean, and in order, especially us folks of German descent.

I loved those backyards, especially mine. I liked the one on Swift Avenue best.

There were endless things to do in those yards and all of us kids spent a lot of our free time there, either in our own yards or the yards of our friends. I will tell just a few of the things we typically did there. Let me use our yard on Swift Avenue as my model.

There was an area near the back of the long lot, near the garage, that my Dad never planted with grass. Instead, wisely, he filled that with stones, sand, and dirt, which he sometimes used in other parts of the yard. But mostly it was a huge sandbox for us kids. We could play in it anytime we wanted to and to our heart's delight. We could do anything we wanted to do back there, except make deep holes someone might fall into or set fires. We could dig, and build things, or just mess around. In the winter, we made snowmen and built forts back there. We could throw balls or snowballs at the back wall of the garage behind it.

At that time, we were allowed to climb the trees, and we didn't have to wear helmets, knee and elbow guards, or any of the protective things kids have to wear now. We were free and uninhibited. But we were careful and rarely fell out of a tree. In all of the years I lived there, I never had anything other than a few scratches....never any broken bones.

When it was time to harvest the cherries and apples, we kids were given tin #10 cans with handles on them and let loose to scamper around in the trees like monkeys and pick the fruit. We could eat all we wanted, as long as we didn't get sick. We looked forward to that all summer. Almost all of the neighborhood kids would take part in that activity, going from yard to yard, picking the fruit for the women to wash, prepare, and can. But we usually stayed on our block.

There was always something tied to one of the trees to swing on. It might be a wooden swing, a rope with an old tire tied to it, or just a big long rope. I loved to pretend that I was Tarzan, swinging through the trees. I learned his loud call and probably drove the neighbors crazy who had to listen to it endlessly. But I was never silenced. The neighbors must have known that I was only having fun and approved of what I was

47

doing. The trees were usually not big enough to make a tree house, but we were content just to climb around in them and sit on the branches.

One time, my dad let us put up a trapeze between the clothesline poles, to use in one of the many circuses we used to put on in our back yard. We also put on plays there. We would invite the whole neighborhood to come and see our productions and charged a few pennies for admission. The neighbors loved our shows and they were cheaper than going to the movies. We also sold them popcorn and lemonade or Kool-Aid.

I also put up a pup tent now and then, or put large blankets and sheets over the clotheslines to sleep out overnight. We did that a lot, too, as the weather and mosquitoes would allow. In the next story, I tell about digging holes in the ground and eating in those holes.

But, there were limits to what we were permitted to do. And our moms and dads were very strict about some things.

We were not allowed to make fires or cook outside. When there was a fry out, my dad made the fires and did the cooking. We were also not allowed to make any bonfires, play with matches, or use candles in the shed or the garage. We did that once, but got in trouble.....so never again.

Our parents were happy when we played in our yards because they could always see us and what we were doing. They especially liked to have us in our yards after dark, rather than playing in the streets and alleys. Those yards kept them from worrying about us or wondering if we were getting into some kind of trouble.

Another benefit that our parents appreciated was that none of the things we did in our backyards cost anything. So, you can see that we didn't have to go far to entertain ourselves and have fun in those days.

Things Taste Better When Eaten Underground

When I was a boy, I liked to dig holes and make tents.

I am sure not all boys did what I did. In fact, I may have been the only boy in Sheboygan who did such a silly thing. I am sure you can understand why a boy might want to put up a tent and sleep in it. We did that all of the time when I was a Boy Scout. But when it comes to digging holes in the ground, you would first think of some animal doing that.

Don't ask me why I did it. I just did!

I used to dig holes all over our yard; little ones, medium-sized ones, and big ones. Sometimes I would put water in them and make them into lakes. I would make little boats and sail them. Sometimes I would put animals or critters in them and watch them crawl or fly out. Sometimes I would make rivers that ran a long way through the yard, and I would make rafts of popsicle sticks and float them down my rivers. My father said I could dig holes in the yard if I always covered them up again before I left the yard or at the end of the day, and as long as I didn't dig them in the grass or in the garden.

The tents I made were fashioned from all kinds of things; old sheets, blankets, or pieces of canvas that I found in the yard or garage. This was before nylon was invented. Sometimes I would put the material over my mother's wash line and stake them down. Sometimes I would hang them from a tree. Later, when I became a Boy Scout, I had my own pup tent. It was a used one, but it served its purpose. I used to put it up in my backyard and sleep in it overnight. I also remember the early days when I was in the Army and on bivouac and had to sleep in tents.... and I loved it!

When I was a kid, my real genius was putting these two passions together. When it got real hot outside, I would dig a deep hole and then put a small tent over it. It was nice and cool underground and the tent kept out the sun.

49

Then I would make a little seat inside so I could sit in my hole. Sometimes I would read down there, or just sit there and think. But when lunchtime came I would often ask my mother if I could eat my lunch in my hole in the ground. She probably wondered about my sanity, but always let me do it. I was convinced that my lunch always tasted better when I ate it underground. But I never found anyone who agreed with me or would join me.

Why did I do this? I don't know. Why do kids do any of the silly things they do? And why do their mothers let them?

Of course, there were rules for this activity, too. By the time my dad was ready to go off to work at night, the tents had to come down and the hole had to be filled up and covered. He would let me keep my pup tent up because according to him a pup tent was a real tent.

And, of course, no food could ever be left in the hole. That might have attracted undesirable animals like rats, mice, gophers, stray dogs or cats, rabbits, or bugs. Any leftovers had to be wrapped up and put in the garbage. The next day I could dig holes again and put tents over them if I wanted to.

Doing this might have been silly. But it sure was fun!

The Shed

We just called it "the shed."

What else would you call it? It wasn't the garage. That was next to the shed and the place where Dad kept his car. It wasn't the house. That is where we lived and was at the other end of the lot. It was just the shed, one of three buildings on our lot on Swift Avenue. It was a storage shed where my dad kept things like his lawn mower, rakes and shovels, hoses, and things he used when he worked and did his chores outside. His other tools and supplies were in a corner of the basement in the house, in and near his workbench.

But to us kids, that shed was not just a place to store things, it was a place to do interesting and exciting things in. It was one of our favorite places to play.

Sometimes the shed became a cave, where pirates came to bury their loot. Other times it was a robbers' den, where thieves came to hide from the law. At times, the shed was made into a theater, where we showed the "Coming Attraction" trailers that Uncle Gilbert spliced together into a big reel that we then played for the kids of the neighborhood over and over. (For those showings, we charged a penny or two.)

The shed sometimes served as the dressing room for those who performed in our circuses and shows, or the actual theater or playhouse where our parents came to see the plays we wrote and performed. It wasn't roomy and it was often very hot and stuffy, but somehow we packed them in. (Those performances might have cost a nickel.)

Sometimes the shed became a store, where we sold things or swapped things, like Lucky Bucks, pins, books, stamps, or baseball cards. On hot summer days, it might become our lemonade stand. And, of course, at one time a part of it was used as the inside hutch for my rabbit. The shed might have been more accurately called "the playroom," because that is what it was used for most of the time. As long as I live, I will never forget our shed.

Usually the shed was just a nice safe and handy place for me and the neighborhood kids to play in and climb on. But, at times, it could be the source of trouble, like when we jumped off the roof and could have broken an arm or leg. We were constantly told "not to do that," but we always did.

It was also the place where the incident happened that made my Dad madder than I had ever seen him.

Like all kids, we experimented with things that were taboo, things we were not supposed to do. Sometimes the older boys would bring those little comic books with dirty pictures or the National Graphic Magazines that showed African women in their scanty native garb. On those occasions, we would close the door, light a candle (something else we were not supposed to do), and look wide-eyed at this "forbidden fruit." Someone would be posted at the door and would call out if any girls or our parents came into sight.

And, of course, like all boys, we tried smoking or got a little taste of alcohol one of the boys had filched from home. We thought we were pretty clever and that we were getting away with something, but our parents always knew what we were doing, or soon found out.

This time, no one had any real cigarettes or corn silk, so we were lighting and smoking rolled up pieces of paper. For some reason, our guard did not see my father coming. He might have been coming out to the shed to get a garden tool. He must have seen or smelled the smoke. He opened the door suddenly and we panicked.

When he saw what we were doing, he was furious. His face was red and he raised his voice to a roar. "What do you think you are doing in here?" he shouted. Everyone dashed out of the shed, scattered, and ran down the alley.....everyone but me. I was caught red handed, with a glowing piece of rolled up paper in my hand. I think this was the only time I can remember that my dad actually spanked me. He only had to do it once. It was a spanking I would never forget. And he warned, "If I ever see you doing that again, I will tear this shed down!" Then he disappeared.

He never mentioned the incident again and neither did I. And no one ever smoked in our shed again.

Many years later, when I was an adult, my mother told me that when he came back into the house he was laughing and said to her, "Mabel, those dumb kids thought I was mad at them because they were smoking. I wasn't. I was just afraid they were going to burn the shed down....and set the garage on fire.....WITH MY STUTZ IN IT!"

Going To The Dump

In Sheboygan, at the time I was a boy, if and when you made a mess, you had to clean it up and dispose of it yourself. What you did when the garbage cans got full was take everything to the dump, which in most cases was just down the street. If you were lucky and didn't have too heavy a load, you might even walk there.

This was before plastic bags were invented and big trucks came around every week or so to pick up your garbage and trash. It was before there was a formal process for recycling. It was simple then and certainly much cheaper. It was also dirty, unhealthy, and smelly. How we did this was a part of our culture, and why we did what we did was largely due to the Depression.

In those days, you did not dare waste anything. If you were a Lutheran or a Catholic, it would have been considered a sin. We Methodists were more practical. It was a good way to use or save some money. But all of us would have felt very guilty if we threw anything away that was still usable in some way. And even then, we hated to let anything go that someone else might find useful. Not too many good things ended up in the dump. Those things quickly found a new home.

Clothing items were handed down from one child to the next in the family or they might be given to relatives or friends for their kids. This was before Goodwill came into being and before the Salvation Army and Thrift stores had their collection points and sales outlets. Rarely would younger children ever get anything new, except as gifts for birthdays, at Christmas, or for the first day of a new school year (we didn't follow that custom in our family.....at our house there were some hand-me-downs, if they were still in good condition and still in style but, at times, everyone got something new.) Being an only child, and a boy, I had no one to get clothes from or to give mine to. Two of my cousins were girls, and my boy cousin, Dick, was always taller and bigger than I was and never fit into any of my clothes. That meant that I had a small wardrobe and had to use everything myself. But that was okay with me. I wore everything until it was totally worn out and no good for anything but rags.

But, every year, usually in the fall I got a new pair of corduroy pants to wear to school and church and a new pair of overalls to wear at other times. Shoes and boots were made to last for years, as were mittens, scarves, jackets and coats, and swimming suits. When I got older, I may have gotten a pair of dress pants and a sweater for Christmas. One of the most exciting days of my life was the day I got my first long pants (not knickers), suit coat, and tie. I never wore a complete suit until I got out of the Army. If or when clothing items were torn or got holes in them, they would be sewed up or patched. Socks with holes in the toes were darned. Shoes and boots were taken to the shoe repairman, to be sewn up or to have new soles and heels put on them. Sometimes, to save a little money, we would go to the five and dime store and get rubber ones you could glue on yourself. They never held very well, but were good enough for old shoes that would have been thrown away anyhow.

The same was true of other things. Anything that could be was fixed by our dads or one of our uncles. For most things, all it took was a hammer, a saw, a screwdriver or a pliers, and some nails or screws, or a nut and bolt. I don't have to tell you that you can't do that any more. Things seem to be made to be unfixable. When motors began to be put on everything, they might have had to be taken to a local repairman. Electronics had not yet been invented. At our house, we fixed our own stuff. My dad was a great mechanic and could fix pretty much anything, if he could get the parts. I learned to fix things, too, like my bike. Then, whatever was left would be offered to the "sheeny," like rags and metal and things like cardboard or wooden boxes. If the sheeny turned it down, an item was useless and ready for the dump.

At every house, at the end of every lot, you would see at least two, and sometimes more, large metal cans with covers on them. We always had two. These were used to collect the things that were destined for the dump. Things were collected there until they were full. One of the cans was for ashes. At that time, everyone had coal-burning furnaces, which had to be constantly cleaned of their ashes. That was my dad's job. Every few days, he would sweep out the ashes that had accumulated below the fire grid and put them into a small bucket. Then he would build and start a new fire. It was an endless task, but one he didn't seem to mind doing. Those ashes would go into the big ash can at the end of our lot next to the garage. The other can was for garbage and trash. Preparing things to put in there was kind of an art. My mom and dad were masters at it. After every meal, after the dishes were washed (it would be a long time before the women would have dishwashers and garbage disposal units or even refrigerators or freezers), my mother would get a big sheet of old newspaper and carefully wrap all of the garbage in it. Actually, there was never much real garbage. Any left-over foods were eaten. So, garbage meant old bones and fat from meats, parts of fruits and vegetables that could not be eaten, and things that had started to spoil or had gotten rotten, things that even the dogs would not eat….the real smelly stuff. This was also before Scotch tape, so these little parcels were tightly wrapped and fastened with either a large rubber band or a piece of string. It was usually my job to take the garbage out to the can. Sometimes I had to hold my nose and chase away the flies.

My dad was in charge of making decisions about the other trash. He hated to throw anything away, but if something was broken beyond repair or he knew there was no longer any possible use for it, he would put it in the can with the garbage. This was before the word recycling was used, even though that is what we were doing….we invented it. But we did not save paper, magazines, or cardboard at that time. Most of it, we found uses for. I don't think the Boy Scouts were collecting old papers for their fund-raising projects yet back then. My dad would never throw away a good piece of wood, a nail, a screw, a nut or bolt, or anything he could use to repair something.

When everything was ready to take to the dump, we were on our way. You may believe this or not, but one of the most exciting things I did when I was a boy was going to the dump with my dad. In the division of labor in their marriage, that was my father's responsibility. He didn't seem to mind me helping him to do it. It was a good time for us to be together and he taught me a lot of valuable things on those trips.

Every town at that time, large or small, had to find open spaces somewhere for dumps. They did not have fancy names like "disposal centers" or "sanitary landfills" back then....you just said, "I am going to the dump" and everybody knew where you were going and what you were going to do there.

At least every week, and sometimes more often, my dad and I would go through our little ritual. We would go out to the end of our lot and empty the cans. We would put the ashes in some smaller bucket, put the garbage in another (or maybe a cardboard box), and the rest of the trash in something else. We would pack all of that in the car. We would usually take my red coaster wagon along, putting it in the back seat.

I don't know how many dumps there were in Sheboygan, because we always went to the same one. It was on a very large piece of land (that must have been owned by the city) in back of the Sheboygan Furniture Company and right down the hill from where my Uncle Gilbert and Aunt Myrtle lived on 13th Street. They were lucky. All they had to do was walk across the street to get rid of their stuff.

My Dad and I always lingered at the dump. I liked to watch the men who worked there. They were very systematic. As people came to the dump, they would inspect what they had brought and separate everything out and make them into big piles. All of the ashes went into one pile and the garbage in another. If we were lucky, we could watch them burn it, which produced a lot of smoke. Combined with the smoke from the many factories in that area, they must have produced tons of pollution in Sheboygan. Nobody worried about that back then.

Then, the other things were sorted out again. Wood went into one pile, metal in another, glass bottles and jars in another, etc. Those are the piles that fascinated my dad and was why we brought my wagon along. Sometimes we must have spent hours there. My dad would go from pile to pile, picking things up and looking at them, discarding most items, but putting a piece of something now and then in our wagon. There was no buying or selling at the dump. Anyone who wanted to claim something and take it home was welcome to do so. My dad was a real scavenger. He sometimes took more junk home than we brought!

When I asked my Dad why he was taking something (it all looked like useless junk to me), he would say, "I think I can find a use for that," or "That might come in handy some day." I remember that when he died and I had to settle things for my mother, I had to dispose of not only his tools, but all of the junk that had accumulated over the years that he had never found any use for. Where did this stuff that nobody wanted finally go? Back to the dump, for someone like my dad to pick up and take home.

It was quite a process, and like everything else that we did in Sheboygan at that time, it was very effective, very efficient, and very cheap. And besides that, it was a whole lot of fun.

I wish we still had dumps. And I wonder sometimes, how do fathers these days teach their boys how to be responsible husbands, fathers, and workers if they can't go to the dump together?

Player Pianos

There wasn't any television yet, and radios had just been invented and were still not as clear of static as radios are now. We did have phonographs, the ones you wound up and that sounded scratchy. It would be many years before long-play records, cassette tapes, videos, and CD's would become common ways to hear music. When I was a boy, recorded music was best played and heard on the "new invention," the player piano.

At first, they were very expensive. We didn't have one at our house, but my grandmother had one. Before her investments went bad and she still had a lot of money, Grandma Huebner bought a big, beautiful, brand new upright piano with the player attachment in it. None of us played the piano, but we loved to get around her piano, put on those long rolls with holes in them and sing together. My cousins and I would take turns pumping it, something we loved to do. It didn't sound like an organ; it sounded a little more like a harpsichord. It must have been the forerunner of the present synthesizers.

I don't remember how player pianos worked, but they were mechanical wonders. Somehow musicians punched holes in those white rolls, and when they went over that gold grid, they made sounds like an orchestra playing. I remember that the sounds were a little tinny, like the music you heard on the merry-go-rounds that were popular at that time. I think they worked on the same principle. But no one cared. We thought they were great. We knew most of the melodies of the songs that were recorded, and the words were also written on the rolls in case we forgot them.

Singing around that player piano was quite a pleasant way to spend a few hours, after a meal at Grandma's house. It beat listening to the men argue in the living room. Sometimes they grumbled when we sang too loud. It was also better than listening to the women chattering in the kitchen. Once Grandma got the piano, we noticed they cleaned up the kitchen faster so they could join in the singing. We kids loved the player piano because it was more than a toy, it was a real musical instrument.

Along with beer and bratwurst, the player piano brought families together, because it was something that people of all ages could participate in and enjoy at the same time. And it didn't require any musical talent. Anyone could quickly learn how to play the player piano. All you had to do was put the rolls on, set a few keys, and pump, and you could make delightful music. As usual, the kids got the hang of it before the adults did.

Because we all gathered at Grandma Huebner's house often, that player piano got a lot of use. I don't know what happened to it when she died. I hope someone inherited it who fully appreciated it, took good care of it, and played it often. Maybe one of the great or great-great grandchildren has it now. But have never seen it since I go

Long Rides

One of the few good things about the depression was that gas was cheap. If you could afford a car (even if it was a cheap used one) and you didn't have anything else to do, you could always go out for a ride. My dad never bought a new car, but in my lifetime in Sheboygan, he had several used ones, always in good condition. My Uncle Gilbert always bought new and bigger cars and traded them in every few years. Outside of the Stutz my dad once had, we liked riding in Uncle Gilbert's cars better.

We boys, who spent half of our lives riding our bikes, considered it a big treat when we could ride in a car. All the adults would have to say was "ride" and we were out the door and in the car before they could get there. It was a thrill to be able to ride in a car...any car. We looked forward to the time when we would own and enjoy our own, something I didn't do until I was 30 years old.

There were two kinds of rides that I remember most - those long rides up to the North Side with my Uncle Gilbert, and those Sunday afternoon rides with the guys. One we had to pay for; the other we got free.

It would happen something like this. It had been a hot day and everyone welcomed the cool breezes that had come up after the sun went down. We would be sitting on the front porch after supper, just talking or listening to night sounds, or playing a game or telling stories.

All of a sudden, Uncle Gilbert would drive up, park at the curb, and call out, "Anyone want to go for a ride?" Hardly ever did anyone say no.

We would all pile into Uncle Gilbert's car and off we would go. We all knew where we would be going, because we had gone the same route hundreds of times. Uncle Gilbert liked to look at the houses on the North Side and ride along the lake from one end of town to the other. If we were lucky, we might stop on the way and Uncle Gilbert would treat us to an ice cream cone or a root beer. We never got tired of going on those rides with him. Maybe this is why we got to know every inch of Sheboygan by the time we were in junior high.

And then there was the other kind of ride.

One of the boys in our class had a car because his father was a farmer and they needed cars to drive into town. One of our older friends also had a car because his father owned a garage and always made one available to him. Both of them were good drivers, but not always as safe and careful as they should be.

I don't think anyone bothered about driver's licenses in those days, at least not when it came to farm kids. Donny had been driving tractors and cars since he was a little kid. Brad, being a little older, had one of his own. These cars were not new or fancy, but they got us to where we wanted to go. And we loved to ride. We didn't care where we went.

On Sunday afternoon, things were pretty dull in Sheboygan, so whenever either of these boys invited us to go out riding, we accepted. But first, we would all chip in some money - nickels, dimes, and sometimes quarters - until we had about a dollar. That was enough for a tank full of gas and we could ride on that all afternoon.

Sometimes we would ride out in the country, often stopping at a lake for a short swim. Other times, we would check out the parks around town to see if there was any action. We might go down to the waterfront and watch the sailboats and wish we were old enough to be sailors and work on one of the coal boats. And now and then, we would go as far as Plymouth, which was about 20 miles from Sheboygan. We liked to shut off our engine and glide down that long hill into town.

I don't remember if we ever took any girls on those rides, but I doubt it. At least not then. This was a guy thing. Their constant giggling annoyed us, they worried about their hair blowing around, they were always flirting, and they were a nuisance and generally got in the way. Riding with girls (or parking with them) was to come later, usually when we got our own cars or went double dating with friends who had one. For now, we were just content to ride with our buddies, any time and anywhere. These days we call that "male bonding."

Boys like cars, and we were boys. Whether they were our cars or someone else's, it didn't matter. We just liked to ride, as far and as long as we could.

I still like to ride, though I must admit I didn't always enjoy those long rides we took on our vacations, on hot and muggy days in the summer, with our five kids.....who were all girls!

School Days, School Days

There was a song we used to sing. If you grew up when I did, then you may remember it....

"School days, school days,
    dear old golden rule days.
Reading and writing and 'rithmetic,
    taught to the tune of a hickory stick.
You were my queen in calico,
    I was your bashful, barefoot beau.
When you wrote on my slate, I love you so,
    when we were a couple of kids."

What wonderful days those were, going to school back in the 20's, 30's, and 40's in Sheboygan, Wisconsin.

In the next stories, I will try to describe just a few of things I remember about those "good old days" when I was one of those "bashful, barefoot" kids.

Sneaking Into The Movies

I was lucky. My father was an engineer and one of my uncles was a movie projectionist. I got to see all of the engine rooms in town with my dad and got into movies free, if I would do it in Uncle Gilbert's way.

Every Saturday afternoon, at the Rex Theater where Uncle Gilbert worked, they had an episode of those wonderful 12-part serials, cartoons, and double features. It was a whole afternoon of non-stop entertainment. My cousin, Dick, and I saw them all, because my uncle sneaked us in.

This is how it worked. We would go early with him and he would take us up to the last seats in the balcony right next to the projection booth. It was about a half-hour or 45 minutes before the show was scheduled to start. We would sit there as quiet as mice, in the pitch dark, until the people who had paid the 10 cents for their tickets came in. Then we would work our way down into the first row seats in the balcony. We liked to see the movies from up there rather than from the ground floor.

If we got brave, we would sneak down to the candy booth before the show started and spend the nickel or dime we had brought to buy candy or popcorn.

It was very exciting to do it that way. The whole thing would have been spoiled if we had bought a ticket. This way, we thought we were pretty hot stuff, putting something over on the Manager, who was paying Uncle Gilbert's salary and getting cheated. Of course, the adults knew what was going on and probably had some good laughs over our ignorance and innocence.

On Saturday afternoons, the movie theaters in town would usually show Westerns to attract the kids, at least one and sometimes two. If you have seen one Western of that vintage you have seen them all, but we loved them. Our heroes then were Tom Mix, Hoppalong Cassidy, and later, the Lone Ranger. We didn't care much for the cowboys who sang. We came to see the cowboys shoot the bad guys and the Indians with their guns.

There would also be another episode of the current serial, always ending with a "cliff-hanger." In the very last episode, the hero usually killed all the bad guys and there was a "happy ending." But cowboys didn't "get the girl." They liked their horses better.

The serial Dick and I liked best was Flash Gordon. But there were lots of others, about guys like Tarzan who lived in jungles, detectives and crooks, cowboys and Indians, and sometimes a woman who got into all kinds of trouble. They were kind of copied from the comic books that were also popular at that time. The adults would laugh at us when we predicted that some day men would fly around in space and maybe even get to the moon. We were sure someone like Flash Gordon would eventually do that.

We liked almost every kind of movie, except the ones that had a lot of kissing in them (until later, when we were older and we would come to the movies to do our own kissing.)

I have wonderful memories of those great Saturday afternoons.... even if I did cheat a bit to get them.

Boy Scouts

After I retired from the active ministry and began attending the services at my church as a layperson, I developed a habit pattern that I still continue to this day. I arrive a little early, get a bulletin from an usher, sit down in the pew, and see what is going to happen that day. I want some time to get myself physically and mentally prepared for the service I am about to take part in. I want to know the theme for the day - the hymns we are going to sing, the Scripture passages that will be read, and what the minister will be preaching about. I might also read the printed announcements and say a prayer or two.

On this particular Sunday not long ago, as I came up the steps into the Narthex, I knew immediately that this was not going to be just an ordinary Sunday. The Narthex was filled with fine-looking young boys, all in uniform. Their shoes looked shined and their hair was combed. I knew something special was going to happen this Sunday because these same boys did not ordinarily look this way. Even before I had a chance to be handed a bulletin, I knew it was going to be BOY SCOUT SUNDAY...something our church always observes every year.

The boys were from our church's Cub and Scout troops. The greeters and ushers were Boy Scouts, and later, Boy Scouts would serve as readers in the service, take the offering, and lead other parts of the service. We had been invaded by Boy Scouts! That was okay with me. I like Boy Scouts. They are good kids and do good things.

As I sat there, my mind wandered back many years to the time when I, myself, was a Boy Scout in Sheboygan. Everything in the service that day reminded me of something I had done or experienced when I was a boy. I loved being a Scout and being one did a lot for me. I relived a little of that time in my life.

The first thing that caught my eye was the cover of the bulletin. Right in the middle of it was a Boy Scout First Class pin, like the one I used to wear so proudly on my uniform when I was a Scout. Above it was this quotation: "The purpose of the Boy Scouts of America,

Incorporated on February 8th, 1910, and Chartered by Congress in 1916, is to provide an educational program for boys and young adults, to build character, to train in the responsibilities of participating citizenship, and to develop personal fitness." A noble goal and purpose.

Then, when I saw those little Cub Scouts in their blue and yellow uniforms, I thought about going to my first Cub Pack meeting, filled with both anxiety and anticipation. I joined as soon as I was old enough to qualify and spent several happy years as a Cub Scout. I waited impatiently to move up into the Boy Scout program, which happened when I was in sixth grade. Later I was a Pack Leader, myself.

My friends at church (which was on the North Side) really put the pressure on me to join their troop. They said it was "much better than that troop on the South Side." In a way, they were right. The church troop had much better equipment, everything was always purchased brand new and in excellent condition, and anything the Scoutmaster asked for, he got. The South Side troop had to make do with things that were often second-hand, patched up and repaired, or made from scratch.

The parents of the boys in the church troop always bought them new uniforms and all the personal equipment they wanted and needed, like knives, compasses, rain gear, hatchets, backpacks, canteens, etc. The boys in the other troop put their uniforms together with pieces from their older brothers and friends. They shared the other necessary items they had all gone out and gathered and belonged to the whole troop.

When the troops went on overnights or to regional camp outs, the church troop had good pup tents and cots, full supplies of cooking utensils and food, the best equipment money could buy, and a special vehicle to haul it in, with their troop name and number printed on the side. The other troop slept all together, side by side, under a huge piece of canvas stretched over a pole. Their equipment was always inadequate and there was no fancy vehicle...their parents had to bring the equipment and them in cars.

I was torn. There were some obvious advantages to joining the church troop, and my friends in my Sunday School class were quick to point them out. I felt honored and pleased to be asked, but I didn't like being pressured and I didn't like their condescending attitudes toward the other troop. That didn't seem "Scout-like" to me. I made my choice and I was never sorry.

I think I joined the troop on the South Side for two reasons. First, it was close to home and my school classmates, who were my buddies, were in it. They wanted me in their troop. And second, I was told that they had "the Best Scout Master in the Council." That turned out to be true. He was!

He was a very unusual and talented man, and he really cared about boys. Of all of the persons who I consider my early mentors and models, I think he stands head and shoulders above all the rest. I think that besides my father and Rev. Jones, he was the most influential man in my life.

He was a man who lived and worked in our community and for the community, and he possessed an amazing collection of practical skills that he tried very hard to teach to us. He taught us how to cook outdoors and how to use tools and equipment. He taught us how to use and maintain knives and hatchets, how to make fires in the rain, and survival skills. He taught us how to pitch and repair tents and live comfortably and dry outside. He took us on long hikes and showed us how to keep from getting blisters on our feet. He taught us how to take care of ourselves and about first aid and water safety. All of this became very useful when I later found myself on bivouac with the Army. Boy Scouts must have made good soldiers.

And he did more than just teach us the basics. He taught us to respect wildlife; plants, trees, and flowers, and birds, animals, and reptiles. We learned the names of them all. He took us out at night to see the stars and could recognize and name all of them. He was a student Indian culture. He taught us how to make Indian headdresses and Indian-style backpacks to carry our gear. He taught us Indian stories, songs and dances and Indian lore. He taught us how to use homemade bows and arrows and about gun safety. We came to have a deep appreciation for these great people who roamed our land a long time before our forefathers even thought of coming here to settle.

This man's talents and skills were endless. But he also taught us values, not in the way our teachers did, but in his own unique way, mostly by example. He showed us, and demonstrated for us, how to be a man....strong, mature, responsible, and committed to the best. We never heard him swear or tell off-color jokes, or say anything mean or nasty or critical about anyone. He had a deep faith, and he and his family went to church regularly. He modeled for us the things he was teaching. He lived what he was and we aspired to be. We all decided that we wanted to be like our Scoutmaster when we grew up. We even told him so, which seemed to please him. I am sure many of the boys in that troop became Scoutmasters themselves when they grew up.

There were many other men associated with the Boy Scouts that inspired us as well, sometimes in odd but important ways.

One of the benefits of belonging to a Boy Scout Troop in Sheboygan was that it was a part of the Kettle Moraine Council and that we got to go out to Camp Rokilio every summer. That's where we met this old man who seemed to be as much a part of the camp as the trees. No one ever knew how old he was, but someone once said he looked like "Father Time."

No one seemed to know his name. We just called him either "Skipper" or "Captain" because he always wore that fancy white Sea Captain's cap with all the Gold braid on it. He also often wore one of those blue pea coats that sailors wear.

We were never quite sure what his job was at camp and we never found out. We knew he wasn't one of the counselors and he wasn't a teacher, and he wasn't a cook or part of the crew on the waterfront. Actually, he didn't seem to do much of anything except hang around and amuse us kids, which was perfectly okay with us.

Skipper taught us to how to whittle, something my great-grandfather liked to do. In the process, he also instructed us how to handle, use, and care for a knife (I think he had some words of wisdom about using hatchets, too.) He always had pieces of wood around that we could practice on. He made some beautiful things himself, which means he was an expert wood carver and sculptor. And everything he made, he gave away.

He was also a great storyteller.

Sometimes we would see him on the front porch of the cabin where he stayed and we would run up, gather around him, and beg him to tell us adventure stories. We liked his sea stories the best. We would sit on the floor at his feet as he would tell us stories about things that had happened to him when he was working on ships and visiting countries all over the world. We got the impression that he had been everywhere. He told us how he began as an ordinary seaman when he was very young, and then worked his way up to First Mate, and finally the Captain of his own ship. He sure had some mighty good yarns to tell. He would tease us by saying that it was too bad that he could not tell us some of his "best stories," but that we were too young yet to hear those. He hinted that these stories had to do with such things as waterfront bars, fights, and "fallen women." We didn't know anything about any of these things yet, so we didn't care. We liked the ones he told us better anyhow. Some of the Captain's stories were hair-raising. Some were thrilling. Some were scary. And some were silly and funny. I doubt if any of them were true, but we loved to hear them and we wanted them to be.

But there was always an air of mystery about the old Captain. We could never quite figure him out or what he was doing at our camp. We wondered what he did all day, and why he seldom showed up at the campfires at night where stories are always told. We wondered why we seldom saw him in our camping areas, or on our hikes, or watching us when we played our games. We know he never slept in a tent. He always slept and napped in the Director's cabin. He was a real loner.

The best time to see old Skipper was at any mealtime. He liked to hang around the mess hall and used to con the cooks and bakers into giving him "samples." He loved to eat and hardly ever missed a meal. When he was not there to eat, we wondered where he was, and were afraid he might be sick. He seemed to have to "go to town" a lot, and "rest" a lot. But then, he was very old and he liked to smoke a pipe. So he might have had to go to town regularly to get his supply of tobacco or some medicine for his cough.

When we did see him in the dining hall, we would pester him until he would go to the piano to play for us, sing for us, and teach us songs. He was not the greatest piano player in the world, and I don't think he could read music, but he didn't have to just to play and sing his silly songs. I remember the eating songs he taught us about the "peas, green beans, and barley grow," and about "all you hungry campers we wish the same to you." But our very favorite song was, "When I Smoked My First Cigar." We made him sing that over and over and over, and we learned all of the words. We never got tired of hearing that song. He warned us not to sing it when we went back home.

The Skipper would eat his meals and then quickly disappear. He would come early for his coffee and breakfast, come back for lunch, and then appear again for supper. And then, we wouldn't see him again until next morning at breakfast. The old man was a lot of fun but he was very illusive. He didn't seem to have any regular duties or keep any regular hours like the rest of us did.

But we never saw him anywhere near the boats or on the waterfront. Never once did anyone ever see the Skipper out sailing. That seemed strange. We wondered why. Wasn't that the most logical place for a Sea Captain to be? I guess it didn't matter. He was a character, and we learned a lot from him.

Anyway, back to that Sunday Service. The most impressive part of the service that day at my church was when all of the Scouts (or anyone who had every been one) were invited to stand and repeat the Scout Oath and the Scout Law. I was surprised that I still knew them both by heart....

"On my honor, I will do my best, to do my duty, to God and my country, and to obey the Scout Law; to help other people at all times, to keep myself physically strong, mentally awake, and morally straight." And then, "A Scout is trustworthy, loyal, helpful, friendly, courteous, kind, obedient, cheerful, thrifty, brave, clean, and reverent." I wondered. Have I lived up to those ideals and principles in my life?

The Sermon was also a challenge, for it was entitled, "Rooted In Values That Last." It was short, to the point, and said in simple language that every boy in the room would understand. It sounded just like the talks that our Scoutmaster in Sheboygan used to give us. I am sure that the values I was taught as a Scout when I was a boy have lasted, and I know I have tried to live up to them to the best of my ability. Whether I have succeeded or not is for others to say. But, as I left the church to go to my car that day, I knew in my heart that I would never have become the man I became if I had not been a Boy Scout in Sheboygan. I might have been okay if I had not been one and I might have been just as successful in the things I attempted to do.

But I am also sure that being a Boy Scout made a difference and enabled me to become a better person than I would have been if I had not been a Scout.

And for that, I am grateful.

The Circus Comes To Town

We were there by 4:00 in the morning. We wanted to be sure we got there before the train arrived. The big circuses had their own special trains, with their names printed on all of the fancy, brightly-colored cars they hauled and the wagons they carried.

When they rolled into town as the sun was coming up, it was a sight to behold. The Ringling Brothers Barnum and Bailey Circus train was the biggest and the best. It was always painted bright red, with lots of green and yellow and other bright colors. Most of the lettering and trim was in gold. Arrangements were made in advance for those trains so they could leave the main tracks as they came into town and park on a special siding reserved for them for the day. The train must have stretched for miles.

Watching the circus train come in and unload was almost as exciting as the performances later in the day. That's why we came to the siding so early, to watch the start of what turned out to be a whole day of activity and entertainment. The first three parts of this show - the unloading, the setting up, and the noon parade - were free. You had to buy tickets for the rest. At that time, the tickets were more expensive than the movies, but cheaper that going to an opera or the Symphony Orchestra. We saved our money for a long time so we could go.

The traveling circuses had to be self-contained and highly mobile communities, providing everything the performers and workers needed to travel in comfort on the road; transportation from town to town, living quarters and sleeping accommodations, and meals. They also needed places to go to relax, to rest, and to dress and prepare for their parts in the shows. Whoever dreamed up and figured out the logistics for all of this was a genius. In one day, everything had to be unloaded from the train, unpacked and set up, and then taken down and packed up again, and loaded back on the train. In between, there were two performances in the Big Top - a matinee in the afternoon and a show at night - and performances all afternoon and evening in the Side Show. It took a lot of organization to put that all together and have it run smoothly.

Everything was done so efficiently. There must have been hundreds of people involved and as many animals. And there must have been tons of equipment, including all of the canvas for the huge Big Top. Then there was the Side Show tent, the Mess Tent, and lots of smaller tents for other things. This is not to mention the thousands of boxes, trunks, and cases that held the costumes, the props, the band instruments, and the food, drinks, and supplies for the refreshment stands and the mess. All of these things had to be packed neatly in countless numbers of individual wagons and cages that had to be unloaded off the train and hauled to the grounds where the circus was set up and back again.

Just think of it. What coordination! What skill! Everyone had to be at the right place at the right time doing what only they could do, putting everything in its exact place to be close and handy to where it was needed and used. And it was all done in a few short hours every morning, in a different city and at a different location. And it had to be done in all kinds of weather, rain or shine. AMAZING! I never got over being awed by the whole process.

When the circus was all set up, it was literally a small tent city, a city on wheels that traveled all over the country, playing one town at a time every day it was on the road. Circuses were really something unique and special. If you have never seen the circus come to town, you have missed one of the real wonders of the world.

Let me lead you through the process as though you were seeing it for the first time through the eyes of a young boy watching it unfold.

As soon as the circus train was settled on the siding, the elephants appeared, ready to pull the circus wagons off the flatcars. Then the teams of horses appeared. They were hitched to the wagons as soon as they reached the ground and off they went. Every time I see those Clydesdale horses pull those Budweiser wagons, I think of the circus.... only in the circus, there would be more than a hundred of those wagons for the horses to pull. They really worked hard. It didn't take long to get all of the wagons off the train and on their way to the grounds where the circus was to set up.

Before I attempt to describe the next step in the process, I need to tell you why people in Sheboygan got so exited when a circus came to town. We were a CIRCUS TOWN because one of circuses at that time was owned by people in Sheboygan and some of our friends were in it. It was named the Sells Sterling Circus. Sheboygan was its home base, though it also had winter quarters in Florida. It traveled in the summer, mainly throughout the Midwestern states. It was not as big as the Ringling Brothers Barnum and Bailey circus, but it had three rings, a sideshow, lots of wild animals, a circus band, and most of the elements that the bigger circuses had. One of our classmates, Betty Heller, was a performer in that circus. Her father played the organ and calliope. Her mother was a performer and had some administrative duties. Betty and her mother rode on the heads of elephants in the Grand Parades. We all thought that was neat and considered Betty a star. We always thought she would end up in Hollywood, like Judy Garland did.

There were lots of smaller traveling circuses, like the Clyde Beatty Circus, that would also come to Sheboygan most every summer. Clyde Beatty was one of the better animal trainers who worked in a huge cage and made lions and tigers do tricks together. He had been in some of the best and larger circuses before he went out on his own. His was only a one-ring circus and was built around his unique talent.

But the circus I am telling about in this story was the largest and best circus at the time. When they made a movie about it, the advertisements said it was "The Greatest Show on Earth." I suppose it was. But back to the process.

Before everything got unloaded from the train, we kids were on our way and had arrived at the circus grounds to watch the roustabouts set up the tents. It was really something to see. The wagons with the tent supplies would always roll in first and would be quickly unpacked. It looked like an army getting ready for combat. The roustabouts would pull things out of the wagons and put them in their places; poles of all sizes, large metal spikes, lots of rope, and big bundles of canvas that got quickly rolled out in patterns on the ground. Somehow the poles found their way into holes in the canvas. The outer poles were raised up first and roped and spiked to the ground. It was fun to watch a small group of men make a circle around a spike and then, with large sledgehammers, take their turns alternately pounding them into the ground. Sometimes they would sing or chant as they did it. That might go on for an hour or so. Then, all of a sudden, the elephants would appear. Somehow they were attached to very long ropes all around the huge spread of canvas. When someone gave a signal, the trainers started to prod the elephants to move out, and the canvas slowly rose to the top of the tallest poles. There were large flags on the poles fluttering in the breeze. We loved to watch that part of the process. It was like magic. There it was, before our very eyes, THE BIG TOP! This is where the main show would be performed only a few hours from now. It was a spectacular sight and thrilling to watch it happen.

While this was going on, other roustabout crews were putting up all of the smaller tents and setting the animal cages and dressing room wagons in places where they would be close to the entrances and exits of the Big Top tent. Nothing was left to chance. Everything had its special place.

At first, when we were too little to do anything but watch, we would just wander around, trying to keep out of the way, and watch with fascination as all of this happened. When we got older, we would "sign on," which meant we would volunteer to work as helpers for the morning. We would never get the heavy and dangerous jobs, but we would carry water and food to the animals, carry messages or small objects, help in the mess tent, or even sometimes help to stretch out the canvas or carry small poles or spikes to where they were needed. But when the guys got hammering with those big sledgehammers, we got out of the way fast!

Whatever we were assigned to do, we happily did. I liked to work in the mess tent, watching the cooks and bakers prepare and serve the food. Because I was small and not as strong as the older boys, I could usually get that job if I asked for it. Everyone connected to the circus came to eat there and sometimes we would meet and get to talk to a performer or one of the clowns. We liked to watch the man who sliced the bread, using only a big sharp knife, but making every slice come out exactly the same.

For our efforts, we would get a free pass to the main performance in the afternoon. We didn't always get the best and most expensive seats, but it didn't matter. In a circus, you can see from anywhere. It was worth working for because the show was always great.

After the circus was up and running, we would go home to have some lunch and rest a little before going downtown to see the circus parade, which was always fun. We would follow it out to the grounds for the afternoon performance, getting there in time to get our seats.

If you have been to a circus (maybe many times) or you have seen one of those circus movies that were very popular at one time, then I don't need to describe the whole circus performance. Instead, I will just tell about the things that I enjoyed and that amused me the most.

I liked the Grand Parade, which was always the first act of the circus, when all of the performers paraded around the whole tent. It was so colorful and such a good introduction to the people we were going to see later on. The band would play a rousing processional march and the spotlights would shine on the persons who would turn out to be the stars of the show. I still play those marches in the Community Bands I play in now and, if I close my eyes, I can still see a grand circus parade pass by.

I liked to see the pretty girls in their sparkling costumes and fancy headdresses riding the elephants, and both men and women riding horses. I liked the gymnasts doing cartwheels and front and back flips.

And, of course, like everyone else, I loved the clowns. There were always lots of them and they made us laugh. Sometimes they would come up and shake hands with us or give us some little gift. If we could get a seat up front, we would take it, hoping some clown might come up a shake our hand.

And, I loved the circus bands. The big circuses would have a big band with many members and a conductor who always stood out in front. They always wore those fancy European-style uniforms, with lots of gold buttons and braid, and hats with plumes on them. I don't think the band ever stopped playing once the show began. It was non-stop music all the way, and those musicians had to be good. They had to play all kinds of music, some of it very hard. But most of the time, they played snappy fast tempo marches. The drummer never stopped playing. When he was not playing with the whole band, he was playing long drum rolls and lots of rim shots when some spectacular act was being performed, and then lots of cymbal crashes as the band played loud chords marking the end of one act and the transition into the next.

I have played with drummers who started out playing in circus bands and they are awesome. I used to dream about some day playing in a circus band myself, playing those marches of King and Fillmore and other composers who wrote music just for circus bands. John Philip Sousa never had a circus band but all of the circus bands played his most popular marches. I still have the joy of playing those circus marches in my Community Bands today. They are always played fast! Those circus drummers were something!

And there couldn't be a performance without the Ringmaster in his black pants, bright red coat, and tall black hat. He would stand in the center ring, blowing his whistle and announcing the acts in his deep bass voice. He was the Master of Ceremonies and did his job well. I decided early on that if I were a circus performer, I would want to be the Master of Ceremonies.......or a clown!

And what would a circus be without those wonderful funny clowns? All through the circus performances, they would come running out and around doing their funny things. They always made us laugh and they got lots of applause. Yes, I would have been happy being a clown, I think! (But it might have been harder than it looked, trying to be funny all the time.)

I also liked the animal acts and their trainers, because they always did things that we had never seen before. The bareback riders, the prancing and dancing horses, those vicious lions and tigers responding to the trainer with his chair and whip, were all exciting. And the elephants... all kids loved the elephants!

And, of course, we all liked the thrilling "death defying acts" - the high-wire walkers and the trapeze artists doing their tricks high above the ground. People used to say that their acts were breathtaking. We were glad there were usually nets to catch the performers if they would happen to fall...but they seldom did.

The whole performance lasted a long time and we always got our money's worth. We were always sorry when it ended. But, there was still more to see and do at the circus after the "Big Show" was over.

The big circuses always had a big Side Show, which was an extra attraction if you wanted to see it and had the money to afford it. They were weird, probably because they were meant to be. The whole point of the Side Show was to peak our curiosity by showing us strange people and things. They appealed to the more dark side of our nature by exposing us to "freaks" and "daring stunts." We never knew what was real and what was fake, and we really didn't care if we were being fooled. Some things were even horrifying and made us turn our eyes away. There was always a bearded lady. Sometimes she was also the fat lady, who was married to the tall skinny man. There was the man with alligator hide instead of skin, and the contortionist who could weave his arms and legs into a pretzel shape. There might be a man who sat on a board of nails or put big pins in his arms, legs, and face. There might be a sword swallower or a fire-eater, a half-man/half-woman, a baby born with two heads (not alive but in a bottle), or some Siamese Twins. Now and then, they would have a mermaid, or some strange animal, or a magician who did tricks. The first time we saw the show, we were captivated and stood or sat spellbound, but as time went on, we soon tired of the things we saw at the Side Show and stopped going. We spent our money on popcorn, peanuts, and cotton candy instead.

The circus and its wonders took up the whole afternoon, and until we got much older or became adults, we didn't come back at night. The circus didn't start to pack up until long after we had gone to bed. It had been a long day and we were tired. After all, we had been up since about 3:00 in the morning. As wonderful as the circus was, enough was enough.

When we got older and did come to watch the circus "tear down," we saw the whole process in reverse, except that we noticed that it took about a third as much time to tear things down and pack them up as it took to set them up. I suppose everyone connected with the circus was tired, too, and were anxious to get back on the train, get to bed, catch a few hours sleep, and roll on to the next town, where the whole thing would start all over again.

I don't remember ever going down to the siding late at night to watch them put the wagons back on the flatcars. When the big top came down, as far as we were concerned, the circus was over. We just watched the wagons leave the grounds and go off into the night. By the time we got up the next morning, if we had gone back to the siding to look where the circus had come in, we would have seen that the circus was gone, without any trace that it had ever been there.

Yes, circuses were amazing; fascinating, exciting, even thrilling at times. Because we enjoyed circuses so much, we were all very sad when, after the war, we heard that there had been a huge fire and the Big Top of the Ringling circus had burned to the ground. I think that happened somewhere in Pennsylvania. The owners decided that they would never perform in a tent again and gave up traveling by train. From then on, the circus performed only in large cities and only in auditoriums or arenas, like the Shrine Circus does now. I took my own kids to one of these circuses once and then stopped going. They did many of the same things as they did when the circus came to Sheboygan. And everything was done well. But it just wasn't the same, and it never will be, not for me.

I decided I would rather remember the circus as it used to be, the kind that I, like all boys at some time or another, wanted to run away to and join.

In a way, I wish I had. Just once!

Carnivals

The big news on TV during the week I am writing this is that, in spite of the hurricane that recently flooded and almost totally wiped out the whole great city of New Orleans, the folks who are left down there are getting ready for and intending to celebrate Mardi Gras this year, as usual. No one and nothing is going to rob these good people of their favorite season of pleasure, overindulgence, and mayhem. You can call it craziness or spirit….it is a little of both, and a whole lot more. Some of the good citizens down there may not yet have homes to live in, food to eat, or jobs to go to, and there are places where the power still has not been turned on. Some of the levees are still leaking and haven't been made ready for the next storm. But the natives down there are determined…it is CARNIVAL TIME!

And when Carnival time comes, everyone stops doing everything they are doing to celebrate and party. If tourists want to join them, they are welcome to come. But bring lots of money, leave your troubles and worries back home, shed all of your inhibitions, and be prepared to wallow in the fun. When it comes to celebrating the carnal side of our natures, no one does it better than the faithful down in New Orleans (except maybe the folks in Brazil).

Carnival is a long and honored tradition that goes back to the Middle Ages. It is really comes out of a religious celebration, in a way. It is the kick-off to Lent, which will eventually lead to Easter.

During the years I spent living in Duluth, Minnesota (as well as in Sheboygan, Wisconsin), the folks did not celebrate Mardi Gras (unless they were on their way to New Orleans.) We were up to our knees in snow, trying to keep from sliding and falling on the ice. Some of the natives were still out in their ice houses fishing or dashing around the countryside on their snowmobiles or skiing up at Spirit Mountain. Our churches had Lent, but the Chamber of Commerce did not sponsor Mardi Gras there like it did the "Christmas City of the North" parade (which was a time-honored tradition in Duluth). In Minnesota, we are

77

lucky if the snow is gone and the sun starts to shine again regularly by Easter morning.

But, because I am a true believer in the value of tradition, I am thinking about the annual visits of the carnivals that came to Sheboygan when I was a kid. They were not as big and gaudy as Mardi Gras, but they were what Webster defines them to be in his famous Dictionary, "traveling commercial entertainment with side shows, rides, and games." Even the most pious Lutherans and Catholics in town couldn't resist them and might even, in their weaker moments, have said they enjoyed them. We Methodists loved them. But they didn't come before Lent. They arrived about the middle of summer, sometime between our great traditional celebrations on the Fourth of July and Labor Day. If we thought the circuses were exciting, the traveling carnivals were even more so. Even if we knew we were being conned, we didn't care. They were fun!

Of course, like the casinos of today, the owners of the carnivals had only one thing in mind....their profits. They did everything they could think of to lure us to their glittery and noisy attractions, where we were teased and tempted to taste all of their offerings and indulge in them fully, leaving as much money behind as we had brought in our pockets and wallets that day.

Most of these carnivals lasted for about a week, and even the most conservative and prudish among us found some reason or excuse to go and check them out at least once before the carnival up and left town again. If nothing else worked, you could always say "I am taking the kids," who demanded to go and needed to be protected from the "evils" that might befall them there. You didn't let kids go alone to carnivals like you might a movie, because carnivals had a bad reputation with some local folks in the smaller towns in the Midwest, because the people who traveled with the carnivals (called "carnies") were known to drink a lot and get into all kinds of trouble. It was even rumored that young girls were not safe with the carny men. They were feared like the sex predators are now. Carnies were also known to cheat and sometimes steal.

After the carnival left, there were always wild rumors about the things they had done during their stay, things that it was later found out were done by our own citizens. Some ministers and priests would not let their members go to the carnival at all, and some church members would almost hide their family members until the carnivals left. Too bad! They didn't know what they were missing.

Actually, and in fact, going to carnivals was a harmless thing to do. I just have to say that I never got hurt in any way by going to them, and I had lots of fun at them. So did most of my friends. But then, at that time, I didn't know much about the sins of the flesh or overindulgence. I just did what came naturally, mostly the spending lots of my hard earning savings in one day on those thrilling rides. Essentially, like the fairs (county and state) that were also popular at the time, you could do four things at a carnival; gamble, go on the daring thrill rides, see the shows, and eat and drink lots of food. You were encouraged to do them all, but if you were a kid you could not do some of them. We thought that was unfair.

We kids liked to go on Saturdays best because that was "Kid's Day," when all of the rides and shows were a NICKEL. You might even have been able to get six ride tickets for a quarter, and a whole lot more for 50 cents or a dollar.

The old fashioned carnivals that came to Sheboygan were all the same, cleverly arranged to give you the maximum opportunities to be amused and entertained and to spend as much money as possible. They were always set up outside of town on some dusty and dirty large parcel of land, usually the same place where the circus had recently been. They didn't need grass and trees. It was always hot out there, because they usually came in the middle of July or early August.

I don't think the carnivals ever traveled by train and the carnies didn't travel together. They probably came in private cars and trucks. This was before the invention of those nice big motor homes or trailers traveling people use these days. When they got there, they would set up their tents, in back of the Midway, to live in, eat in, and do their personal things in during their stay. They often brought their families and kids along. It must have been miserably uncomfortable back then. But the people who traveled with carnivals were rough and tough survivors. They had to be. Many of them spent their entire lives on the road.

When you entered the Midway, as it was called, you walked through a large opening, or sometimes a fancy arch, with the name of the carnival on it. The word SHOWS was almost always in it. Everything was strategically placed on a long oblong strip. You could just walk around the whole oblong path to see and participate in everything that the carnival had to offer. You could spend a whole morning, afternoon or evening doing that just once. If you wanted to go around another time, you probably had to stay into the evening. That's when the teenagers and young adults liked to come with their dates. The Midway was pretty at night and was kind of romantic after dark.

First, you came to what were called "the games of chance" or "the games of skill." There were lots of them and all kinds. You could see the prizes on large shelves just waiting to be claimed. The carnies would yell at you as you went by, trying to convince you that it was "easy to win" and telling you how "wonderful" their prizes were. No one ever used the word "gambling." It didn't matter if you won anything (from the carnie's point of view), it was just a whole lot of fun trying. I still hear folks who go to the casinos or Las Vegas now say what the folks in Sheboygan said then, "I don't go to gamble, I just go to play the games and see the shows."

We kids just bypassed that whole section (we were not allowed to play the games unless we were with our parents or an older adult) and went right to the rides, which were clustered together in the whole middle section of the Midway. The carnival rides then were pretty tame compared to what they are now in the theme parks like Valleyfair, the Six Flags parks, or any modern State Fair, but we loved them, sometimes got dizzy and sick to our stomachs, and might have thrown up now and then. Human beings were not designed to go on such contraptions but seem to love to do it anyway. I guess risk is part of life. But most of those rides were perfectly safe. There seldom were any accidents.

The placement of those rides was cleverly done. First, there were those cute little rides for the younger and smaller kids. Usually they were nothing more than sitting in or on something and going around in circles. Parents of little kids were suckers for those things and left lots of money there early on. We passed those by. Then there might be a big Merry-Go-Round right in the center. Kids of all ages, and even adults, liked to go on those. There was a charm about them. They were colorful, the horses and other animals gently went up and down, and that funny circus music was always playing. Whenever I go to Como Park in St. Paul with my grandchildren, I always take them on the Merry-Go-Round they have there that has been preserved and is over 100 years old.

Toward the back of the ride area were the more daring and exciting rides. You had to be a certain age or height before you could even ride on them. Some of my favorites were the Tilt-a-Whirl, the Caterpillar, and my very favorite, the Whip! At the end of ride section, there would always be a big Ferris Wheel, the very favorite ride of everyone. You couldn't leave the carnival ground without having at least one ride on the Ferris Wheel. Young couples loved it because the boys could put their arms around the girls, to protect them when they pretended to be scared. You might even steal a kiss when your car was way up on top and no one could see you.

Then, last but hardly least, were the shows. They took up about a third of the grounds. There was something for everybody, but not everybody could go in all of them (namely us kids, who wanted to). We usually skipped the big sideshow (we called it the Freak Show). The circus sideshows were always bigger and better, and we got to feeling guilty when we stared at those poor creatures who couldn't help it that they were different and strange.

We kids enjoyed The House of Horrors, The House of Mirrors, and the animal shows. But we wondered why we were not allowed to come in and enjoy the shows with the prettiest girls and the best music. We could watch them outside when they performed on a big platform to tease people to come in. Why couldn't we come in and watch the whole show? We didn't really know what those shows were about…..we were too young at the time.

And then, somewhere in that section, was my very favorite attraction….the Penny Arcade. Since nothing in there was considered gambling, we could play in there to our heart's content. I used to stay there a long time and left a lot of my pennies. I got a big kick out of the movie machines, the ones where you cranked the lever around and watching the police chase the criminals, the cowboys shoot the Indians, people throwing pies at one another, and women in their underwear. These carnival arcades must have been the forerunners of the present Video Arcades the teenagers now love so much and spend so much time in and money on. The games in the penny arcades were all simple "games of skill," and, if you won, you could win some modest prize or a couple of free games. They were fun, but probably not worth the money we spent on them.

Later, when I got to be an adult, I would always stop at the Penny Arcade at the Minnesota State Fair. My daughters were not impressed and were not interested in going with me, but I had fun putting a lot of my pennies in those old machines. I was sad to learn that the arcade is no longer there. They replaced it with a Butterfly Museum. I love butterflies, but....it's not quite the same!

Scattered throughout the grounds were small stands where you could buy just about anything to eat or drink that was available at that time. Just like the State Fair now, people ate and drank their way through the Midway. I did too. I never liked cotton candy, but I loved Cracker Jacks, popcorn, peanuts, and anything with ice cream in it. I would usually put some money in my secret pocket to get a hamburger and some pop about lunch time, and maybe some lemonade, made with REAL lemons, throughout the day. And, of course, I would have several ice cream cones or bars. When my parents were with me, they would treat me to those things so I would have more nickels to spend on rides and other things.

And that was it. All of a sudden, you realized that you were back to the game tents again, only on the other side, and on your way out. You had made the full circle. The vendors on that side tried extra hard to get you to play their games, sometimes getting downright rude. It was their last chance for them to get the change you still had left in your pockets. And they usually succeeded. Most people left the carnival with empty pockets and wallets. But they didn't care. They had expected to spend all of the money they had brought. I was smart. I saved at least one last nickel for a final ice cream cone. My family and I almost always went to the carnival on Saturday. That way our money went farther. I would take my savings, maybe a dollar of more, and spend it all. I figured it was worth it for a full day of entertainment and fun.

People in Sheboygan, whether they would admit it or not, loved the Carnival as much as the people in New Orleans do, because they needed and wanted to take a break now and then from their daily routines. They were hard workers and needed time to relax and let loose a little. They didn't care if they got conned and wasted some of their hard earned cash. The carnivals that came to Sheboygan were fun and harmless.

I suppose there will always be carnivals of some sort or other, big and splashy ones like the Mardi Gras in New Orleans and Brazil or the modern State Fairs, and many fancy theme parks, like Disneyland in California or Disney World in Florida, Dollywood in Tennessee, or the Six Flags in various parts of the country. And I know there are still some of those very small ones that travel all over the country and now set up in the parking lots at the Malls or in community parks.

The carnivals traveling around today might be similar to the ones that came to Sheboygan when I was growing up, the ones we looked forward to with great expectation and enjoyed so much, but I am certain they are not the same. But that's okay. I am sure the kids now love their carnivals just as much as we did.

So, let's give a cheer for the carnivals!

May they long endure!

The Bread Board

Our first assignment in Shop was an easy one. Everyone was to make the same thing....a bread board. The shop teacher told exactly us how to do it. We were to find a piece of wood, of any size and shape, plane it until it was the thickness we wanted it to be, and then sand it to make it nice and smooth. I think we put something on it at the end to make it shiny and preserve the wood. I remember we were told "never to paint it."

No sweat. This was going to be a breeze. And it would make a nice Christmas present for our mothers. We all eagerly went to work.

I found my piece of wood. It was about 14" long and 7" wide. It was about 1" thick, but we were told by the teacher that the ideal bread board was about 3/4 of an inch. Some boys put a handle on theirs, but I decided not to. I just put a hole at the top so my mother could hang it up if she wanted to when she was not using it.

With a wood file, I could easily round the edges, which is what we were supposed to do first. Then, I measured it very carefully and marked it, and started to plane it. It looked so easy, but turned out to be a little tricky. I planed it and I planed it. Those curly pieces of wood flew everywhere. It was getting smooth, but when I measured it, it was always thicker (or thinner) on one side than it was on the other. So I planed some more. I planed and I planed and I measured and I measured. The board kept getting thinner but never came out even on all sides. It was 3/4 of an inch on one side, but a little more on the other, or less. It never was quite the same all over. I was coming very close to 1/2 of an inch in some places so I had to be careful.

I worked and worked, planed and planed, and measured and measured, but it never came out the way I wanted it to. I was getting discouraged and our teacher warned us to be very careful when it got close to the thickness we wanted. So I planed some more, though slower and more carefully. By the time the board was the same on all sides, it was down to about 1/4 of an inch, about a 1/2 inch thinner than I wanted it to be. But I decided to quit while I was ahead. I breathed a sigh of relief and quit that part of the project.

The sanding was easy. First we used rough sandpaper and then fine sandpaper, until it was very smooth. Finally, we put the finish on it and set it out to dry for a couple of days. The bread board was finished!

My first project in Shop was done and I took it home. I didn't really like what I had done, and I had to admit to myself that it did not come out the way I had hoped and expected it to. But our teacher seemed to be satisfied and told us we had all done a good job. He also said that we were now ready to move on to the next project, one a little harder and more complicated than the bread board had been. I was ready to move on.

A few weeks later, I took out the bread board and looked at it again, more carefully this time. It wasn't all that bad. And after all, it was the first time I had ever done something that involved the planning, the tools, and the skills like that. You can't be perfect the first time you do anything. I began to feel just a little twinge of pride. I had done it and I had done it all myself. That was something to be proud of.

I knew my mom would like it. Mothers are always proud of anything their children make for them, and usually say so. Whether they like it or not, or use it or not, they always show it to the other moms and brag about you. Yes, it was okay. I would give it to my mom for Christmas.

By the end of the semester, we had finished working with wood and had done a lot of neat projects using metal. The first project we did in metal was a sugar scoop out of a tin can. That turned out better than the bread board. We were told that the next semester, we would make things involving electricity.

As Christmas drew near, I wrapped the bread board and the sugar scoop up in colored paper and hid the package in my closet. On Christmas Eve day, I put it under the tree. When Mom opened it on Christmas Day, there were tears in her eyes. She seemed very pleased with my humble gifts and said so. I was very pleased, too.

I never saw her cut any bread on the bread board (she just hung it up in the kitchen), but she used that sugar scoop almost every day of her life. I remembered still seeing it in her kitchen when I got back from the Army years later. Then, probably in one of their many moves, they both disappeared.

When it came time to sign up for my classes for ninth grade, I did not choose to take another Shop course again. I signed up for the Typing class instead. In my heart of hearts, I knew that I was never going to make it as a carpenter or a cabinetmaker. I was not destined to be a man who made a living working with his hands. I was destined to get a job that was more mental than manual.

And that is what I did.

Shop Or Sewing,
Typing Or Printing

It didn't make any sense, and it wasn't fair. But that's the way it was then.

After all of those years of boys and girls being in the same classrooms, studying the same things, with the same teachers and in the same way, suddenly, when we got to Junior High School, the sexes got divided for some of the required courses.

Boys had to take Shop and girls had to take Sewing. Girls could not take Shop and boys could not take Sewing. Since Cooking was a part of the Sewing class boys didn't get to learn how to cook either, at least not in school. That was tough if you decided to remain a bachelor, unless you continued to live with your mother. And where did the guys who became cooks and chefs learn their art? On the other hand, girls didn't learn how to use tools and fix things, which might have come in handy if they didn't get married, became widows, or when their husbands all went off to fight the war. This kind of division of labor might have made sense when our grandparents first got off the boat and came to Sheboygan to live, but it ceased to make sense to our generation.

The next set of rules were just as silly. Only girls were allowed to take Typing in the ninth grade. Boys could take another semester of Printing or Shop (we all had to take Printing in the eighth grade, which was considered an advanced Shop course), but could not take Typing. Why not? I guess somebody thought that because most, if not all, secretaries at that time were women, boys did not need to know how to type. But what about guys like me who majored in Journalism in college? Did we have to go on typing with only two fingers, like reporters used to do, just because we were males? Why couldn't we use both hands? It was all pretty dumb when you think about it now.

But fortunately for us, when we got to be ninth graders, some smart person changed the rules. I think it was the Principal of my school (who was also the Orchestra Director) who allowed both boys and girls to take some of the classes.

For the first time, ninth grade boys were allowed to take Typing if they wanted to, instead of Printing or Shop. But there were still double standards, even under the new rules, which were only half fair. For example, girls still could not take Printing....and some of them might have. It would be a long time yet before students would really be treated as equals.

So, this left us boys with a hard choice. If we wanted to take Typing, we couldn't take Printing anymore, something we all really liked to do. I remembered that I agonized over this for a long time, but finally decided to take Typing. It was one of the smartest decisions I ever made in my life.

First of all, I became a very good typist, almost as good as the best girls. And I liked the course. The teacher was great! A lot of the guys laughed at me, but I didn't care. I was learning a new skill which was to benefit me for the rest of my life....though I didn't know it then.

As it turned out, I got to go to college after the war and ended finally ended up in Journalism School, where knowing how to type was as important as having computer skills is now. I typed all my papers in every class and I typed all of the copy I wrote for newspapers, magazines, and radio. Everything I handed in was neat and easy to read. I am sure I got a few A's instead of B's for that alone. I bought my own typewriter while I was at the University of Wisconsin, which I carried around everywhere for years. Now, of course, I use a computer, like all professional writers do. And they don't just teach typing anymore, they call it "keyboarding."

But I could have missed it! I have always been grateful that the schools in Sheboygan turned out to be a little more progressive than most schools were back then, and that I was at the right place at the right time when they changed the rules.

To tell the truth, I didn't really want to take that Typing class; I would have enjoyed taking Printing much more. But I did take it, and I am glad that I did. For some reason, I sensed that it was the smart thing to do. If I were a student today, I wouldn't have to make such a choice. I would start learning how to use a computer at a very young age.

I must admit that the way they did it in Sheboygan (until we got into the ninth grade) didn't make much sense and it wasn't fair. I am just glad the educators in Sheboygan came to their senses before it was too late for me.

Gym And Recess

Do schools still have gym classes? Do they still have recess? I hope so, because we always looked forward to those activities when I was a kid.

Kids can only sit so long and then they have to let off some steam. And it is not enough to train the mind, we also have to train and develop strong young bodies and well-rounded personalities. The educators in Sheboygan when I was growing up were smart; they made Gym and Recess important parts of every day. They made them part of the curriculum, just like the ancient Greeks did.

It didn't matter that those ugly gym suits were not attractive, that we did a lot of sweating and got smelly, or that we had to take lots of showers and got athlete's foot often. And it didn't matter that the boys were divided from the girls. Gym was fun! It was meant to be. That was the whole idea. We got to run around those big gyms, climb ladders and ropes, do chin-ups and push-ups, throw balls around, and do all kinds of crazy things with our bodies. But, we also learned a lot of good things, as well.

Gym was not for just the good athletes, it was for everybody, boys and girls alike. And it proved to be helpful to me when I got into the Army. I loved to do all of the physical things soldiers have to do. To me, it was very much like being back in Gym. I knew how to do all of the things we did on the obstacle courses already except, of course, crawling on our bellies in the mud, and getting shot at with live bullets.

You didn't have to be good at some sport and you didn't have to compete with the biggest and the best in your class. Everybody got to play. Everybody got to be on some team. And, in good weather, we got to go outside and everybody got to play the games, not just the good players. The goal was not to win, but to have fun and stay fit. That was fortunate for guys like me who were strong and agile, but very small and light. I could not compete in competitive sports. I was one of those who would have been left out if we hadn't had Gym. I would have missed a lot.

And Recess was even more fun. It was a time to do anything you wanted to do, with no direction or instruction or interference from adults. If you wanted to swing, you could swing. If you wanted to play marbles, you could play marbles. If you wanted to get up a quick game of ball, you could do that. If you wanted to jump, run around, stand on your head, just be silly or tease the girls (the ones who wanted to be teased), you could do those things, too. It was your time to do as you pleased.

Or, if you just wanted to sit quietly under a tree and do nothing, nobody would bother you. As long as you did not hurt anybody or get hurt yourself, the adults let you alone. It gave us great freedom and I am sure it was good for our health.

That's why I hope my grandchildren are still having Gym and they get some time every day to have Recess. Good grades, test scores, and good academic learning and achievement are all fine and good, but that is not all there is to life. Kids have to learn how to have fun, too, if they are to become mature, healthy adults some day.

Watching The World Series

When they say that baseball is "the Great American Sport," I have to agree. At least it was in Sheboygan.

I grew up playing baseball, watching baseball, and listening to baseball games on the radio. To us, baseball was just as necessary to our well being as eating, sleeping, and breathing. We did like basketball, football, and soccer, too, but not as much as baseball.

People in Sheboygan were crazy about baseball, especially my Uncle Bernard. When he was listening to the Chicago Cubs on the radio (which he did every chance he got), you didn't dare talk to him, bother him, or even come near him. He was in heaven. He got so engrossed in those games that he didn't even smoke or drink beer until the game was over.

There were several ways we enjoyed baseball. First of all, we played it.....usually on a vacant lot. Second, we went to see our semi-pro team play it.......at our very nice local ballpark. Third, we listened to it on the radio. There wasn't a Major League team in Milwaukee yet so we were all Cubs fans.

And then there was the WORLD SERIES. This was a long time before the Super Bowl football games, the Final Four basketball games or even the restored Olympics. The World Series was THE EVENT of the year. And it was a big deal! Everything stopped for those World Series games, even school.

Here's how it happened when I was a kid in Sheboygan.

When classes were dismissed to "see the game" (which were always played in the afternoon because they didn't have lights yet) we could either run home, if we lived close enough, and listen on our radios, or we could go out on the front lawn of the school and watch it across the street at the corner grocery store, which was a whole lot more fun.

The grocer always put up a huge board on top of his roof. Someone put numbers and images on it as the game progressed. He would also rig up some kind of loudspeaker to amplify the radio broadcast. We could not only hear the game, but see it as it progressed. We could see it on the makeshift field that was outlined on the board just as it was being played on the playing field at the ballpark. We could watch the batters go around the bases when they got a hit. And we could keep track of the strikes and balls, hits and runs, and write them down if we wanted to. There were big numbers put up on the board as the scores advanced. It was a crude forerunner of the fancy score boards we see at the ball parks these days.

It was the next best thing to being in the stands watching the game and it was really neat!

Most of us heard and watched the whole game and cheered and whistled and carried on just like fans in the stands do now. But it was all done in front of our school and it was free, thanks to our friendly grocer.

The only drawback was that, as now, it was usually the New York Yankees or Dodgers who most often played and won the series, instead of the Cubs. I guess some things don't change over time!

Bullies

Every school has its bullies. Even in Sheboygan we had them, and the one we had in our school was one of the worst. It took some time before he got tamed. I understand now why bullies do what they do, but we didn't then. We just thought they were nasty and mean, and we stayed as far away from them as we could.

Bullies are such a pain. They never pick on people their own size. They always pick on the little kids, who are younger, smaller, and weaker than they are. That's why they get away with the things they do.

Actually all bullies are cowards. They are afraid to take on the kids that are as big and strong as they are. Bullies are never fair. It is no wonder that the other kids never like bullies and won't have anything to do with them. Bullies must be very lonely. They don't have any friends, not even other bullies. And they know that if they play by the rules they will lose. So, they always play dirty so they can win.

We had this bully in our school and he tormented everyone, even the girls, which really was out of bounds. You could tease and pester the girls at that time, but were never allowed to abuse them in any way. But this bully never bothered me or the guys I hung out with, most of who were younger, smaller, and weaker than he was, because we had our friend, Wesley Jerving, to protect us. Wesley was just as big and strong as the bully was, so he never took Wesley on and he never teased or tormented any of his friends. If he had, Wesley would have taken care of him fast. He would have lost big time.

As the bully got older, he got worse and if he wasn't stopped, someone was going to get badly hurt.

Our third grade teacher, who was a kind, fair, and patient woman most of the time, could get tough when she had to. She had finally had it with the bully. She decided one day that enough was enough and decided to solve the problem once and for all.

She announced to the class that day that there was going to be a "contest" (which was actually a no-holds barred fight) between two of the members of our class at recess. We were all invited to attend. The winner would get a nice prize. We didn't know that she had set this up with Wesley, and he had agreed to be one of the "contestants." The other "contestant" was to be the bully, who was not terribly excited about doing this, but could hardly refuse. His reputation was on the line.

We all got excited when the bell rang for recess and we rushed out to the place where the event was to take place. The word had gotten around and kids from other classes joined us. We formed a big ring around the two boys to mark the boundaries. Our teacher loudly announced what the rules were to be and the two boys shook hands. That was the last time they did that.

Then, she blew a whistle and the contest began. We all cheered and yelled our heads off. The Principal and Assistant Principal must have heard it in their offices, but they were in on the plan and didn't move. They had had it with the bully, too.

At first, it was a fair fight. It started out with wrestling. The two boys rolled all over the ground and tried to pin each other down. But it soon turned into a more serious fight with bare fists. The bully, of course, was the first to break the rules of no kicking or biting or pulling of hair. He tried to do all three, and anything else he could think of to hurt Wesley. But Wesley was too fast and too good a fighter for him. He scarcely touched Wesley.

Wesley was the first to draw blood. He hit the bully hard on the nose and blood spurted out all over the place. And then Wesley hit him again and again. The bully kept bleeding as he got punched in the nose and face. He also got some good blows to his stomach, jaw, and head. He was a mess. Finally, Wesley punched him real hard in the stomach and knocked the wind out of him. The fight didn't take long. The bully fell to the ground and refused to get up. He had had enough and called it quits.

After counting loudly to ten, our teacher blew a whistle and the fight was over. We all went back to class. Wesley got the prize. The bully went to the nurse's office, where he didn't get much sympathy, but did get cleaned and bandaged up. She was sick of him, too.

The bully didn't come back to class for a couple of days. His mother wrote a note to the teacher saying that he was sick with the flu. When he did come back, he was very quiet and meek as a lamb. He apparently had learned his lesson. It was the last time that the bully ever bothered anyone in our school. He just sulked away when he saw anyone coming, and he sat alone anytime he was not in class and in his assigned seat. I almost felt sorry for him. The wind had been taken out of his sails.

When school started the next fall, he didn't show up the first day of class, or the second, or the third. When we asked about him, we were told that he was gone. His family had moved out of town. We didn't miss him, and there weren't any more bullies to take his place. I guess the word got around about the "contest," and about Wesley.

That was the end of bullying in our school. If there were fights, as there always are when boys reach puberty, they were fair and even matches between guys who wanted to fight it out. Those were played by the rules that the boys had made up themselves.

I suppose that schools still have bullies, but I wonder how many of them also have a Wesley?

Can Boys Be Cheerleaders?

One day, I read an article in a magazine called, "Can Boys Be Cheerleaders?" Apparently in some places, this is a very controversial issue and there are big debates going on about it. Of course, being from Sheboygan, I know that this is a silly question. I know the answer. Of course they can. Boys make good cheerleaders. I know....I was one.

Because I was always very small and couldn't compete well in physical sports, where big bodies and large muscles were required, I had to find other ways to make my mark. One of them was playing in the band. The other was cheerleading. In both cases, I got into all the games free.

I was always very peppy, full of energy, very agile, had a good loud voice, and commanded attention and respect from others. I think I was born to be an entertainer and a leader, and I made an ideal cheerleader.

It is true, I was not as cute as the girls on my squad, but the girls thought I was cool. Even the boys thought it was okay for me to do this and followed my directions. The guys on the team were glad to have us out there whipping up the crowd, cheering them on.

I was fortunate that my school allowed anyone, whether a boy or girl, to try out for and become a cheerleader. At that time, cheerleaders didn't just wave pom-poms and wiggle around. We really led cheers. We made most of them up ourselves. I suppose there was some kind of quiet and subtle sexism involved that we were not aware of. For some reason, few boys ever turned out for cheerleading. So the ones, like me, who did were always in the minority. We didn't mind, and neither did the girls. These girls also turned out to be the girls who liked to dance with us. We had rhythm.

At election time, all of the girls voted for me to be the Captain of our squad. The girls didn't seem to mind taking directions from me. Being a cheerleader gave me my first taste of teen popularity. I learned that the visible guy, the guy out front, got all of the attention....and the prettiest girls.

When I was in junior high, I led the cheering for the basketball and football games. In high school, I played in the band for those games so I did not join a cheerleading squad. The girls weren't happy about that. They said they missed me. And to tell the truth, I missed them, and the fun of leading the cheers. But, by that time, my passion was playing the drums.

Cheerleaders didn't wear skimpy outfits then. We wore nice slacks and neat letter sweaters. And we didn't do fancy tricks or dance around. We weren't there to entertain or put on a show. We were there to get the spectators to cheer their heads off for our team. And they did...... LOUDLY! We had those long funny horns to amplify our voices.

I can still remember how much fun it was getting out in front of the bleachers, urging the crowd on. We never sat down and we were never quiet and, at the end of the game, we were tired and sometimes hoarse. But it was a great ego trip, being out there in front and supporting our team. Sometimes we even went on a trip out of town with the team. Those were usually special games or to tournaments.

I am glad that our school in Sheboygan was ahead of its time and did not discriminate. I wanted to be a cheerleader, and it would have been hard to convince anyone that I was a girl.

Going To School All Summer

When school was over for the year and summer vacation began in early June, the country kids disappeared and went out to work on the farms. We city kids didn't see much of them, if at all, until school started again after Labor Day. We city kids were suddenly at loose ends and needed to find things to do.

So, to keep us city kids busy and out of trouble, some wise adults (either from the recreation department or the schools) organized and conducted summer programs at the schools around town. It is hard to explain or describe what this was like because it wasn't a summer school as such. We didn't have to come to class, take tests or get any grades, and we didn't have to come if we didn't want to. But it wasn't just idle play either. We learned how to do lots of things we wouldn't have learned how to do otherwise. And it wasn't like recess; things didn't just happen. It was all planned and carried out in a very orderly and efficient way.

There were always lots of adults (some teachers and lots of college kids that got hired for the summer) helping us kids have a good time. The kids who didn't come were really missing something.

Most of these planned activities happened in the mornings, before it got too hot and muggy. In the afternoon, most everyone wanted to be at the beaches or in the parks. Now and then, there might have been a field trip to some place in the afternoon or a program or activity at night. But, the "playground programs" usually shut down about noon and we went home for lunch. I don't remember if this program lasted all summer or only until August. Regular school started again right after Labor Day. Lots of families took their family vacation just before that.

My friends and I liked these summer programs. They usually took place in the playgrounds in back of the schools, where we were used to having recess during the school year. We would come early, right after breakfast and before the planned activities started. We might play some marbles before the leaders arrived and the organized programs began. Or we would just swing, horse around, play some catch, or get a game

98

of scrub ball going. But when the adult leaders came, we would quickly join a group of our choice.

There would be a time for sports, like baseball, soccer, or volleyball. There might be a time for crafts or quiet games, or a story time for the little kids. There were groups for those interested in music or some activity that required a special skill. Sometimes a group might go on a trip or go to the lake to swim. There was something for everyone. I don't remember what we did on rainy or stormy days. I suppose we moved to inside the school and used the gym and classrooms for the activities.

As the summer went on, the groups got smaller. Kids, including me, were always disappearing for a week or so to go to camp or on vacation. The playground program was fun, but of course we did other things in summer, too, like going to the beach, swimming in the river, riding our bikes around town, or playing in our own yards and neighborhoods. Some kids never came to the summer programs at the school, and there were days that my friends and I did not show up either. But it was neat that they were there for the days we didn't have anything else planned.

Groups from the playground would take part in parades and festivals and put on shows, concerts, or programs for our parents and people in the neighborhood. People loved to come to them, and they were always free. All you had to bring was a folding chair to sit on and maybe a jacket or raincoat, just in case the weather suddenly changed.

I don't know who paid for all of this, but for us it was free. And I don't remember that you had to sign up in advance. We just showed up, and when we did, there was always something interesting, fun, and often exciting to do, and many skilled and creative leaders to help us do it.

I have lots of great memories of the fun we had on those summer days!

Ballroom Dancing

Would you believe that I was the best boy dancer in the ninth grade?

Well, I was! That was not my opinion. That's what the girls I danced with said. I was the best dancer because most of the boys in the ninth grade were either too shy to dance with a girl, thought dancing was stupid and only for sissies, or had never had the chance to learn how to dance. Don't feel sorry for them. They had their chance. They could have done what I did. I just made a wise decision they didn't make.

However, I can't take all of the credit for this, or claim that dancing was one of my natural talents or skills. If I was the best boy dancer in the ninth grade, as everyone agreed I was, I have to give the credit to the girls.

You see, at that time, part of our school day a couple of times a week was an activity period scheduled between the end of lunch time and the beginning of afternoon classes. Everyone could sign up for an interest group of their choice. Not everyone did, but you were a fool not to. In the seventh and eighth grades I always signed up for the Chess Club. I was a good chess player and found it a challenging game. At that time I loved to play chess and most often won my matches.

But when I got to the ninth grade, some of the girls ganged up on me before I could sign up for the Chess Club again. They told me that during this year the school would be sponsoring some dances and they needed some boys who knew how to dance to dance with them at those dances. They flattered me by telling me that I would make a very good dancer because I had "natural rhythm" and they told me that if I learned how to dance they would dance with me at those dances. Flattery won out. It was an offer I could hardly refuse.

So.....I signed up for Ballroom Dancing, where we were taught by a couple of good professional adult dancers hired to teach those sessions. It turned out to be a whole lot of fun, the girls were not only pretty but also great dancers, and we learned all of the new steps and the right moves. I was one of the few boys to join the class, which was their loss and my gain. Once learned, it was a skill I have enjoyed using all of my life. I did not regret that I had not chosen to play Chess rather than dance with those lovely girls. It was the age when we began to recognize that girls were very different than boys in many wonderful ways.

Ballroom Dancing was a great activity. I took it all fall, and then signed up to continue it through the winter and spring. By the time the dances started I was a "dancing devil." Again, that's what the girls said.

To make a long story shorter, at the ninth grade dress-up dance at the end of the year (the boys had to wear white shirts, suit coats, and ties, and the girls had to wear long party dresses) I was not only the best, but the most popular dancer on the floor. It was really an ego boosting night and one of the most memorable events of that ninth grade year. I long ago forgot what happened at our graduation, but I will never forget what happened at and after that ninth grade dance.

The gym was beautifully decorated, they hired the best big dance band in town, there were endless refreshments, and near the end of the dance they turned the lights way down low so we could "dance close." The adults said it was just like the dances they had at their country clubs.

When I arrived at the dance, my dance card was soon filled with girls' names and I got to dance every dance that night with some pretty young thing (we were not permitted to have dates or come as couples.) I must admit that I got some sadistic pleasure watching the boys who had called me nasty and degrading names for joining the dance class as they stood around on the sidelines with sullen looks on their faces, burning with envy, and itching to get some girl in their arms. They should have listened to the girls! This turned out to be a whole lot better than Chess.

And then there were some other rewards for my hours of practice besides becoming a good dancer. One of these was something I had been wanting and waiting to do all year. I got to please Betty Heller and get her to do some things every boy in class would have given almost anything to be able to do.

First, she agreed to dance with me for the first and last dance set, and two others in between. Everyone agreed that Betty was probably the best girl dancer in our class, so getting her for that many dances was something! Sometimes when we were partners the other kids stopped dancing, made a big circle around us, and watched us perform our fancy steps. I think she would have danced every dance with me that night if the other girls had not demanded to have a turn.

And, better still, she agreed to let me walk her home.

And, she let me buy her an ice cream soda on the way.

And, she let me hold her hand until we got to her door.

And.......well, we won't go into that.

Let's just say that, like Gene Kelly, I danced all the way home. I would have done it in the rain if it had been raining.

Joining that Ballroom Dancing class and learning how to be a good dancer sure paid off. It was one of the smarter and better things I have done in my life!

The Dances At The Yacht Club

One of the other things I went to see and take a picture of when I was on my revisit tour in Sheboygan was the Yacht Club. It is still in the same place, is the same size, and looks exactly the same as it did then. As I stood outside looking at it again it brought back many fond and happy memories, mostly of the many dances that I attended there when I was in a student at Central High School.

If the truth were told, the boys who quit their Boy Scout troops and joined the Sea Scouts when they got to high school, had less than pure and sometimes mixed motives. Some of them might have been seriously and sincerely interested in sailing. Others were only or more interested in dancing. I must admit that though I wanted to learn how to sail, my interests tipped primarily toward dancing. I thought I was some cool dude in my sailor suit and cap and hoped the girls would be impressed too.

When I got to Central High School (in my Sophomore year) the word got around among the boys that if they were a Sea Scout they could come to the Friday night teen dances (after the football or basketball games) at the Yacht Club that were sponsored by the members of the Yacht Club. There were also several other dress up dances held there for the Sea Scouts and the girl of their choice several times a year. Like sailors all over the world, we Sea Scouts loved to dance, and were good at it. Like sailors everywhere we also liked girls. For you to understand why this was such a big deal I have to tell you a little more about what happened on Friday nights at our school or around town.

Friday night was the big teen night in Sheboygan. While the parents were out shopping Downtown, or at the neighborhood tavern having their beer and fish fry, their sons and daughters were at THE GAME. In fall it was football. In the winter, it was basketball. And, because we always had good teams at Central and were contenders, none of us ever wanted to miss a game. You had to be pretty sick, grounded, or pretty weird not to go to the Friday night game. I always played in the Pep

103

Band or Marching Band, so I was always at the game playing. I never missed a game and we won most of them the years I was in school there. I think our basketball team even went to the State Tournament one or all of those years. We might have even won one.

But the festivities did not end with the game. Whether we won or lost, we would spill out of the stadium or gym like lemmings and descend upon the town. Most of the kids headed for the nearest ice cream parlor or hamburger joint. Some of the older kids, who liked to dance, would head for the YMCA, where there was always an "after the game" dance on Friday nights. But those of us privileged enough to be in the Sea Scouts, and our date for the night, would head for the Yacht Club, which was right on the shore of Lake Michigan. We could walk to all of these places, or take a bus. Not many of us had cars or the use of one. Sometimes Yacht Club members would pick us up at the school and drive us home after the dance. That was even better!

The Yacht Club was (and still is) one of the fanciest and beautiful places in town, known for its fine dinners, polished dance floor, and bar and lounge (which was off limits to anyone under the age of 21.) It was a great place to take a girl if you wanted to show off how important you were. It was rumored that only the prettiest girls in school got to go there. So, on most Friday nights, after the game, that is where my Sea Scout friends and I could always be found.

They had a great big Juke Box there with all of the latest popular dance records on it, and they always turned the lights down real low to create a romantic setting. There might have even been a little hugging and kissing going on. If there was, no one seemed to notice or care.

There were always lots of chaperons there, but they were really unnecessary. There was never any bad behavior at those dances. We felt like adults when we were there and acted accordingly, or better.

Those were great nights and great dances and I will never forget them. Even the best ballrooms that we went to later could not quite match the Yacht Club in Sheboygan, right on the shores of Lake Michigan.

It was the best place for dancing that I ever danced or played in.

The Glenn Martin Orchestra

I must have been born to be a performer. I seemed to be destined to spend at least parts of my life in show business; mostly as a musician, an actor or a comic, and then later as a teacher and preacher. Some my relatives thought I took after Grandfather Martin, who was an actor and artist and huckster most of his life. He made his living in one form of show business or another. So, I came by it honestly.

I have always had a passion to entertain. It was in my genes. My life proved I had the talents and skills for it. They came out best in making music.

I always had a natural sense of rhythm, perfect pitch, great timing, and a flair for ad lib. Some said I was a ham. I came alive when I was on a stage or a bandstand. You can call it ego if you like, but I would rather think of it as a love to perform, entertain, and make people happy. It started early and is not yet over. My first professional career was as a musician. Now I just play for fun.

I was also destined to be a leader, usually being chosen to be the Director, Producer, or Conductor of the things I got involved in. It was not that I wanted to be in charge or control people and things all the time. I just seemed to have the knack of putting and holding things together and bringing out the best in talented people.

I think my passion for show business began in Kindergarten, when we were all expected to play some kind of noisemaker in a rhythm band. We also learned how to sing simple songs. At home, either in my backyard, shed or garage, I used to write and put on plays, programs, and circuses. The poor parents in our neighborhoods had to come and see them. And pay a few pennies or up to a nickel to see them. In a way, I was already a professional way back then. It is true that "there's no business like show business." I learned that at an early age and never forgot it. I thoroughly enjoyed being a small part of it.

In either the first or second grade, I got my first big chance to perform on stage for an audience. I was chosen to be the Director of the Harmonica Band. My teacher dressed me up in a bright little cape, with a pair of matching long pants and hat. I really look sharp. Then I was given a long stick to direct with and I got up in front of the players and kept time. We made a mighty sound.

A few years later, I joined the Boys Choir at church. At that time, I had a good tenor voice. We had a very good adult director. I was just one of the singers. In that organization, we wore beautiful bright red robes, with a short surplus over it and a very big white bow around our necks. We sang once a month in church. We weren't the Vienna Choir boys, but we were very good. Everyone at the church said so.

As I wrote the last two paragraphs, I came to realize that one of the reasons I might have enjoyed performing so much is that we got to wear all those fancy costumes. Another reason might have been the chance to use our imaginations and to create characters much different than us, like the one I played in the sixth grade.

During that year our class put on a play, and I got my first big break as an actor. I was given the lead in "Jack and the Beanstalk." Of course, I was Jack. I think my friend Wesley Jerving was the giant. In one scene, I had to climb up the beanstalk, which went right up to the ceiling. It was pretty scary and had I fallen, I might have broken my neck. I learned from that production that there is nothing in the world better to raise one's self-esteem or tickle one's ego, than the applause of an audience.

And so it went......bands, orchestras, drum corps, choirs, plays and musicals, concerts and programs. I spent a lot of my growing up days on some stage. I even got a silly nickname, "Penner." He was a popular radio comedian who used to say, "Wanna Buy a Duck?" The kids got to calling me that, because I used to imitate the radio Penner, making his silly sounds and saying that silly question.

But it wasn't until I was a sophomore in high school that I entered "the Big Time." I formed an eight-piece dance band that was called, of course, "The Glenn Martin Orchestra." All dance bands were named after their leader at that time. The leader's initials were always painted on our bass drum heads, along with ours, which caused some problems when you played with more than one band.

I recruited seven other guys to help me make music. It was the big band era and the style was swing.

Jerry was the lead alto player and arranged most of our music. In a real sense, he was the Musical Director. Donny played tenor sax (and sometimes accordion), and Warren was the other alto sax. Then there were two brothers, Billy played trumpet and Andy played string bass. Joe played electric guitar (we didn't have a piano), and I was in the back playing drums. I also served as the MC. Once the band was formed, we got a pretty young girl by the name of Jeannie to be our vocalist.

We sounded very good, if I don't say so myself, and soon became popular around town. But before we began to play for dances, we worked hard getting organized. In the winter, we practiced in houses, but when the weather got nice, we practiced up on the second floor of that old red barn in the back of our house on Kentucky Avenue. People came from all over the neighborhood to listen to us. But only "invited guests" were allowed to climb the ladder and come up into the area that used to be the hayloft. However, those who did had to be quiet and there was no horsing around. As we got better, dancing was sometimes allowed. No barn dance fiddlers and guitar players ever swung like our band. We were so hot I was afraid we might burn that old barn down!

Our first public appearances were at a few school dances, before we got a regular gig playing alternate Sunday afternoons for the popular Sunday Tea Dances at the Catholic Church. When we all joined the Sheboygan Musicians Union and became "professional musicians," we graduated to private parties, dance halls, and supper clubs, and started to get paid. It wasn't much at first, but it was the status that counted. We did that for two years, until we graduated. There were two other bands like ours in town and we enjoyed the friendly competition for popularity and jobs.

At that time, it was my hope, dream, and intention to become a professional musician and to lead my own orchestra full time. My plan, after graduating, was to enlarge the band, go on road, make recordings, play on the radio, and become rich and famous. If the other Glenn (Glenn Miller) could do it, why couldn't I?

But it was not to be. The war came along and we all went off to join the military and fight for our country.

Who knows....if that had not happened, I might still be leading the Glenn Martin Orchestra!

The Sunday Afternoon Tea Dances

As I have said many times before in my books, we teenagers in Sheboygan loved to dance and we danced a lot, especially when we got into high school. Along with skating and swimming, it was probably our favorite pastime. That's probably why we got to be very good dancers. Another reason was that we were able to dance to such great music, both local and live, or on the jukeboxes that were all over town.

We not only danced a lot, but we also bought lots of records and knew all the tunes. This was the 40's, the peek of the "Big Band Era," when Swing was King and Benny Goodman was the "King of Swing." Our other favorite bands, besides Benny, were Glenn Miller, Artie Shaw, Harry James, Gene Krupa, and hundreds of bands like them that played the hotels, nightclubs, and ballrooms all over the country. You could also hear them nightly on the radio.

Those big name bands seldom came to Sheboygan, but now and then we would travel to Milwaukee to see them and dance to their music. The best place to hear them was at that huge ballroom at the State Fairgrounds in Milwaukee. I will never forgot the night that Glenn Miller was playing there and we all jammed into Donny's car and drove down there to see him.

Swing was our kind of music! We were all "Jitterbugs."

The older folks liked to dance to Old Time music, and each ethnic or nationality group had its own kind of music and dancing that they would play at weddings and parties. You didn't hear much Latin or Country music in Sheboygan, there weren't too many good Jazz Bands around, and Rock music was still ten or more years away. If you went to a public dance or a ballroom when I was a teenager, you would probably dance to Swing music. And that is what our band played most of the time.

There were some very good local bands in Sheboygan and, by the time we were sophomores at Central High School, three of us had formed our own dance bands. I have already told you about mine. Two of my good friends had theirs. Joe Bifano and I (both drummers) had smaller (7-8 players) bands, and Dick Hoertz had a bigger band (11-12 players.) At that time, all dance bands were called orchestras, even if none of them had strings.

Because teens were not supposed to be in places that served alcohol until they were 21 (though our bands were allowed to play in such places for adults), there were a lot of teenage dances sponsored by the schools, churches, and social clubs. And anywhere there was a jukebox there was also a small dance floor. There were plenty of places to dance. But, it was a treat when there was a dance with a live band, and that's where Joe, Dick, and I came in. At that time, the three of us and our orchestras furnished most of the music for teen dances.

By far one of the most popular teen dances in Sheboygan during those years (1940-42) were the Sunday afternoon Tea Dances at St. Clement's Roman Catholic Church. It was one Catholic church in town where Protestants were not turned away, but welcomed, at least for three hours a week. And on a Sunday yet!

I don't know why they called them Tea Dances. They didn't serve any tea. It must have come from the custom the British have of drinking tea in the middle of the afternoon. These dances started at 2:00 p.m. and ended at 5:00 p.m. It was three solid hours of non-stop dancing, either to the music of the live band for the day or a jukebox during a few short intermissions.

For a long time, Joe's band and my band alternated every other week. I don't remember if Dick's band or any other bands ever played for any of those dances, but I don't think they did. I think Joe and I kept this gig for ourselves. I don't know why. Maybe the other bands had joined the Union by that time and wouldn't or couldn't play these gigs because of the strict Union rules. Anyhow, Joe's orchestra and my orchestra played lots of those dances over those two years and enjoyed every one of them.

I don't remember if the dances were free or if the church charged a small admission. They did sell popcorn, pop, ice cream, and snacks. I don't remember whether we got paid for playing or played for free. I don't think it mattered. We loved to play and, even when it was not our turn, we loved to come anyhow and dance. If you were a teen and liked to dance, St. Clement's was the place to be on Sunday afternoons.

The church basement was always packed. That's where a lot of the kids, especially the boys, learned how to dance. It was a healthy, happy, safe, and lively atmosphere for boys and girls to mingle, and a perfect place for them to go on those long, boring Sunday afternoons. The only other alternatives were going to a movie or one of the bowling alleys.

Unlike some dances now, everyone at these dances was well behaved. They had to be! The priests, who were the chaperones, saw to that. Those priests were usually nice guys, but they didn't take any guff from anyone. If anyone got out of line, they were asked to leave. If you got a bad reputation for bad behavior, you didn't even get past the door. The priests were forgiving at Confession on Fridays, but they ran a tight ship on Sunday afternoons. No Hail Marys or Our Fathers could get you into the dance if you didn't follow the rules.

When I was revisiting Sheboygan, I stopped at St. Clement's Church and took a couple of pictures. The church it still there, on the corner across from the big government building, a few blocks from Downtown, and right up on top of the hill that comes from the lake. It looks exactly the same as it looked then. Those Catholics built their churches to last.

As I stood there thinking about how we danced those afternoons away at that wonderful place, and remembered that it was at one of those dances that we first heard that Pearl Harbor had been bombed by the Japanese, I wondered if they still have dances there or if those dances died, too, when we went off to war. If they do still have Tea Dances there, I am sure that the kids no longer dress as nicely as we did, do not dance as well as we did, and the bands are much, much louder than we were.

The Gig At Lauer's

I will make this story short and sweet, because other stories about my musical career already appear in my other books. If it did not fit in this section it might have been my last "boyhood" story in this book, because it is about something that happened AFTER we graduated from high school.

Shortly before we graduated in June of 1942 our band got hired to play for the summer at Lauer's. It was a plum job and other more experienced bands wondered how we got it (by that time we had a clever manager who was a super salesman.)

Lauer's was a popular nightclub out at Crystal Lake (near Plymouth). My friend, Dick Hoertz, and his orchestra, was hired to play at the other club across the street from Lauer's. I forget the name of it. On some nights and on weekends other bands came from Sheboygan to play for the dances at the Ballroom down the road. All of these places were always crowded. As they used to say in jive language, "the joints were jumpin" all the time. Even though Sheboygan bordered the great Lake Michigan, the folks in Sheboygan loved to go out to the smaller lakes where they had cottages, or just to swim at the many beaches. Teenagers flocked out there once they got their own cars and had licenses to drive them. They came during the day to lay out in the sun and at night to dance. Lot's of marriages got started at Crystal Lake.

We started our gig at Lauer's the night after we graduated, which was a Friday. Mr. Lauer was anxious for the weekend business. We didn't have much time to get out there, unpacked and settled, and set up, but we made it. We were dressed up, on the stand, and ready to play before the Friday night crowd began to gather.

This gig was a good deal. We played for dancing every night except Monday, and a Sunday matinee. We had all day Monday off and often went home for the day and to sleep in our own beds overnight. But I expected everyone to be back by noon on Tuesday so we could rehearse new music all afternoon. We always wanted to play new and fresh music every week.

Each of us got $21.00 a week, could eat whatever the cooks had left over in the kitchen after the nightly gig, and were given a wonderful full course Sunday Dinner before the matinee. That was big money at the time (it was more than my father made.) We were also provided with a cabin to stay in (owned by a lady school teacher who had very strict rules for conduct). It had a nice swimming beach and a rowboat we could use. It was in easy walking distance from the club. We played there through Labor Day. What more could we ask for?

For this important job I bought a brand new drum set. It cost me over $150.00. We all bought some very nice looking uniforms; dark pants, white shirts, cream-colored coats, and maroon bow ties (we all tucked a hanky to match in out coat pocket). A local clothier, who was one of our most enthusiastic supporters and a great dancer, gave us a good price. He said he "wanted us to look nice."

Jerry made lots of new arrangements of all kinds and styles of music and they were well-rehearsed and ready to play (he made more arrangements as the summer went on.) Unlike other bands on gigs like this, we rehearsed, as well as played, every day. We worked hard but we considered it fun. We came there to play and play we did, literally night and day. We stopped playing only to eat, sleep, and have a little fun on the beach. Some of the guys grumbled from time to time, usually when they would have liked to have more time with some girl that was staying at a cottage nearby. I guess I was pretty intense and a little hard on them. But at the time, music for me was everything.

I won't tell you about the girls who used to flock out there all summer, or the after hour jam sessions we used to have at Lauer's with the guys (the bands at that time were all guys.....except for the girl singers) from Dick's band and the guys, mostly from Chicago, who played at the Jewish resorts and clubs at Elkhart Lake close by. My drummer friend, Joe Bifano (who played with Dick that summer), and I often had drum contests to impress the other drummers from the "big city." We held our own. Sometimes those sessions began about 1:00 a.m. and lasted until the sun came up. It was a great way to learn how to play jazz and we did. We played that summer with some very fine musicians.

I could write another book of stories about the things that happened that summer. But I won't. School was over for us. Adult life was beginning (even though for most of us it would take three more years before it would be legal.) We had left Sheboygan, and we were off to make our way in the world. Most of us would never come back to Sheboygan again to live and work. It was a great summer and one of those once in a lifetime experiences.

Then, three months later, The Glenn Martin Orchestra would be no more. Too bad. It was really a good band and I am convinced we would have made it to the big time if we could have stayed together and gone on the road after we left Lauer's. We had some good offers, but we couldn't take them. We went off to war instead.

But then, if that hadn't happened I would not have gone to college and Seminary, become a Minister, found the girl I married, and had all those nice kids that I had.

I guess the Lord had bigger and better things in mind for me than I had. There was still a lot of life to live after the gig at Lauer's.

Chairs

Working For A Living

In Sheboygan, when I lived there, most people in Sheboygan would emphatically deny that there was any class or caste system in that fine city. They would say that their ancestors came to America to get away from such things. They would say that in Sheboygan everyone was not only born equal, but had equal opportunities to become successful in whatever they wanted to do. People wanted to believe that Sheboygan was a classless society, or close to it.

Of course, this was not true. Like every society anywhere in the world, your place in Sheboygan society was determined by the family or ethnic group you belong to, your gender or race, or the amount of money and property you had. Mostly, your place in Sheboygan was defined by the work that you did.

Like I have said many times before in my books, in our town, most boys, when they grew up, did what their fathers did. I did not, but I still learned well the values that were taught to me by watching my father, my relatives, and their friends do their work. I am glad I did. The things I learned were to come in handy when I grew up and had to support myself and my family.

We Martins were blue collar and working class all the way. And proud of it! None of the members of my dad's side of the family were doctors, lawyers, bankers, owners, or even teachers or elected officials. And they weren't managers or salesmen either. None of my male relatives on my dad's side of the family were teachers or professional people, or worked in offices or stores. None of them were farmers. My grandfather on my mother's side of the family was a barber. He was the only one in his family that I know of that had his own business. The rest of our men on both sides of the family worked for wages. The women were all "housewives" and mothers.

The men in my family worked in factories. They got paid by the hour. And they did hard and dirty physical work, work that required some skill but mostly strength and endurance. And, at first, and for some all of their lives, they did not have Unions to care about and protect them and their jobs. Some of them died from work related illnesses. I doubt if any of them got pensions.

Though my dad eventually became a Chief Engineer and the boss in the power plants where he worked, he started out like all of the others, doing manual labor. Even when my dad got to the top of his profession and could have, he never wore a white shirt, suit, and tie to work. He wore work clothes that working men purchased at Sears or J.C. Penny's.

The only time you would see my dad dressed up was in church on Sundays, or at weddings, funerals, or parties. On Monday he would be back in the engine room in his work clothes again.

My father was not impressed by "being the boss." He didn't just sit in his office, like some bosses did, smoking the cigars salesmen used to give him to get his business. He could usually be found down on the floor with the other men, checking out a troublesome furnace, fixing something no one else could fix, or cleaning out a boiler. That's why he came home so dirty after most shifts.

He was a good boss, because he set a good example, and because he considered himself one among equals. I never heard any of the men who worked with him call him, "Mr. Martin." He was just "Bill" to everyone. My father felt most at home being one of and a part of the "working class." My dad always identified with those he called "the little guy," and the little guys who worked for him not only respected but loved him. When he died, all of those little guys came to his funeral and had tears in their eyes. Those are the ones who told me how lucky I was to have a father like my dad, that "Bill Martin was a good man!"

Fortunately, my dad did not expect me to "follow in his footsteps," but he did insist that I would never forget that the road to success in any occupation came from observing the working class values he had grown up with; hard work, discipline, loyalty to the company, and giving a "day's work for a day's pay." That was what he believed, it was his creed, and he lived out those principles and values every day of his life. I admired him for that. And I hoped I could be as good a man as he was.

I was not to become blue collar. I was destined to wear white shirts and suits and ties. I did not get dirty on my jobs. I used my mind more than my hands. I spent most of my time with professional and creative people. And I was most often in charge - the manager, the boss, the employer. I did get called, "Mr." or later "Rev." I had lots of degrees and all the credentials I needed to get "to the top" of the professions I had chosen for myself. But I never forgot where I came from and what I had been taught as I was growing up in Sheboygan. I think I was successful in the things I did because I was well disciplined, well organized, loyal to those who employed me, and gave more than day's work for the pay I received. And I always spent a lot of time with the "workers" I worked with and not the guys of my professions who joined the Country Clubs.

It is a good thing I grew up in Sheboygan. I shudder to think of what might have happened to me if I had been born and raised with "a silver spoon in my mouth" instead of on lots or German rye bread, milk, cheese, and vegetables and fruits from my mother's gardens. And I am glad I had a dad who was not afraid to get his hands dirty, if that was required to get the job done.

Things Made Of Wood

I love things made of wood, be they wonderful works of art, furniture, or whole houses. Maybe this comes from my love of trees or the fact that there is not only a beauty about wood but also a utility and permanence. It can be used to make so many things, and, if properly cared for, almost lasts forever. Or this fascination with wood may be something I learned from my father and great grandfather, who both, in their own ways, were workers of wood, not carpenters, but more like artists.

My Dad was always making something out of the orange crates he was forever bringing home from the grocery stores. He made model sailing ships, miniature houses to put under the Christmas tree, and all kinds of other good things. He also helped me make scooters and little cars.

My great grandfather did wood sculpturing (he called it whittling) and was a kind of cabinetmaker. When he came to stay with us during the winter my dad would get him big blocks of wood, out of which he would make such things as wooden pliers that worked, a large box with a ball inside, or a linked chain. All with only a knife and solid blocks of wood. My dad would also get him a large supply of orange crates and he would make small shelves for the women, who loved them. His specialty was a corner knickknack holder. These always had three shelves of different sizes, and they were given a fine shine with a choice lacquer. He always gave away everything he made free. I am sure that whoever got them considered them prize possessions. By this time they should be valuable antiques.

But, my love of wooden things probably also comes from the fact that I grew up in Sheboygan, which was known for the fine furniture that was made in the several factories around town. Making chairs (and other furniture) was one of the major industries in Sheboygan at the time. My Uncle Gilbert's twin brother Chet worked in one of those factories. Chet's factory specialized in making fine chairs. In fact it was named the Sheboygan Chair Company. These Sheboygan chairs were sent and sold all over the world. Chairs were one of the four things Sheboygan was known for. Recently someone wrote a book about the history of furniture making in Sheboygan. The Sheboygan County Historical Society published it and has it in its collection. It is very interesting and told me a lot of things about this industry that I never knew.

I remember the Sheboygan Chair Company factory very well because it's large production plant was right down the hill from where my aunt and uncle and cousin lived. We used to play right near the fence that surrounded it. They wouldn't let us kids inside to watch the chairmakers work, but in summer they would open the windows and doors so we could see inside. There was probably a time when I might have seriously thought that I would like to work there when I grew up. But I never did. I also suspect that this is where my dad might have gotten some of the scrap lumber he always had in the basement and in the garage. If it was from there, it was the best quality money could buy. Oh yes, there is one more connection. That same great-grandfather, spent his working life as a traveling salesman for a Chair company (not one from Sheboygan but in New York state someplace.) ~just like Scottish blood flows through the Martin veins, there may be wood in the Martin genes, too.

Just like cheese, and brats and beer, Sheboygan was known for its chairs.

Factories

Though Sheboygan was built right on the shores of Lake Michigan, it was not a port city. The only big ships that came into our harbor brought coal that was used in the factories, or maybe some sand and gravel that was used in construction. No ships came to Sheboygan from foreign countries like they do to Duluth where I recently lived. And though Sheboygan was surrounded by farmland in all directions, Sheboygan was not considered rural or farmland, either. Sheboygan has always been a good-sized city, with about 40,000 people, and it was essentially an industrial city, much like Milwaukee or Chicago, with factories of all kinds and sizes throughout the town.

Most of the local men, and some single women, worked in those factories. Factory work at that time was steady work and it paid well. Those who did not work in factories worked in jobs that provided services to the people who worked in the factories. Sheboygan was a factory town.

This was all due to the development of mass production and the assembly line process. I know it started in England with the woolen mills, but Henry Ford had a lot to do with it here. Factories could turn out large quantities of goods in a hurry, and at cheap prices. Some men worked in the same factory for their entire life. Almost all of my male relatives on my father's side worked in factories, and so did my father, though he did not work on an assembly line.

The biggest factory, which was right outside of the Sheboygan city limits, was the Kohler Company, which made toilets, bathtubs, and other bathroom furnishings. It still does. Mr. Kohler came from Germany and built a whole town, named Kohler, around his large manufacturing plant. Many of his workers lived there. Many others lived in Sheboygan, Sheboygan Falls, and maybe even Plymouth. It was also one of the places where they had one of the country's first big strikes, which I will tell about later in this book.

One of Mr. Kohler's son-in-laws, named Vollrath, owned the Vollrath Company in Sheboygan. It was perhaps the largest factory within the Sheboygan city limits. The Vollrath Company made kitchen supplies, like pots and pans and dishes. It was called enamelware because that is the material it was made of. My father worked there in the power plant most of the time when I was growing up. It is only after I had graduated from high school that he accepted another job.

I cannot remember all of the products that were made in Sheboygan when I was a kid, but I do know about some of them.

I do remember there was a tannery down on the east bank of the river. It was just called, "The tannery" by the people who lived near it. It was the place where they cured hides for the making of leather products. It was a smelly place and it really fouled up the river that dumped its runoff into. The people who lived near the tannery plant were always praying for a west wind. At that time there were no pollution controls and no one seemed to worry about what happened to the fish in the river. Wherever all that foul stuff went, it didn't seem to affect Lake Michigan, which was always fresh and blue.

There were also all kinds of machine shops that made metal and electrical parts for engines and appliances. Some of them were owned by companies from Milwaukee, Chicago, and Gary, Indiana. Welders and machinists were always in demand in Sheboygan. Some of my friends went to vocational school to learn those trades. After the war my cousin worked in one of those factories for a time, before he moved to Manitowoc.

Near our house on 14th Street there was a company that made clothing items like sweaters and jackets. Before she got married my mother worked in a factory that made stockings for women. There must have been lots of others that made things to wear. The Leverenz Company made some of the finest shoes made anywhere in the world. I went to Sunday School with Billy Leverenz, who probably would have taken over the company one day, if he hadn't been killed in the war. His brother became its president after the war.

The Kingsbury company made beer; there were lots of small cheese factories and sausage factories, and some large bakeries that made most of the bread that was consumed in Sheboygan. They might not have been considered factories by the owners of these businesses, but many of them used some kind of assembly line to produce their products.

And then there was the Verifine Company, which was, like its name, a very fine company and a good one to work for. This company handled milk and dairy products, but they also made lots and lots of ice cream as well. The last time I was there the building is still there, and it is still making dairy products, but now it is called "Land O' Lakes." There was even a company in Sheboygan that made Jell-O, before it was called Jell-O and Jack Benny made it famous.

Those factories were usually very large, sometimes taking up blocks of land and could be several stories high. They were not very attractive. In fact, some of them were very dirty and ugly. But they were not made to be things of beauty; they were constructed to produce the most goods, in the fastest time, and at the cheapest prices possible. My father spent most of his working life in power plants that supplied the power and electricity for some factories.

Because of these industries, Sheboygan was always a very prosperous community. Those factories made a lot of stuff, and most of what was produced were consumer products that people needed all of the time and in large quantities. Sheboygan did not suffer as many of the ups and downs and rises and falls that some other industries and communities did that were one industry towns, like the auto and steel industries, or communities that depended completely on the income from such things like mining ore or cutting lumber or processing other natural resources. We lived in a mining town for three years, and believe me it was very different from living in Sheboygan.

Thanks to those factories, which maybe at times produced more dirt, smoke, and pollution than would now be allowed, it was a healthy, productive, and desirable place to live. Even though I chose never to work in one, and never did, I could not have lived the kind of life I lived without the products and resources those factories provided. I didn't know or appreciate that at the time. But I do now.

All Those Pots And Pans

One of the fringe benefits of my dad's working at the Vollrath Company was getting all of those neat pots, pans, and dishes, either very cheap or free. They were seconds that could not be sold, but we didn't care. Sometimes we couldn't even find the little chip or scratch that disqualified them for shipment and sale. My mom's kitchen was full of things that had been made at Vollrath. So were the kitchens of other women in Sheboygan. Vollrath's wares were just as popular then as Tupperware was when we set up housekeeping.

I never quite figured out how these products were made. My dad probably tried to explain it to me, but I never caught on. I think each article was first shaped out of some kind of thin basic metal, maybe tin or an alloy of tin. Then it was covered with some bright colored something that they called enamel. I think it must have been brushed on. Then it was baked in an oven to make it hard. It is sort of like the ceramic things that artists make now. Once it was done it was very hard and almost indestructible. You could chip off the enamel but you couldn't break them.

About the only artistic design that was put on these articles was maybe some spots of white on the colored surfaces. But mostly all of these pieces and sets were plain bright blues, reds, yellows, or other colors. They were very pretty, but they were not made for beauty, but utility. After the war started Vollrath probably made things for the military.

The factory turned out this enamelware out day after day in huge quantities. My dad used to work the night shift so I suppose the factory was open around the clock and the production assembly lines never shut down. Maybe factories were closed on Sundays. I don't remember. Then everything had to be packed and shipped from the plant to retailers all over the country and maybe the world. It took a lot of workers to do all of that. It was a good steady business, Vollrath paid well, and it was a good place to work. I don't know what the Vollrath company makes now, but I know the factory is still there. I saw it on my revisit, on the same corner lot where it has always been. It looked the same as when my dad worked there, except it may have had a new coat of paint or two since then.

The products that the Vollrath Company made were well designed and well made and they were practical, easy to carry around and easy to clean. Not only did the women use them in their kitchens, but they used them in the lunch boxes they sent with their husbands when they went off to work. In summer, you would see Vollrath ware all over town in the parks and picnic areas. And there wasn't any waste. You never threw any of these utensils away, like people do now to paper or plastic plates and cups. Vollrath ware was always taken back home and used over and over again. It never seemed to wear out. It was made to last forever.

We were lucky dad worked there, because my mom probably had more pots and pans and dishes from Vollrath than any women in our whole family, and maybe even more than any other woman in town.

Those Awesome Engine Rooms

My dad spent half or more of his waking hours in engine rooms. That's because he was a power engineer by profession. And I spent a lot of my free time in engine rooms, because every time my dad would take me some place to do something he would always stop at some engine room to see his friends on our way home. I got to love engine rooms. To a kid they were awesome. And only kids whose dads were engineers could get into those sacred places.

Think of it, first of all the colors in an engine room are eye-catching; shiny black polished metal, mixed with gold, and sometimes red, green, and yellow. And there are steps, walkways, and ladders everywhere, daring you to climb them at great risk to your safety. Then there are all kinds of mysterious things that only a trained engineer would be able to identify and understand; things like wheels and rods of all sizes going around and around and back and forth, valves, pipes, pistons, clocks, w thermometers, and gauges of all kinds. Everything means something, everything shows something, everything measures or indicates something. They tell the engineers at a glance exactly what is going on all over the building that they are furnishing utilities for. And they immediately tell them when something is not working or has gone wrong.

You would think engine rooms would be dirty places to work in. But they are not. They are usually clean as a whistle. The engineers might get dirty, but that is when they are shoveling the coal into the furnaces, cleaning out the boilers, or fixing something that is greasy or oily. They may get dirty but they keep their engine rooms and the machinery clean.

Engine rooms are not as noisy as you might think. There are lots of sounds, but the engineers get used to them and when you are in there for a time, what you hear is more of a steady hum or a puffing or hissing sound. And there are the whistles and bells that all mean something. But those sounds are much different from the loud clashes and bangs that you would hear if you were on the assembly room floors where the products were being made or put together. Of course, in engine rooms there is always lots of steam, coming from everywhere. That is what powers the machines.

I came to love engine rooms and sometimes begged my dad to take me to one, even when he did not plan to go there. They are pleasant and mysterious places. You always wondered how everything worked so smoothly. You marveled at how smart those engineers had to be.

When you stepped into those engine rooms in Sheboygan you could immediately feel the POWER! But, after all, that is what an engine room is, a place that produces power. There was also always lots of water in the engine rooms I used to visit. That water was turned into steam, which was needed to run all of the machinery in the factory or plant. Nothing could be made, nothing could be produced, nothing could run without the power that came from the engine room. And there wouldn't have been any steam without the use of huge amounts of water and coal. Maybe now it is all powered by electricity, and oil or natural gas or nuclear energy might be used instead of coal.

But it is the engineers who make it happen. My dad was one of those engineers. Folks said he was one of the best.

Wow!

I never got tired of going into those engine rooms with my dad. It was more exciting than doing what some other kids did with their dads, like playing baseball or going fishing. Any dad could do those things. Only a dad who was an engineer could get you into an engine room to experience the miracle and mystery of POWER!

Ships, Harbors, And Docks

One of the most vivid memories I still have of my boyhood in Sheboygan, is of those rare and precious times, when my father would take me down to the harbor to watch the large ships come to unload their cargoes at the docks. I have mentioned this before in some of my other books, but now I would like to describe, in some detail, what that area of town was like and how important it was to the welfare and prosperity of our town.

I had a professor in college once who used to tell us that "A person's character is formed by the place where he/she lives." I have learned that this is true. There are mountain people and desert people, river people. and ocean people, and I suppose there are people who love to live in jungles. Some people like to live in big cities; others like to live in small towns or out in the country. And then there are wilderness people, usually men, who like living alone. We, who were lucky enough to live in Sheboygan, were Lake Michigan people. That lake influenced everything we did. This was confirmed for me just recently when we found ourselves living again in Duluth, right on the shores of Lake Superior. It felt very much like living in Sheboygan when I was a boy. It was sort of like coming home.

Lake Michigan is a beautiful body of water and it dominated our lives in many ways. It influenced our thinking, our daily activities, and our values more than we realized. Only those who live next to a great body of water would understand what I am talking about. Everything else in our lives may change from day to day, month to month, or year to year, but 24 hours a day, 7 days a week, every month, and every year, from birth to death, that lake is always there. Like God, the lake is an ever constant, and ever lasting presence. It is something to fear at times, yet something that offers security, dependability, and comfort most of the time.

If the basics that form and sustain life on this planet are earth, wind, fire, and water, then people who live in Sheboygan have three of those four right under their feet and before their very eyes, from the day they are born until the day they die. For me, it was the water that held the greatest attraction. I loved Lake Michigan and missed it when we lived in Minneapolis and became river and prairie people. And for some reason I never really liked the ocean, though I was surrounded by one when I spent time in the Army in Puerto Rico, which was an island.

Later in this book I will tell about the beach that ran along Lake Michigan, which stretched out for hundreds of miles in both directions, North and South. But for now I want to tell about the harbor, which was right in the middle of town, separating the two halves.

The beach was broken up at this point by huge cement breakwaters that went out into the Lake for about a mile, creating a passageway into the harbor. On some of them there were small lighthouses, there to guide the ships into the harbor at night or during impending or actual storms. All along that harbor there were high walls made of either cement or heavy timbers. It was a straight shot from the lake into the harbor and toward the land. But then, at one point, it turned and the water flowed South toward the Reiss Coal Company yards. That is where the huge mounds of coal were piled. This was all man made and the lake constantly tried to unmake it. It didn't seem to like that harbor.

The whole process was very efficient. The big vessels carrying the coal (or cargo) came in from the Lake and into the harbor. I often wondered where they came from. All of a sudden they would appear on the horizon, like out of nowhere. They quickly came into the harbor, were unloaded, and just went out into the lake again and disappeared, leaving those huge piles of coal on the docks. It was all kind of mysterious and exciting. Your mind could make up stories of where those ships came from and where they were going next.

According to current standards and sizes these coal boats were not very large, but to a young boy they looked monstrous. They were very long and always painted a kind of reddish brown. There were white structures, on both ends. We were told that that is where the crew was housed and ate and where the engine room was. The rest of the ship was flat, where the coal was. We couldn't see the holds from the shore.

My dad and I would stand for hours at the end at the harbor and watch the ships come in. First a ship was only a speck out on the horizon, but then it got bigger and bigger as it got closer and closer to shore and into the harbor. And then, of course, as it came almost to where we were standing, it was huge! The men aboard, who looked like my little toy soldiers, would wave to us in greeting as the ship passed by. We would wave back and shout things to them. Sometimes they would throw something to us that we would try to catch.

As the ship would pass by us we would move farther down to the docks and watch as the ship was unloaded. The huge cranes would come down and dig up huge piles of coal, come back up, turn to the right or left, and dump its load on an increasingly larger and growing mound. It would take a long time to unload in those days, and we rarely stayed to watch the whole process, or for the ship to go back out the channel and back out into the lake.

As we stood there and watched, my dad might tell me more about my Uncle Harry or some friend of his who worked on one of those boats, and he would tell me that some day maybe he might get a job as an engineer on one. It was a dream he was never able to fulfill.

I learned from him that the coal would now be trucked out to the factories, like the one where he worked, where it would be shoveled into the furnaces, to make the fires, that heated the water, to make the stream, that would turn the turbines that produced the power that was needed to run the machines in the factories. I didn't know it then, but I was getting a first-hand lesson on the docks of how the whole production system for making goods worked. It was an early lesson in economics. All of this took place just a block or so from where my Grandpa Wisch had his barbershop. Sometimes we would stop to see him on our way home.

I never got tired of going to the harbor and the docks with my dad. Any time he said, "How would you like to go down and see the ships come in?" I always immediately said, "Yes!" and headed for the car. I loved to go anywhere with my dad, but going to see the ships was the most exciting thing we ever did together. It was one of things I missed when we both left town.

The lake, the harbor, and those big ships were almost more than a little boy's mind could grasp, but it was enough to make me wonder if some day I might become a sailor like Uncle Harry. I never was. I became a soldier instead.

The Kohler Strikes

There were two Kohler strikes. One took place when I was a kid and in grade school. The other took place, after the war, when I was an adult and no longer lived in Sheboygan. Both of them were terrible and should never have happened. Neither of them solved the problems they were supposed to solve. There weren't any winners or losers, just a lot of pain and suffering. And Mr. Kohler's dream of creating a perfect community turned out to be a nightmare. Members of our family were deeply involved in both of them.

Sheboygan did survive. Cities have a way of doing that, in spite of mistakes their citizens make and the foolish things they do. But during the last years when I went back to visit my mother and see my relatives no one any longer talked about the Kohler strikes. All of the persons most affected by the strikes are gone and not even memories seem linger. Or is it just denial? The strikes are facts of history, but I think the people who live in Sheboygan and Kohler now would just as soon forget them. It is just as well. I only bring them up again here because they were an important part of my life story, especially the first one.

It would take a whole book to review and rehearse the facts and events of that momentous strike. I suppose someone has done that, but I have never seen any of those reports. I am not sure I want to. The issues at that time were complex, feelings ran high and got out of hand, and the people involved did cruel and harmful things to each other. If cooler heads could have prevailed and the interests of the community had been made a higher priority than personal selfish interests, the strikes would never have happened. But they did. And Sheboygan was never the same after them.

I am glad I was a kid and not an adult when the first one took place. And I am glad I was long gone before the second one began. But I do know that those strikes affected everyone who lived in Sheboygan while they were going on. No one escaped. All of their lives and relationships were changed significantly, and some lives were ruined or lost. Some of the Sheboyganites who were involved at the time did recover from the first strike, but some of them, who were still in Sheboygan during the second, did not make it through the second one very well, including members of our family. Some people either finally left town or died earlier then they would or should have.

The first strike (which is the only one I am going to tell about) affected us directly, because most of the men on my father's side of the family, worked at Kohler and found themselves on both sides of the conflict. Fortunately my father had left Kohler and worked at the Vollrath Company by that time and was not directly involved in the strike. He was not one to take sides. But I am getting ahead of the story. Let me back up and tell how important the Kohler Company was to the people of Sheboygan back then.

Some of my earliest memories of being a kid in Sheboygan are of listening to my uncles and grandfather talk about Kohler. The men who worked there always had a love/hate relationship with the Company, because their lives were dominated by what went on there. Kohler was at the vital center of their lives. They depended on Kohler for their jobs, which was their only means of support. They could have gotten other jobs, but they would not have been paid as well. The best jobs were at Kohler, so you would think they would have been grateful to be able to work there. But they weren't. They had all kinds of mixed feeling about their employment and their employer.

Like working men everywhere, they grumbled and complained constantly; about the work rules, about the conditions at their work stations, about the pressures they had to work under, and about their managers, supervisors and straw bosses. But mostly they complained about their pay, the small raises they got from time to time, and the bonuses they got every year at Christmas, which were always less than they expected or thought they deserved.

That was the dilemma. They generally thought that Mr. Kohler was next to God and that the Kohler Company was the greatest place in the world to work. But they didn't know, ever see, or like Mr. Kohler, and they were always talking about "quitting and getting a better job with a better company." So the issue of forming a local union was a hot one and you were expected to take sides. Some of my uncles were for a union. Some were against it. I think my grandfather didn't think it was a good idea, but "would go along with it" if there ever was one.

My uncles who wanted to form a union thought Kohler was a terrible dictator; "cheap, cruel and heartless", and that the plant was a "sweatshop." In a way they were right. Mr. Kohler was in charge and ran the show. If you didn't want to do things his way you could leave and find work elsewhere. And some of the working conditions were bad, or downright dangerous. The pro-union workers complained that they were treated like "slaves" and worse then "stray dogs." The believed that the only way they could defend their rights and get what was due them (by which they meant shorter hours, easier work, more pay, and higher bonuses at Christmas) was to form a union. They were ready to sign up and they demanded that a vote be taken.

In these family arguments my father tried to stay neutral, which was not an easy thing to do. He usually was quiet during these arguments about Kohler. If he did say anything it was only to cool things down and calm the uncles. But he was never successful. The arguments continued and got hotter and hotter as it came close to the time where there was to be a vote. The women noticed that the drinking at this time increased. The pressure was on.

A shrike at Kohler had been coming on for years. It was going to happen and nothing could stop it. It was only a matter of time before something would cause the "bubble to break" or the "cover to fly off." An explosion was due. Unions were forming in all of the factories in all of the cities all over the country. Mr. Kohler couldn't hold out forever. His dream of a peaceful utopia in the middle of America was fast coming to an end. And, at that time, it was hard to keep labor disputes from getting violent.

There was a kind of fatal progression and momentum to these first strikes, as though some mysterious hand were directing them from above. They started peacefully, with petitions and complaints, which led to talks and walks and the holding of signs. As time went by and nothing happened, frustration set in and there were some acts of vandalism and some destruction of property. At first no one got hurt, but if all else failed, both sides were determined to fight it out in the streets, which they often did, because foolish things were done, by both sides.

Strikebreakers were hired by the companies. Soon they were armed. Police were frequently called in when fights broke out. Soon people started to get hurt, and finally some got killed. When things got completely out of hand, governments stepped in and the troops were called out. Order was finally restored. There were some nasty strikes at that time. And no one seemed to be happy after they blew themselves out and were over. Labor relations and conditions only seemed to get worse.

It didn't take long that particular year for talking to move to action. Some of the men in the Kohler plant circulated petitions asking the company to allow them to form a union. Of course, Mr. Kohler refused to accept the petition. The men got angry and threatened to strike. They warned that if that happened there might be violence. Mr. Kohler told them if they did dare to strike, he would fire them all, hire replacements to take their places, hire guards to protect his property, and call in the police if he had to. All of these things he promptly did. There was no chance for any negotiations, no talks, no mediators. It was a declaration of war. The "loyal workers" were given guns and those who wanted a union armed themselves and prepared for the battle. There were a lot of hunting rifles around and plenty of ammunition.

Though I was not there in person I will never forget that fateful night. How could I forget it? From then on the event became part of Sheboygan history, legend, and lore, and it was rehearsed and relived, over and over and over by those who refused to forgive and forget. It was terrible, something that no one would ever have thought could happen in such a peaceful community like Sheboygan. And certainly not in Kohler, the perfect city, second only to the Garden of Eden or Paradise.

But, it did! IT SURE DID!

When word got out to the men who wanted to form a union that Mr. Kohler had hired a "bunch of thugs" and armed both them and workers who had pledged to "stay loyal," the pro-union men quickly got their guns and gathered outside across the street from the plant. They came late that afternoon, just as the sun started to set and it was growing dark. The pro-Kohler men and hired guns were on the inside. The plant had become a fort. The anti-Kohler, pro-union men were on the outside. It was like something out of an ancient war where a city was under siege, or a movie about one of the European revolutions, where all of the peasants got cut or gunned down.

First there was only shouting back and forth. Some of the men on both sides were obviously drunk. The language got profane and nasty.

Then the voices got louder and more angry, and the men on both sides started to throw things, like bottles and bricks.

Nobody knows what happened next or who fired first, and it is a good thing no one could be named or blamed.

Suddenly all hell broke loose and there was a long shootout. Guns blazed and bodies started to fall.

It lasted a long time and many men in and out of the building were seriously wounded. There was no one to stop the fight. The few policemen that the City of Kohler had hired to keep order were nowhere in sight. It was a battle royal, totally out of control. It went on for hours, with only breaks in the action to reload.

By the time it was over I think eight or nine men had been killed. I don't remember anyone telling me how it stopped or who stopped it. Maybe the men on both sides just ran out of ammunition or lost interest in continuing such a senseless and useless fight. In time, everybody just disappeared.

That's often how these things end. All of a sudden it is just over, and only the wreckage and the bodies are left behind. Those who were there when the sun came up the next morning said that it was like a scene out of "Gone With the Wind." The beautiful grassy and tree covered strip between the plant and the shopping strip across the street was covered with trash, discarded clothing, bottles, and blood.

Those who stayed out of curiosity watched as military units from the National Guards or the regular Army came marched down the street and set up an encampment on the grass. I think the Governor had called them out when the firing began. They put up tents, stacked their rifles, and quickly went off to set up guard posts around the plant. The troops remained there for about two weeks. I know because my dad and I went out and saw them. The strike was over. There wouldn't be any unions at Kohler for several more years. Soon everyone was coming to work again as if nothing happened, and people all over the world were buying new toilets. What an irony!

To a kid my age it was all pretty exciting. And confusing. I can remember asking lots of questions, but no one would answer them. The adults just told me that I was "too young to understand." They were right. I was. My dad didn't know what to say so he kept pretty quiet, just shaking his head, and saying such things as, "O my God!" or "How could something like this have happened?"

Fortunately, none of my uncles, who were on both sides that night, armed and shooting at each other, were harmed or killed. They were more stunned than anything, like they had been awakened from a bad dream. They were in shock. At first, when they got together again for a family occasion, and they retired to the front room to drink their beer and smoke and talk, they were very quite. They didn't have their usual lively argument about something, or talk about Kohler at all. They sort of pretended that it had never happened. They drank a little more beer than usual.

But later, as time went on, they did talk about it now and then. They told each other where they were and what they did during the strike, and how sorry they were that this was the way things had turned out, and how no one ever meant it to go so far. They also agreed that nothing had gotten settled, that everyone had suffered, and that they had better just do their work and forget about a union for now. They must all have been glad that they were still alive.

Years later a union did get formed, and eventually all of my uncles belonged to it. But it didn't happen because of or in spite of the strike. That strike was over, if it ever was really a strike at all. It all ended in a hail of bullets. Nobody wanted to talk about it anymore. In time, the elder Kohler had died and one of his sons was running the company. He might even have become a Governor for a while, or at least a Senator.

The second shrike, the one after the war, was much worse. It was a big one, involved the national Teamsters Union, and it lasted for years. At times it really got out of hand and spilled over into the community. A lot of property was destroyed in and around Sheboygan, and a lot of people got hurt. It cost lots of money and the government got involved. I don't remember how that one ended. I wasn't there anymore.

This time, my uncles were all on the same side, and they all suffered together, which didn't help them much. Most of them slowly died from either silicosis (from working in the sandblast room) or alcoholism (made worse by the shame and guilt they had to live with.)

I was glad I was no longer in Sheboygan when the second strike took place. And I am glad I was not an adult for the first one.

Bootleggers

It was a kind of cottage industry. Almost all of the men in Sheboygan at some time or another were engaged in it. But not many men sold any of it. They just used what they made for themselves, and maybe a few friends, when they came over to their house and wanted to take a nip. It was illegal. So everyone was really careful. I am talking about "bootlegging," which was something that was done during prohibition. This is a true story of something that happened, right in our own neighborhood, at that time.

The rumor started going around that the man and woman who lived next door to us on Swift Avenue were bootleggers. That would have made sense, given what the people who lived on the block had been observing. All the clues were there, but as yet none of the evidence.

By this time, as prohibition lingered on, and people were getting more and more thirsty for booze and there was more and more bootlegging going on, even in our beloved town, and by people who ordinarily considered themselves to be law abiding citizens. They didn't see themselves as some Al Capone or like the moonshiners in the South who made hard whiskey. They were not in it for the money. They just liked to have a little something around that was stronger than root beer or Coca Cola. They just made their brews as a hobby and their own pleasure, things like beer, wine, and a little bathtub gin. It was usually hidden from the children, and the police.

Of course there were a few who found out that there was a good and ready market for their products and that it was an easy way to make a few extra bucks on the side. Bootleggers are not born, they just get carried away and make more stuff than they can use for themselves. So....they begin to "share it with my friends." It was suspected that this man and his wife were among those few.

Now put it together yourself and you will understand why the people on our block were so suspicious; the drawn shades both day and night, the strangers going in and out, the big mean dog, and the strict privacy.

Wouldn't it make sense? And besides, they were foreigners (Germans), who hardly spoke a word of English. They must be up to no good. The older immigrants didn't like or trust the newer immigrants then either.

The rumor persisted through one of those long winters when people who came to their house regularly wore those long overcoats that were very big and oversized. The people on the block wondered what might be carried inside. If they weren't bootleggers they must have been spies of some kind. Something was definitely going on in that house.

I wouldn't be surprised if there might have been some quiet conversations going on between the officers down at police headquarters and some of the people on our block. We started to notice that that there were more cops on our beat, and they seemed to be patrolling our block more often than they used to. This was before the days of squad cars, so they were doing it on foot. We were not a high crime area, so why were they there? You know how those rumors get started and spread.

They were all convinced that something fishy was going on, and some of the people on the block decided that what was going on "right under our very noses" was a well organized, thriving, and prosperous bootleg business. They didn't have any proof, but you know what they always say, "where there is smoke there must be a fire."

My own reading on this behavior would be that there was a whole lot of wishful thinking behind this, and maybe a little envy and jealousy.

Sheboygan wasn't always the most exciting town to live in. We didn't have the action of those high crime cities like Milwaukee and Chicago, where daily there were big bank robberies, mayhem, and even murders. (There weren't such things as serial killers and sex offenders and terrorists yet, or at least they weren't called that.) All of the crime we had was local and not something to make movies about. If there were any crimes being committed in our beloved town, it was due to drunkenness, starting fights in taverns, or some petty thievery. Someone would get locked up in the jail for a night or so, and then let go. The real gangsters were in the big cities. We never expected Al Capone and his gang to come to Sheboygan to do business, though they might have.

So wouldn't it be exciting, if some night, the police would come and storm the house next to ours, haul out that couple in handcuffs, destroy those stills they had in the basement, and take the couple off to jail? That would get headlines and front-page space in the Sheboygan Press! It might even be reported as far away as Milwaukee or Green Bay.

As for the couple, it would be "good riddance." Nobody liked them anyhow, except my mother, who used to talk with the woman in German over the back fence. I liked their dog, even though it had bitten me once, when I got too close to him and teased him. If they had gotten arrested, it would have made a lot of people happy, and it would have "served them right" for coming into our nice quiet and safe neighborhood and "causing all that trouble and scaring everyone out of their wits."

But that didn't happen. The folks on the block were bound to be disappointed. None of the rumors were true, quite the contrary.

As it turned out the couple next door were not bootleggers. Far from it. The neighbors would have known that if they had taken the time to get to know these nice people. Though they were very shy and kept to themselves, they were just a couple of scared immigrants like the rest of them once were, trying to get by and make a living. When we got to know them they were friendly and often kind and helpful. They were even Lutherans in the old country.

When the police reports finally came out, they clearly, officially, and finally verified that they were NOT bootleggers, nor had they ever committed any other crime.

Mom, Dad, and I knew that already.

Actually, as it turned out, the bootlegger among us was another man, a few blocks away. One day, the back of his house blew up and the police came and took him away. I often wondered where the people on the block got their supplies after that?

The Cost Of Things
In The Good Old Days

One summer day, one of my daughters was begging me to raise her allowance. She was going into junior high in September and she was pleading with me to raise it because it was not going to be sufficient to buy the things she said she needed and wanted when she started school.

Like parents of my generation usually do, I was being self-righteous and unreasonable, telling her that I thought her present allowance was ample and that she was lucky to get any allowance at all. I told her that I never got an allowance when I was her age, because I earned all of the money that I got to spend. I suggested that she might find some way to earn some money herself. That went over like a lead balloon.

When that didn't work, I tried to persuade her that what I was giving her now was surely enough for her needs and that if we could sit down and work out a budget for her spending I could prove it and she would agree. Of course, she didn't. She kept telling me that things "cost more now than when you were a kid." As it turned out, she was right!

But, still convinced that I was right, we started to compare costs of specific items then and now and I soon discovered that things certainly did cost more for my kids than they did when I was a kid her age in Sheboygan, a whole lot more, even when we factored in the higher wages and income, inflation, and the changed value of the dollar.

Just for the fun of it, I would like to share with you what some things did cost back then (in the 20's and 30's). You can do the numbers and make the comparisons yourself. But I warn you, it may cost you a much higher allowance than you now so generously give.

To be fair, let's start these comparisons with the income side.

For instance, all during the depression years, my dad worked 12 hours a day six days a week. For this he got a monthly wage of $70.00. His employer didn't take out Social Security (there wasn't any during most of his working life), tax withholding, union dues, or any of the things they do now, and the employer did not pay for health benefits or pensions. He was on a strict hourly wage, like most workers were then. His check always came to $70.00 and I don't ever remember his getting a raise when I was still living at home. He was lucky to have a steady job.

But as they would say in Sheboygan, that was just enough "to make ends meet." Married women generally did not work, so the wages of the man was the total income for that household. Single working women probably made about half the amount the men made. Young girls who still lived at home often had to give most or all of their income to their fathers for room and board. Young single men might rent a room in some private home for less than a few dollars a week. It started to get expensive when he got married and started to have kids, often many.

I started to earn my own money when I was very young. You had to wait until you were 16 to hold down a steady job, but you could do other things to make some money. I started out delivering magazines. I did that one day a week and earned about 34 cents. Later I delivered papers. I did that every day, except Sunday, and made one or two cents per paper. That usually added up to a couple of dollars a week. I thought I was doing very well. When I got into high school I worked in the summer at an A & W root beer stand and got paid 20 cents an hour or about $8.00 a week, unless I worked overtime and made a little more. That was good money and I saved most of it. At the end of the first summer I worked there I bought a brand new bike for $20.00. I also got all of the free root beer I could drink, but had to pay a nickel for a black cow (a root beer with ice cream in it).

When I became a working musician (when I was about 16) I started to make "big money." I could earn anything from $2.00 to $5.00 for a gig. I used to play on weekends and sometimes made almost 1/3 or half as much as my father did that week. My first full-time band job, during the summer of 1942, was at a summer resort (which I already told you about)\ where I paid $21.00 a week (I should have taken a leader's fee like the Union guys did, but I didn't), plus lodging at a cottage, one meal a day, and Sunday dinner.

Later, in the fall of 1942, when I went to Milwaukee to job around and do casuals, I would get paid $8.00 to $12.00 for a three to four hour gig. At that time workers on other jobs were lucky if they made 33 cents an hour and could make as much as $15.00 or $20.00 a week. Is it any wonder that I wanted to be a musician?

In Madison, after the war (1948-49)), while I was going to college, I worked with a band on weekends at a supper club and got paid $25.00 for the weekend (Friday, Saturday, and Sunday nights and a Sunday afternoon Tea Dance), plus a good Sunday dinner. That was a lot more than my friends made for full-time weekly jobs doing other things.

While I was in the Army (for three years) I got $42.00 a month, all of my clothing and equipment items, and room and board. I didn't gamble, smoke or drink, and I didn't chase women, so I saved most of that. I remember buying a War Bond each month for $25.00. By the time I got discharged I had saved enough money to buy myself a new drum set.

Because I was an ex-GI when I decided to go back to school, I qualified for the government program called the "GI Bill." This paid for our full tuition, our books, supplies, and fees, and $70.00 per month for living expenses. Because I always was able to supplement this with my earnings from band jobs, I always had money left over at the end of the month to put in a savings account in the bank. I was not wealthy, but I was well off for my age.

So, from an early age, I always had money to buy things and learned the value of money and how to manage it. I was also a saver and always had money in the bank. I knew the value of money, and still do.

This is how I spent it.

I started out buying penny candy, and moved up to 5 cents for a double dip ice cream cone or a Terry's hamburger. A coke or root beer was also a nickel. Movies cost a dime, as did a chocolate eclair. I loved chocolate eclairs, even though they cost so much. A real treat was a banana split or a malt for 15 cents. A Big Little book was a nickel, most magazines were also a nickel or a dime. That sounds cheap, but it wasn't then. You could get a whole meal at a restaurant for a quarter. The first records (the old two-sided 78s) were anywhere between 39 to 69 cents. A model airplane kit was 25 or 50 cents, depending on the size. I bought lots of both. And so it went. My parents bought me my clothes and shoes, but I paid for all of these other things myself.

As I grew older, and began to earn more money, I made bigger and more costly purchases with the money I earned or had saved. I bought my own roller and ice skates, bikes, and drum sets. My first drum set (which I bought while I was a sophomore in high school) cost me $15.00 (it was used.) My second set, which was brand new, cost over $100.00. It did not have any cases to carry it in. The brand new Slingerland Radio King drum set (complete with cases) that I bought when I got out of service cost less than $400.00. Now, that same set would cost at least $3,000.00. Now my drum equipment, which includes a complete set, cymbals, and cases and carts, is insured for over $6,000.00. So, you can see the difference.

Here are a few more examples of what adults paid for things when I was a boy.

They could get a full tank of gas for about a buck or less, our rent for a flat was $18.00 a month, and violin lessons were 50 cents a week. I don't know what a ton of coal or a large chunk of ice cost, but it must have been cheap. And then there was food. We ate well, and often out of the garden, but I don't think my mother ever had any more than $20.00 a month to spend on food. Add to that the monthly electric and phone bills, payments on the car, and payments on some necessary things that to be purchased on time, and you can see that things were cheap. But there was a lot to pay for each month with those small fixed salaries. And people were committed to paying their bills on time and in cash. I didn't buy my own clothing until I left home so I don't know what those prices were. And shoes. Shoes always seem to be expensive. It was only after I got married and had five kids, and was on a limited salary, and my wife did not work outside the home, and I didn't play band jobs anymore, that I realized how hard it must have been at times for my parents to figure out how to "make ends meet," even when prices were as cheap as they were. And what did they do for Christmas? And birthdays? And special things? As you can see, for my folks, there wasn't much left over for entertainment, or giving to church, or for taking vacation trips, things we just now take for granted.

As people like me look back we wonder how they made it. It must have been hard for them at times, especially if they had large families. But they did! As a boy I seemed to have had everything I needed, always had some kind of a job, and always had money to spend or save. I think living through the depression was more a question of attitude than it was of economics. If you complained a lot about what you didn't have or couldn't afford, you could get pretty miserable and unhappy. But if you were grateful that you had a job and could pay your monthly bills you could live a happy life.

I was lucky to have lived in the kind of home I grew up in. My dad always had a steady job and he could be proud of the fact that he was a good provider. I came out of the depression grateful that I had experienced it and learned from it. But my mother came out of the depression feeling cheated and bitter. All of her life she worried that she would not have enough money to pay her bills, which she always did.

My father never talked about it.

The 8th Street Bridge

Every city or town that has a wide river running through it on its way to a lake or ocean, must have a bridge or bridges. Some of them may be large high bridges that also carry a major road or highway. Some of these are lift bridges that must open and close when even the smallest craft must pass beneath them. In New England they like those small wooden covered bridges that usually go over a small stream or creek. They were built for wagons pulled by horses and not modern cars or trucks. The bridges I am talking about are made of cement and steel.

When we were still living in Duluth, Minnesota, they were celebrating the 100th Anniversary of their beloved and famous Aerial Lift Bridge. People come from all over the world to see it. I know a lot about that bridge because one day an old guy (who looked almost as old as the bridge itself) gave a talk to our Duluth Kiwanis Club and told us all about how it was built and how it works. When they refurbished it, they said it cost about a million dollars to do it. But it is one of Duluth's main tourist attractions and probably will pay its way. One of the things the old guy giving the talk said was that this Aerial Bridge was the only bridge like it in the world. I don't believe that, because our 8th Street Bridge in Sheboygan, Wisconsin looks a lot like the Aerial Bridge in Duluth and served the same functions. But I didn't want to tell him that because I didn't want to hurt his feelings.

The bridge in Sheboygan, at least when I lived there, was simply known as the "8th Street Bridge" and it has been there as long as anyone living in Sheboygan can remember. It not only connects the South and North parts of town and divides the town in half, but frequently holds up traffic for frustrating periods of time when it has to be raised and lowered. You can avoid the bridge by going across town on 14th Street, but most people didn't and probably still don't do that. They just came down 8th Street hoping to get across the bridge before it had to do its thing and let a craft of some kind go through. Or, maybe folks were just more patient then. That's the way we always came when we went up to see my grandma.

The 8th Street Bridge, which was a minor inconvenience for motorists, was a major and exciting attraction for us kids. We never got tired of watching the 8th Street Bridge go up and down. On boring days we would hop on our bikes and ride down to the harbor just to see the bridge. It had a special attraction for me because it was right down the street from my Grandpa Wisch's barbershop, and I got down there often.

I think part of the fascination for us kids was how the bridge worked. As one was coming down the street from either direction, walking or riding in your car, all of a sudden a loud bell would ring and big red lights would start flashing. Everyone knew that this meant that some vessel was coming toward the bridge and needed to go up into the river or out to the lake. Then those long white and black striped wooden barriers would come down (we always thought they looked like Zebras), blocking the traffic on both sides of the bridge. We liked to ride right up to those barriers on our bikes to get a good view. We were always tempted to duck under them and get right up to the lip of the moving platform, but we knew that was dangerous and that we would get severely punished if we dared to try.

Very slowly, on both sides, the platform that served as the roadway would start to rise, until it had reached the height that the operator determined was necessary to allow the vessel coming through to clear. There were big wheels with teeth on them on both sides of the bridge and huge metal cables that made the whole thing work. We kids never quite figured out how it all worked.

Then, after the craft had passed through, the platforms would slowly come down again, the barriers would go back up, the lights would stop flashing, and the bells would stop ringing, and the traffic (sometimes backed up for blocks) would start flowing normally again. It always worked exactly in the same way, day in and day out. There was another bridge somewhere else up the river, but it must have been higher because it was not a lift bridge.

Another thing we kids liked to do on that bridge was endlessly ride across it on our bikes. The metal on the surfaces of the roadway made the tires on our bikes make a funny noise, kind of a loud humming. There was no other way or place in town where we could make that sound. It was really neat. Of course, there were walkways on either side of the roadway so people could walk across the bridge at any time of the day or night, and high metal railings to guard them. That is one place my dad and I liked to go to look out into the harbor and lake. You could get a wonderful panoramic view from up on the bridge.

I don't remember what happened in the winter, if the harbor froze over so vessels could not get in and out of the channel. Maybe the bridge did not have to go up and down in the winter. But someone would have to plow the roadway and someone would have to shovel the snow off of the sidewalks. We still had to use the bridge. It was a necessity. We couldn't get from here to there without it.

Now and then, like kids do, I wondered what it would be like to jump off the bridge into the water below. But I was too chicken or smart to ever try. Now and then someone did. But we did do another dumb thing we were not supposed to do. We would load up our pockets with stones and then go out to the middle of the bridge and throw them in the water, watching them go down and splash in the water below. We were very careful not to hit anything. We would count how many seconds it took to reach the water and tried to estimate the distance the stones traveled.

One day, as I was walking across the bridge I got this terrible urge to throw something into the water. The only thing I had in my pocket that day was a nickel. Without thinking I took it out of my pocket and flung it as far as I could out and into the water. As soon as it left my hand I realized how stupid that was. I had just thrown away an ice cream cone, a coke, or a hamburger. I never did that again.

You would have thought that eventually we kids would get tired of watching the bridge go up and down. But we never did. There was something about that process that continued to fascinate us. To this day I still like to watch aerial or lift bridges open and close or go up and down. Maybe some day I will understand why.

When I was a kid we always hoped that some day the bridge would get stuck. We wondered who would fix it and how. But it never did, get stuck that is. At least not while I was there. We did get held up for about two hours in Duluth once. It was right after the 4th of July fireworks at the waterfront. The big ships got held out in the lake while the fireworks were going on and were all lined up eager to get in and dock. When the bells rang and the light flashed and the barriers came down we were five cars away from getting across the bridge. There was nothing we could do but wait until all the ships came in.

It was very late and we were eager to get home, but we got out of our car, went down to the channel stood by the railing and watched the huge ships come in. It took two hours but I don't remember ever having a closer or better view of those ocean-going vessels. As I stood there, I thought about the bridge in Sheboygan and relived some of my boyhood again.

When I was on my revisit trip to Sheboygan, I purposely went down to see what had happened to the 8th Street Bridge. For some reason it didn't look quite the same as I remembered it, and neither did the whole area around it. I couldn't figure out what was different about it and it didn't really matter. It was still there and it was still doing what it was designed to do. It still works the same, and I suppose it always will, as long as the river is there and boats need to get out into the harbor and from the harbor into the river. And as long as it is the best way to get from the North Side to the South Side, and visa versa.

Del Fredrichs' Garage

Every town has a few people in it that the town cannot do without. These persons are not the town leaders, and they are not prominent citizens or have any titles. They don't hold any office and they don't have a lot of money. But they perform the essential services that keep things running smoothly and they do what they do quietly and without expecting any praise and little reward. These persons just go about their business and do their thing day after day, efficiently and well. They are the saints among us, though they certainly would not consider themselves to be anything special. They are people with huge talents unusual skills, but small egos.

There were people like this in Sheboygan when I was growing up, and I think my dad knew them all. One of these was Del Fredrichs, the father of a good friend of mine. He and his family lived right across the street from the school I attended. He and my dad were a lot alike.

Dad often said that Del Fredrichs was the best auto mechanic in the world, and when he couldn't fix something on his car himself (which wasn't very often), he would always take it "out to Del." Why would he take it anywhere else?

Del was a plain and simple man, and he was always dirty. I never saw him dressed up, ever! When he would come home from work at night, his wife, a lady who was neat and clean to a fault, would not let him come into his house until he had taken off all of his clothes in the outer hall and taken a bath. I don't know how much formal education Del had, but it didn't matter. He was a natural, a master craftsman.

But this story is not about Del; it is about his shop. His shop was a fabulous place. I would stop doing whatever I was doing and cancel anything I planned to do if I could go with my dad out to Del's shop. A trip out there was an adventure into a mysterious and captivating land.

I don't think Del's garage had a formal name and I don't remember there being any sign on the building to identify what it was. It didn't need one. Everyone knew what and where it was. It was Del's garage!

Actually what it was, or more correctly had been, was a small airport, out on the edge of town. One time somebody got the bright idea there ought to be an airport in Sheboygan and for a few years there was one. Real airplanes were housed out there and for a time there were scheduled flights out of there, and maybe even a small flight school. I think it was called "The Sheboygan Airport." But that didn't last long. There were either not enough planes, or flights, or frequent flyers to justify the high costs of doing business. It soon went belly-up and Del bought the whole airport and turned the hanger into a garage. It turned out to be an ideal place to fix cars in.

Del never advertised his business. He always had more cars to fix than he had time to fix them. Del was always busy and he didn't make appointments. You just brought your car out to Del's place and he "worked you in." No one complained if they had to wait until Del was ready to fix their car, and there weren't any fancy waiting rooms with free coffee and donuts. You just hung out and shot the bull with other waiters until it was your turn. You weren't there to be entertained, you were there because of the quality of Del's work. Everyone knew that if Del fixed your car it was really fixed. And he fixed them cheap. And no one ever got a bill. And no one got credit. You just paid Del cash when you had the money, or I am sure there were times when he didn't get paid at all. Some of the farmers probably paid him in chickens, eggs, and milk. Del did well, but he wasn't interested in making a lot of money. He liked fixing cars and took a great deal of pride in his work.

When you brought your car to Del you never said something fancy like, "Mr. Fredrichs, I would like you to determine the cause of the trouble I seem to be having with my car, and when you find out what it is, would you be good enough to please give me an estimate of the cost and arrange for its repair?" All you needed to say, like my dad always did, "Hey Del, how about fixin' 'er up?" He always did.

But, more about his shop. I want to tell you why we kids were so fascinated with it and why we were so eager to go out there with our fathers. We were almost happy when their cars broke down and they had to take them out to Del's to fix them.

First of all Del's garage was huge. It had been an airplane hanger after all. Second, it was always cluttered. You have never seen so many car parts in one place in your life. His inventory, both new and used parts, was huge. Third, it was always dirty, oily, wet, and greasy. Del never cleaned anything until he actually used it and put it in a car. He wasn't interested in a clean garage. He was only interested in working cars.

It was said he never used new parts unless he absolutely had to, or a customer insisted. He could always find the right part and he knew where everything was and how to get his hands on it. He knew how to rebuild engines and create and build parts from scraps. How he did that was one of the great mysteries in Sheboygan.

And then, lastly, Del did all of his own work. He would hire a couple of young guys to do things like change tires or oil, wash, or grease the cars. But when it came to repairing them, he wouldn't let anyone touch a car but himself.

And, just like the old Jew shoe repairman I told you about in another book, Del guaranteed his work 100%. If you had any trouble with your car after he fixed it (accidents did not count and sometimes parts got old and worn out and had to be replaced), or were not completely satisfied with the work he had done, you could bring your car back and he would do the work over again. FREE! Del was not only a master mechanic and machinist; he was a magician.

I often wondered who fixed the cars in Sheboygan after Del died. I doubt that he ever retired. What would he do with his time?

Trains, Buses, And The
Interurban To Milwaukee

I loved to ride on anything, not just on my bike, my roller or ice skates, or the many scooters and small play cars I used to make. I also loved to ride in cars and on buses (I don't think we ever had street cars in Sheboygan), and my uncle's milk wagon that was pulled by horses until he got a truck. When we were in town we rode the buses. But when we took trips out of town we always rode the train. I loved to ride on those trains. It was the most comfortable way to travel at that time. If airplanes had been in common use then, I would probably have loved to ride on them too. But they were to come later, after the war. I also liked to walk.

During my boyhood, if you wanted to get out of town and take a trip somewhere, you usually rode on a train. You could take your car if you wanted to, and many people did. But as far as us kids were concerned, riding on a train was a real treat and a whole lot more fun. It was also the most convenient, cheapest, and most comfortable way to travel long distances. We were lucky. There were lots of trains running in and out of Sheboygan at all hours of the day and night. Sheboygan was an important stop on all of the passenger train routes.

There was a beautiful big train station running almost through the middle of our town. It was right at the bottom of the hill coming from 14th street going east toward 8th Street. It was about a block away from the Penn Avenue Bridge that ran across another part of the river that finally found its way into Lake Michigan. That whole area was full of tracks, railroad cars, engines, and buildings related to the trains in some way. It was an important part of town. Everyone knew where the train station was and how to get there. It was the kind that smaller towns used to have that later were turned into restaurants or museums.

All of the important trains stopped in Sheboygan on their way to or from Green Bay on one end and Chicago on the other. At Chicago you switched to trains going across the country. It was also where they hooked on the Pullman sleeping cars and the dining cars. AMTRAK still does that. I am sure some of those trains went all over the country, stopping at most every little town along the way. But I never traveled that far, until later, when I was in the Army and eventually traveled from coast to coast several times.

One of the major stops for all of the trains was Milwaukee. I used to go down there from time to time to see some of our relatives. Once the trains got out of Sheboygan they would follow the coastline up Lake Michigan. When you looked out of the window on those rides you could always see beautiful views of the lake. Many of the major railroad companies at that time had trains running through Sheboygan. At one time or another as I was growing up I rode them all. I remember names like the Milwaukee Road (which was always painted orange), The Great Northern (always painted yellow and green like the Green Bay Packers). And then there was the Silver Streak, at that time the newest, fastest, most beautiful train in the country. I don't know what train company it belonged to, but I think it was the Burlington Railroad. All of the trains hauled both freight and passengers.

I don't have to describe the trains to you. If you have ever ridden on a train you will have sat in the coaches, eaten in the diners, and may have even spent a night or two in a sleeping car. You might have even had one of those fancy compartments, like now and then the Army would furnish us. If you haven't ever been on a train you owe it to yourself to take a ride on one of the modern AMTRAK trains. Take the one going out West. That is the best one. You can take the one to LA or the one going to Seattle. The scenery is different once they split and head south or north.

The other train we loved to ride was called the Interurban. It was kind of an ugly duckling. It was sort of a streetcar, ran by electricity, without an engine to pull it, and with only a car or maybe two at a time. It might be called a short train. I think the one we rode only ran between Sheboygan and Milwaukee, or it might have gone as far as Chicago and might have started in Green Bay. I don't think I ever road it farther than Milwaukee. It would be something like the commuter trains that you will find in some of the big cities, mostly on the East Coast. I used to ride those from Boston up to Fitchberg when I was going to the Seminary and working at a church on weekends. Whatever the Interurban was, it was fun to ride. I can remember taking frequent trips to Milwaukee with the Boy Scout Drum and Bugle Corps, either going to an American

Legion convention or to the Wisconsin State Fair. The Interurban was a neat way to travel. Now those trains are called Commuters.

My other vivid memories of that train station in Sheboygan, and those trains, were the times our Drum and Bugle Corps marched the new recruits down to the station to get on the trains which took them to their first assignments. I will never forget the day that I was one of those recruits and ended up at Fort Sheridan, Illinois for my induction. Then, three years later, I probably took the train back to Milwaukee again to enroll at Milwaukee State Teacher's College. From then on I was more inclined to ride the Greyhound buses that were cheaper and took over most of the train routes to the smaller towns. I didn't like them as much as the trains but they took me to the places I needed or wanted to go.

Anyhow, I have and always will love riding on trains. Over the years Margaret and I, or our whole family, took several long trips on the AMTRAK trains. It is still a treat!

My First Ride On
The Moving Stairs

This momentous event did not happen in Sheboygan. It took place in Chicago. It was too early for Sheboygan to have one of them yet, though Pranges had one later. It was an experience I was never to forget. Doing something for the first time is always exciting. This was especially so, because it was new and novel and you couldn't do it just anywhere. At that time you had to go to Chicago or one of the big cities around the country to do it. I am talking about the first time I rode on that wonderful invention called an escalator, or as it came to be more commonly known, moving stairs.

Rarely, but now and then, we would take a trip to Chicago, which was always a big deal because it was the farthest place I ever traveled to until I graduated from high school. Milwaukee was fun too, but Chicago was not only a different city, but a whole different world.

My great-grandfather Martin was living there during those years and we went to see him. He was very old, single, and staying at the home of nice Jewish lady by the name of Ethel. It was rumored that she had been married to my grandfather, who had deserted her, and that my great-grandfather was taking care of her. That could have been true. My great grandfather was still employed, working as an aide at a hospital, and boarding at Ethel's.

Grandpa was a nice old guy and Ethel was an excellent cook and a lively lady. She used to take my mother and me sight-seeing to very interesting places when we were there, like some of big museums and art galleries, or the zoo, or the open market, or a big movie theater downtown called the Chicago Theater. They usually had stage shows there and all of the big bands traveling around the country played there. We always went to her favorite store, the big Marshall Fields store downtown, to do some shopping. Needless to say, we always had a great time with Ethel. For a kid at that time going to a big city like Chicago was like going to Disneyland is today, except we got there by train rather than plane, another part of the adventure.

It was at this big Marshall Fields department store, the largest in the Midwest and one of the largest in the whole country. They had just started experimenting with the newly invented moving stairs. On one of these visits I got to ride them for the first time.

They were really something. They looked like other stairs, except they were made of a very shiny silver metal. On the sides of the stairs were railings made of some kind of black material. The difference between these stairs and ordinary stairs is that everything moved, constantly. You got on either at the top or bottom and just rode them up or down. At first it was a weird sensation. I don't remember how many there were throughout the store or whether they went to all of the floors. If there was more than one set of moving stairs I road them all, many times.

Like all kids, when they have a new toy, I was totally absorbed by the experience. While the women were shopping, I just road up and down those stairs, it must have been for hours. After that, whenever we were in Chicago after that, and Ethel asked us where we wanted to go, I would shout out loudly, "To that big store downtown.....to ride the moving stairs." It was always one of our stops, and my very favorite. I never got tired of riding on those escalators.

Of course, very soon, all of the apartment stores had escalators, including Pranges in Sheboygan. They became commonplace and no one got excited about them anymore. Except me. For some reason, they captured my imagination and I have never gotten over it. To this day, whenever I am in a store or shopping mall, if they have elevators and moving stairs, I always choose to ride the moving stairs. And I still get a tiny thrill every time I do it, because it makes me think of Ethel and my grandpa as I am going up or down.

Cheese

The Cheese Capitol Of The World

I think I know why Plymouth, Wisconsin, a small town about 23 miles west of Sheboygan, was known as the "Cheese Capitol of the World." It was because Plymouth was in the "Dairy State" and Sheboygan County, which probably had more cows per acre than any place in the country. Wouldn't that make sense? Lots of cows! Lots of cheese! Those cows produced more milk than all of the people in the county could consume, so those smart farmers who lived around Sheboygan, used what was left over to make lots of butter, cheese, and ice cream. They probably made more money selling other dairy products than they did from just selling milk or maybe they just learned how to make good cheese in the old countries they came from.

It is my opinion that Plymouth got the honor of being called the "Cheese Capitol of the World," just because the Kraft Cheese Company used to have its headquarters there. But that was not really fair. There were hundreds of other small cheese factories all over the county, many in our area, that made as good or better cheese than Kraft did, and that cheese was shipped all over the world. I think at one time there were more than 150 small cheese companies in Sheboygan County. I don't know how many there are now.

As I have said before, one of the four things Sheboygan was known for was the fine cheese that was produced in and around there. Sheboygan only became the "Brat Capitol of the World" much later.

One of the reasons I am writing this story about cheese is that I would like my grandchildren to know that we once had a corner on the cheese used in one of their favorite dishes long before they arrived on the scene. When they come to visit, and their grandma asks them what they want to eat, you can bet your bottom dollar that the first thing they will say is, "macaroni and cheese." When we go to the Country Buffet to eat, the first thing they put on their plates is a huge helping of macaroni and cheese.

I still do love cheeses of all kinds, if they are the good farm-made, small cheese factory kind and not that processed stuff that looks like limp plastic or rubber that the Kraft Cheese Company now produces in Chicago and places other than Plymouth. But I don't like cheese on my apple pie, the way every person who comes from Wisconsin is supposed to eat it. I am told there is a law that in Wisconsin all of the restaurants have to serve a slice of cheese on a piece of apple pie. I don't know if that is true. I think it might just be a custom or a marketing trick.

I am sure that cheese is still big in Sheboygan, only second in popularity to brats and beer. It was even bigger when I was a kid. It was almost unpatriotic not to like or not to eat cheese in my hometown. So we all ate lots of cheese. It was also cheap and handy and lasted a long time, if properly stored.

But now that I don't live in Sheboygan anymore, I can allow myself the right and privilege of eating cheeses that are not made in Sheboygan County. And, if you won't tell anyone, I will admit that I love that white cheddar cheese from Vermont that I get at my grocery store's deli best of all. It is just like the cheese that a friend of mine used to send me every Christmas that was made in New York State. I feel a little guilty when I buy other cheeses, but they are so much better than most of the white cheddar they now produce in Wisconsin. It is almost as good as the white cheddar that a friend of mine introduced me to that is made in Belgium and sold in one of the shops in Canal Park in Duluth. Kraft never made anything like this, even when I was a kid, and before they started mass-producing everything.

Yet, I must admit, that every time I visit Sheboygan, I try to stop at one of those little roadside cheese stores and bring back a few packages of the cheeses still made the old fashioned way in Sheboygan County. I know that this cheese comes directly from the cows, because I can see them grazing in back of the cheese factory.

Brats, German Hard Rolls, And Beer

I don't know why they made such a big deal in Sheboygan about making cheese. They made just as much (or more) sausage, bread, and beer.

Now they no longer call Sheboygan (or Plymouth) the "Cheese Capitol of the World." That all changed after the war and the Kraft Cheese Company moved its headquarters to Chicago. Now it would be more accurate to call Sheboygan the "BRAT Capitol of the World." Now, in Sheboygan, BRATWURST DAY is bigger than the 4th of July and people come literally from all over the world to celebrate it. On that day, the smoke from the fryers covers the whole town, polka music pours from the speakers, and there is only one smell......brats cooking! It is a pungent and mouth-watering odor like no other, that is, if you like brats. If you don't, you better not come to Sheboygan during the summer, and certainly not on the Annual Bratwurst Day.

Those old German sausage makers who owned the butcher shops when I was a kid should have lived to see this. They knew all along that they made the best brats in the world, but they would have never been so bold as to say it out loud or make a marketing slogan out of it, like the sausage makers do now. But it has been true all along.

There is no brat better anywhere in the world than a brat made in Sheboygan. Even the brats we buy now at our supermarkets that are made in Johnsonville (which is near Sheboygan) are not quite like the ones that were made in Sheboygan when I was growing up there, at least not according to my mother, who had eaten and loved brats all of her life. And my mother used to tell me that the brats they made when I was growing up were not as good as the ones they made when she was a child. She said that is because "now they have too much filler in them." I didn't like brats when I was a kid and seldom ate them, so I could not tell the difference. Now I think the ones they make in Johnsonville are great! So much for good taste.

Whenever people got together back then, for a party or a picnic or just for a backyard outdoor meal in the summer, there would have to be at least three things; brats, German hard rolls, and beer. It didn't matter what nationality, race, religion, or gender you were, those three were a must. After that, you could bring anything else you wanted to enhance the potluck.

If you were Italian you might have brought some pasta dish.

If you were Greek you might have brought some soup.

If you were German or Polish you might have brought some sauerkraut, mustard, catsup, pickles, or raw onions to put on your brat.

If you had kids, who didn't always like brats, you might have brought some hot dogs or hamburgers for them.

And then, of course, there would have to be all kinds of good desserts. Everyone seems to love dessert.

Brats always had to be cooked over an open charcoal fire. If they were fried in a pan, like the women had to do if they cooked them in the winter, they never tasted as good. My dad always said that it was not the "secret spices" that gave Sheboygan brats their unique flavor, as the German butchers liked to claim, but the smoke and the bucket of beer he put them in when they were done. Whatever it was, there is no flavor like it. I wonder what my dad would think of those cookers they use now, the ones that do not even use charcoal. How can brats taste right unless they are saturated with smoke from a charcoal fire? And soaked in beer?

My dad knew all of the tricks for making a perfect brat. He taught us that we must constantly keep turning the brats as they are frying in order to keep the skins from breaking and the precious juices from coming out. He also taught us that we must never turn the brats with a fork or tongs. You must turn them with your fingers, dipping them first in cold water or beer to keep them from getting burned. He had tough fingers with lots of calluses on them from working in the power plant. Most of us mere mortals are not so lucky. We get a lot of red fingers when we first learn how to do it the "right" way.

No one could fry brats like my dad. He was an artist. When he was at a fry out anywhere, he was always elected to do the honors. I learned my lessons well. In my own family, I always fried the brats, in the same way my dad did. And they came out perfect every time.

I hate to admit it, but when I was a boy I didn't like brats. And I didn't like onions and sauerkraut and a lot of other stuff we Germans were supposed to think were so great. But the one thing I did like and could never get enough of were those wonderful German hard rolls, made from secret recipes of the old German bakers. They got handed down and passed from generation to generation but were never written down. Those rolls were also great to put hamburgers on, like Terry always did. But somewhere along the line those secret recipes did not get passed on or must have died with one of those old bakers. You can't get rolls exactly like that in any bakery in Sheboygan anymore. Believe me, I have tried.

So, that's the tradition I grew up with. It was a kind of culinary art and ritual that got played out week after week, year after year, all over Sheboygan and the countryside surrounding it. It was brats, German hard rolls, and beer. If you didn't like that menu, you were not only looked upon as being very strange, but were in danger of getting very hungry in summer.

And, of course, then there was beer....lots and lots of beer. I didn't like beer either, and still don't, but it didn't matter. We kids were not allowed to drink beer anyhow. I always liked root beer better, and still do.

Much of the beer was made right in Sheboygan, in a brewery only a short distance from where my Uncle Gilbert and Aunt Myrtle lived. A lot of beer was consumed in Sheboygan so that brewery worked day and night to turn it out. To the people in Sheboygan, drinking beer was like drinking milk, tea, coffee, or wine in other places. And brats and beer always went together. As the song says, "you can't have one without the other." Before they began to import the better known and more popular beers from places like Milwaukee or St. Louis, most of the people in Sheboygan drank the local beer made at our very own Kingsbury Brewery, that is after the law was changed after prohibition. During prohibition, a lot of men (including my father) made their own beer in their basements for their own use. But when the law got repealed, that home art lost its luster. The beer Kingsbury made was much better anyhow, and their beer was cheaper to buy than it had been to make. You could get it on tap at every tavern, in kegs for picnics and parties, and in bottles for home consumption. Beer in cans was still years away. Some of the men (including my father) continued to make homemade wine and homemade root beer, but they stopped making the bathtub gin and that terrible whiskey.

Almost everyone in Sheboygan, male or female (except me) liked to drink beer. It was the Sheboygan way and the drink of choice. You didn't ask why. If you were from Sheboygan you just did it!

So there you have it.

If you were born, raised, and lived in Sheboygan, you had better like brats, German hard rolls, and beer.

If you didn't, you better just move away….like I eventually did.

Taverns, Bars And
Beer In Copper Kettles

If you were thirsty for a beer there was always a tavern nearby. There were also bars, but these two institutions were not the same. There were some important differences and it was wise to know what they were so you didn't get into the wrong place.

A TAVERN was a place where you went to meet, eat, and play cards with your friends. They were nice, clean, pleasant places. It you got thirsty, it was okay to have a beer. You could also get a free hard-boiled egg, a big dill pickle, or some raw ground beef and onions on a bun. But that was not the main reason you went to a tavern. You went to a tavern primarily to socialize. Unlike the taverns in jolly old England, you couldn't sleep overnight there. If, by chance, someone started to drink too much, started a fight, or broke any of the furniture, they would promptly get "thrown out on their ear" by the bartender or proprietor. I know that happened at taverns because my Uncle Bill Furman owned one on the North Side and I got to go there now and then and saw for myself what went on in such places. They usually didn't serve meals at taverns, except maybe a Friday night fish fry.

If you wanted a little more action or intended to get drunk, pick up a "loose woman," do some serious gambling or start some trouble, you went to a BAR. They were often rough places and not in the better parts of town, where men went to be macho, show off their muscles, brag, chew tobacco, tell dirty jokes, and drink lots of whiskey. "Ladies" did not go to bars. If you were a woman, single or married, and went to a bar without a male escort you were asking for trouble and frequently found it. You could get the same things to eat and drink at the bars as you got in the taverns. Come to think of it, these were the places were the first junk food was served.

Bars always had a loud jukebox but only a tiny dance floor. The sailors who frequently came to town headed for the bars as soon as they could get off their ships. They were not looking for a simple friendly card game. And they didn't come to dance. They came looking for "the broads" and sometimes a good fight. The most lively bars in town were always found on the waterfront.

So you see, if you wanted to take your family for a fish fry on Friday night and took your kids along, you would not go to a bar, you would go to your favorite tavern. Kids were not allowed in bars.

And then there were the bars out in country. They were called ROADHOUSES, probably because they always looked like houses and were always two stories high. At night, there was always a red light shining outside to mark the location and intent of the place.

The rooms upstairs in these places were not for drinking or sleeping. Roadhouses were not motels. Once I was told by an older guy that some young girls from Chicago lived up there. I never saw any of them in any of our grocery stores or shopping at Pranges, and I always wondered why they didn't stay at a nicer place, like the Sheboygan Hotel across from Fountain Park, during their stays. I was also told that some of the roadhouses had gambling, which must have been legal at the time. I don't really know first hand what went on in those roadhouses, because I have never been to one.

Then there were the NIGHTCLUBS or SUPPER CLUBS, which had some of the same features and functions as a tavern or bar, but they were more like a fine restaurant, which many of them were. But they also had large dance floors and floorshows, sometimes nightly or sometimes only on weekends. They had both jukeboxes and often, live bands. When I became a professional musician, I often played in these establishments. Those were good gigs and always paid top dollar. But it was expensive to go to these clubs, probably because they were so fancy and offered so many amenities. Many of them quickly went out of business because the average person in Sheboygan could not afford to go to them often enough to support them. They were usually located right on the edge of town and on some major road. They always had big bright fancy signs to mark their location.

And finally, there were the BALLROOMS. The main reason for going there, of course, was to dance. People of all ages in Sheboygan loved to dance and danced a lot, especially to polkas, waltzes, and old-time music. It was not a great town for jazz, but it was a good place for the up and coming swing bands to play. The ballrooms at that time were always very large and most often near small towns or out in the country.

Of course, because steady and strenuous dancing causes people, mostly men, to "work up a thirst" there was a lot of beer and hard drinks consumed in between dance sets. The women at that time were smart. They would usually drink Coke and nurse a bottle or two through the whole night. The only time they would drink beer or something stronger was when the guys were doing the buying. Sometimes the young guys would bring their own bottles and go out to the car and take a swig during the time the band had intermission. They probably did that at the infamous "Dreamland Ballroom" right outside of Sheboygan. Maybe that's why there were so many fights out there on weekends.

When I got to be a professional musician I played in all of these places.......starting in corner taverns when I was 16, and later in nightclubs and ballrooms as I got older. I never enjoyed playing in bars and turned down those jobs when I could get something better. Those bars were always too darn smoky! And the people who came there were often rude, crude, loud, and nasty. They were not there to listen to good music.

But, you didn't have to go out to any of these places to drink your beer. Most of the beer consumed in Sheboygan was consumed right in the home, usually at mealtime. That's where my dad and mom did most of their beer drinking. My dad even had an interesting theory about that. I called it "the copper kettle theory."

My father always claimed that beer tastes better if it comes from a copper kettle. I never believed that, and I don't believe that to this day. But I was only a kid and I was not ready to argue with my father about something that important. Kids didn't disagree or talk back to their parents in those days.

I just shut my mouth, took the 15 cents my dad gave me, went over to the tavern (which was on the corner in back of our house), and got dad's beer in that pretty copper kettle he always sent with me to bring the beer back home for his supper. That amount of beer was just the right amount for my mom and dad for a meal. They didn't need any for me. I drank either milk or Kool-Aid.....and you didn't have to put either in a copper kettle.

Dad swore by his theory and it was one of the few things he would argue about if anyone did not share his conviction. When other men said that beer tasted just as good or better out of bottles or kegs, or insisted that beer always tasted best coming right out of the tap at the tavern, my dad would disagree. What he liked the best was the beer he sent me to get for him and bring home in his own familiar and special copper kettle. So, why argue? It was his 15 cents.

The only other person I ever saw with a copper kettle was an old man who lived up the hill from the A & W root beer stand where I worked. Every day, he would come down that long hill (several blocks) with his empty copper kettle in his hand. We would see him go into the tavern at the bottom of the hill. In a short time, he would come out of the tavern and we would continue to watch him as he carried the kettle full of beer all the way back up the hill. It would take him almost an hour to complete the whole trip. He was not steady on his feet, and often used a cane when he was not fetching his beer, but he never spilled a drop.

So maybe dad was right. Maybe beer did taste better out of a copper kettle. The old man and dad would have agreed on that.

Verifine Ice Cream

If you lived in Sheboygan back in the 30's and 40's you would have eaten Verifine Ice Cream....lots of it! You might eat it in a cone or a dish, or as an ice cream sandwich, or on a stick dipped in chocolate. If you were lucky and had the money, you might even treat yourself to a sundae or a banana split, or you might have one of those nice rich creamy malted milks they made at the drug stores. The basic ingredient for all of the above was the wonderful creamy ice cream that Verifine made day after day at its plant right close to the Vollrath Company, a few blocks from the baseball park, on the street that went way out to Kohler.

It was like the old song says, "You scream, I scream, we all scream for ice cream!"

We didn't really scream, but we ate lots of ice cream in Sheboygan when I was a kid. And none of it was fat free!

But whatever shape or form your ice cream treat took, the ice cream you ate in Sheboygan was probably made by the Verifine Dairy Company. They also handled milk and other dairy products, but their ice cream was what made them so popular, and made them most of their money.

No doubt about it. Verifine made fine ice cream. I think now the company is called Land 'O Lakes.

In Sheboygan, the Verifine Dairy Company had a monopoly on ice cream. If you wanted to eat ice cream, you would have to buy a Verifine product or go to Milwaukee to get some other brand. It was as simple as that.

At first, as I remember, we could only get three flavors; vanilla, chocolate, or strawberry. But by the time I left town to make my mark in the world, there was one ice cream shop on Geele Avenue that stocked 36 different flavors! I'm sure I tried them all. At one time, you could get triple dips, and you could get three different flavors on the same cone. I know that one of my favorites was orange-pineapple. Then, there were those wonderful cones, now called sugar cones. They were all made by the Schuckert Company. Like Verifine, they had a monopoly on those cones.

Now I like to buy my ice cream from Ben and Jerry's or Baskin Robbins. It has to be shipped in from the East Coast. But if I still lived in Sheboygan, you can bet I would buy my ice cream from Land 'O Lakes. It is called loyalty!

One of the reasons I got excited about having well paying jobs when I was a kid was that I started to have enough money to buy more expensive ice cream products, like one of those fancy dishes you could get at a drug store or ice cream parlor that cost 15 cents. I liked those ice cream sodas and those big creamy malts, but most of all, I loved those banana splits. One of the most vivid memories I have of my Aunt Harriet was of her taking me and my cousin, Dick, (and sometimes her cousin ,Wayne) to the finest ice cream parlor in town, the one that was up on 8th Street near the Sheboygan Theater. We always ordered a banana split. That was a real treat….it was fancy and it was expensive. If it was an extra large one, it might cost up to a quarter.

Banana splits were always served in a pretty long glass dish. The people who made them were real artists. First, long slices of fresh bananas were placed longwise on the sides of the dish. There were never any blemishes or brown spots on them. Then, there were three scoops of ice cream on top of the bananas - one vanilla, one chocolate, and one strawberry. On one scoop there was a chocolate syrup, on the second one a strawberry syrup, and on the last one a pineapple syrup. It was always eaten with a long handled spoon.

If you ever have had a banana split like that, you would never forget it, and you would yearn to have more. It was as close to heaven as you were going to get in this life.

Out in the country, people often made their own ice cream. But I lived in the city and had to buy mine, which I did almost every day in the summer time, and as often as possible the rest of the year.

I grew up eating the best ice cream made in the world, and I have been addicted ever since!

Riding With The Milkman

In Sheboygan, we thrived on simple pleasures. One of the really exciting things I remember doing when I was a young boy was riding with the milkman. I had that privilege and pleasure because my Uncle Milton was a milkman and he had his route in my neighborhood.

At that time, your milk and cream came in glass bottles and was delivered right to your door. The dairy companies hired men to do it. Delivering milk became an honored profession for a time. It looked like a nice clean job, the hours and the pay were good, and it must have been a better way to make a living than working in a noisy and dirty factory. At one time, I thought I might like to become a milkman like my uncle when I grew up. It was that or being a fireman, policeman, or teacher. That was before I decided to be a musician.

The process worked like this. Every night, before they went to bed, the women would put the empty bottles out on their back porches, or in some other known and handy place. They would always wash them before they set them out. With the bottles, they would leave a note for the milkman telling him what they wanted to buy the next day. The milkman would come, read the note, leave what was ordered and take back the empties.

I don't know if the women left the exact amount of money for the purchase or charged it and paid for it in some way later. All of the merchants at that time allowed people to buy on credit. People trusted one another and vendors almost always got paid. Records were kept in order books and no bills were issued. It was a nice, simple way to keep track of things.

The milkmen started out very early in the morning, sometimes when it was still dark. I suppose they had to get down to the dairy to load their wagons and complete their routes early enough for the women to have their milk and cream before breakfast. My uncle would pick me up at my house when he started his route and drop me off in time to walk to school. I know when I rode with my uncle and "helped him" (by carrying some of the empty bottles), it was well before I had to get to school.

At first when I did this, my uncle had a wagon drawn by a horse. In the winter, it was a sleigh with runners on it. Later, those all disappeared and were replaced by trucks. They were not as much fun. They were always white (I suppose, to match the color of the milk) and had the name of the company painted on the side. These vehicles weren't very big, but they carried a lot of bottles. In the beginning, I don't think they sold any other dairy products, just milk and cream. Men liked to use cream on their cereals and in their coffee. Women could whip it and put it on puddings, cake, and pies. We kids drank a lot of milk. On the top of the milk, there was always a layer of cream. That had to be mixed into the milk before we drank it. Sometimes, in the winter, the cream on top of the milk would freeze, pushing the cardboard little cover into the air. I thought that was neat.

The other thing I remember was that the milkmen always wore some kind of white uniform and had an official looking white hat or cap. When you saw them, you could not mistake them for anyone other than a milkman. At that time, men took a great deal of pride in their professions. I used to brag to the other kids that my uncle was a Milkman, and that I got to ride with him on his route. That made me a kind of local celebrity.

I don't remember too much about Uncle Milton. He was tall and handsome, and rather quiet. He was married to my Aunt Ella on my dad's side of the family. He did have a son whose name was Richard (I always called him Dick). His last name was Meyer, so he must have been German. Unlike most of my other uncles, and like my dad, he did not work at Kohler or Vollrath. I do remember that I enjoyed being with him and he seemed to like my company.

But then, suddenly, all of those adventures stopped. One night, Uncle Milton drove his car over the edge of the quarry into the water and drowned. I remember someone in the family saying one time, "I guess Milton wasn't able to pay his gambling debts." I was just a kid. I didn't know what that meant. And I never heard the whole story about his death. It didn't matter. Uncle Milton was gone and my days of riding with the milkman came to an end. I went on to other things, and never became a milkman.

I wish we still had milkmen. And I wish we still got our milk in glass bottles and had it delivered to our door, cold and ready to put on our cereal.

Somehow it seems that milk tasted better that way.

Fessler's

Everyone called him Mr. Fessler. He must have had a first name, but I never heard anyone call him by that, so I don't know what it was. My mom always called him Mr. Fessler, my dad always called him Mr. Fessler, and, of course, I was expected to call him Mr. Fessler. At that time, we called all adult males over 21, "Mister."

I was very fond of Mr. Fessler, not just because he was a big friendly man who always had a smile on his face, but because every time I came into his store he would let me pick out and give me a free cookie. He did that for all the kids. Unlike some other store owners and managers in town, Mr. Fessler really liked kids. He always stopped to talk to the kids who came shopping with their mothers, getting down on his haunches and chatting with them eye to eye. He also liked to pat us on the top of our heads and tell us what good children we were and how glad he was to see us.

Most married women did not work outside the home and did all of the shopping. Single women usually still lived at home and may not have done any grocery shopping at all. Their mothers did. Most women wanted to shop during the day when their husbands were working and their children were off at school. And the women didn't shop every day, like some women do now. Most women shopped once a week, with their biggest shopping trips coming right after payday.

Mr. Fessler must have had a wife, but I never remember ever seeing her or meeting her. They lived in the house right next to the store. And he must have had some kids, but I didn't know them either, probably because the Fesslers lived on the North Side and the kids went to different schools than I did.

The only place I ever saw Mr. Fessler was in his store, which he both owned and managed. He was there all the time. I don't think he ever took a day off or ever took a vacation. But his store did not stay open 24 hours a day like supermarkets do now. All stores had hours then, opening early in the morning and closing early in the evening. Like most of the other stores in town, Fessler's would also have been open on Friday nights, closing at 9:00 p.m., and might have had shorter hours on Saturday. All businesses were closed on Sundays. The Fesslers must have had a life outside the store, but I don't remember seeing them often around town or at activities or events. Maybe after working all week, Mr. Fessler was content to stay home when he was off.

Because Sheboygan was a factory town everything was organized around the working shifts of the majority of workers. Most factory workers worked one of two shifts - from 6:00 a.m. to 6:00 p.m. or from 6:00 p.m. to 6:00 a.m. Only clerks in stores or banks and professional people had different hours. This was before the time of 40 hour weeks and weekends off. Mr. Fessler and his employees put in long hours, but I am sure he paid them well. If the store was open, Mr. Fessler was there. It was his life.

If you did not know that Mr. Fessler owned the store, you would never have guessed it by looking at him. He looked just like one of the clerks, in his long white apron over non-descript clothing, waiting on customers and helping people find what they came to buy. He must have done his bookwork at night because any time you came into the store during store hours you could find Mr. Fessler out on the floor. He was always busy, always cheerful, and always ready to do anything to please. It was his store and he was proud of it. Talk about customer service! Mr. Fessler might have invented it.

The store was just called FESSLER'S. I think that name was in large print over the front entrance. But this store didn't need a sign. Everyone in Sheboygan knew where Fessler's was, because it was one of the first of what would later be known as supermarkets. When his store opened, it must have been the largest food store in town. It combined the old butcher shop, the produce market, and the bakery in one space and under one roof. Then it had all of the new canned and packaged products that were coming onto the market, along with specialty items like nuts, candy, garden seeds, and some plants and flowers in season. He might even have sold Christmas trees. Anything that was edible could be found at Fessler's, if it was in season and available, and more. And at good prices.

As the years went by, more and more things came pre-packaged, but at Fessler's there were still a lot of products that could be purchased in bulk; like milk and dairy products, juices, pickles, honey, rice, sugar, flour, nuts and candy, and lots of cookies (those were in boxes or big glass jars with covers on them.) That's were I headed when I came into the store. First I got my cookie, then I went to find and join my mom. Sometimes I would just wander around the store. Kids couldn't get lost at Fessler's. Mr. Fessler knew who you were and whom you belonged to. He kept his eyes open for stray children and pets.

I am sure that my mother also shopped in the other Mom and Pop stores and the butcher shops closer to home, and I know that she would sometimes buy fruit and vegetables at the Farmer's Market outside of Pranges on Friday nights, but she did the bulk of her shopping at Fessler's, even though it was on the other side of town.

Maybe one of the reasons for shopping there was that her credit was always good there. She only had to pay Mr. Fessler once a month, right after dad got his paycheck. She always paid in cash and in full. Her purchases were all recorded in a little record-keeping book with her name on it. Every regular customer had one.

Another thing she liked about Fessler's was that it had a pharmacy (we used to call it a drug store) connected to it. You could just walk through a door between them that was always open. I think one of Mr. Fessler's brothers owned that. It really was "one-stop shopping."

However, perhaps the best reason for shopping at Fessler's was that if you ever bought anything at Fessler's that was not completely fresh and of the best quality, you could bring it back and exchange it, no questions asked, and your money was refunded or you could exchange it for something else. Mr. Fessler wanted his customers to be 100% satisfied.

Let me tell you a few more things that people liked about shopping at Fessler's, things that you hear people complain about missing when they shop in the big self-service grocery stores we have these days.

Mr. Fessler stressed quality and service. He expected his clerks to dress neatly, be pleasant and courteous, and to "bend over backwards" to please the customers. If any clerk couldn't answer your question, serve your need, or find just exactly what you wanted, he or she would call Mr. Fessler and he would take care of it himself.

Mom especially liked the butcher shop at Fessler's. Not only was all of the meat fresh (none of it was packaged in advance), but it was cut and trimmed to your specifications. Some of the best sausage makers in town began to bring their products to Fessler's. And if you wanted a soup bone or some scraps or bones for your dog, those would be thrown in free with your purchase. Your meat was always wrapped up carefully and nicely in clean white paper and then in newspaper, with a string wrapped around it.

Fessler's was a great store!

Many years later, when I came back to Sheboygan to visit my mother, I frequently went to shop with her at Fessler's. By that time, there were bigger and fancier stores in Sheboygan that were closer to her where she could have shopped. And the old store was getting to look a little faded and jaded around the edges and did not carry the variety and quantities of products that the bigger stores carried. But loyalty meant a lot in Sheboygan. As long as Mr. Fessler was alive and she could get there, mom continued to shop at Fessler's. I can remember him growing very old, but he always looked the same, and he continued to come to the store every day.

I think that maybe the last time I saw Mr. Fessler was at the wedding reception party that my relatives arranged for us the first time we came back to town after Margaret and I got married. We had gotten married in Minneapolis so they were cheated of a church wedding and a typical Sheboygan reception, so they decided to put one on themselves. They wanted to meet "Glenn's wife." That was in 1950 and must have been in the early summer, close to the 4th of July. They rented a hall, had tons of food and kegs of beer, hired a band, brought lots of gifts, and had a great party. There must have been over 100 of my relatives there, as well as some special friends and guests. Mr. Fessler was one of those, though we did not know he was coming.

This time he didn't look the same. He was not only very old, but very thin and frail. People had to help him walk and it seemed that it was hard for him to see. He just sat quietly on the edge of the crowd. I had told Margaret about him and his store, and was proud to introduce him to her. He wished us the best and presented us with a gift. It was a beautiful table lamp. We had it for a long time and carried it from place to place as we moved all over Minnesota. I don't know what finally happened to it. It might have gotten broken or we might have given it to one of our girls when they moved out. When we received it, it was a very precious gift because we were told that Mr. Fessler had picked it out himself.

I have often wondered what happened to his store after Mr. Fessler died. When my mother moved to the nursing home, she didn't need to shop any more. So on our visits to Sheboygan after that, we seldom stopped to do any shopping at the stores there. If we did, it was always on the South Side. I don't remember ever going back to shop at Fessler's or even trying to see if it was still there.

Unfortunately, those stores and that way of life passed away a long time ago and I don't expect they will ever come back, which is too bad.

I miss stores like Fessler's, and I miss men like Mr. Fessler. He was one of a kind!

Terry's Famous Hamburgers

It almost brought tears to my eyes. I could hardly believe it. Terry's is gone? Not closed, not moved to a better location, not out of business......just gone, the whole thing. It no longer exists! There is nothing left of Terry's for anyone to see and remember.

How can that be? We always thought that Terry's would be there forever, for our children, grandchildren, and great grandchildren to enjoy as much as we did.

What I am talking about is a famous restaurant that was almost an institution in Sheboygan. You could almost say it was as if they just tore down the Empire State Building or the Statue of Liberty in New York or the White House in Washington, D.C.

Okay, I am exaggerating and being overly emotional, but to us, Terry's was darned important. And now it is gone! I know that because a friend of mine sent me a newspaper article that reported that Terry's had been demolished to make room for some highway construction project on Calumet Drive. How sad!

Another cherished place in Sheboygan has now become a memory.

You might wonder why anyone could get so excited and sentimental about a little hamburger joint, so I will tell you about Terry's and why it was such a special place to us.

Terry's was one of the most popular places in Sheboygan, because Terry made the best hamburgers (and brats) you have ever tasted. Everyone who lived in Sheboygan went to Terry's regularly, and people who visited Sheboygan make at least one stop at Terry's while they were there. It might have been one of Sheboygan most popular tourist attractions. If you came to Sheboygan, you had to go to Terry's before you left.

After my own house, my school, and my church, I suppose I spent more time at Terry's as I was growing up than any other place in town. Wherever the action started, it almost always ended at Terry's, which was open day and night, around the clock. I spent a lot of happy hours there. And, as the kids would say, I ate tons of the best hamburgers I will ever eat there.

Terry's was the place to go…..for any meal of the day, for a last bite on the way home at night, or after you had completed doing whatever you were out doing at any time. Actually, I am surprised that brats became so famous in Sheboygan. I think a Terry's hamburger was always better than any brat. Terry's was a place, but it was also a tradition, and now it is probably a legend in Sheboygan. I can hear the old guys, who might still hang around in the barber shops or in some corner tavern saying to the young guys, "Yes, I did that.....I always did....when I wanted to get a great hamburger I always went out to Terry's."

Terry's sure wasn't a five-star restaurant. It was more often called a "hamburger joint." You wouldn't find white table clothes, napkins, or candles. You wouldn't go there for a wedding reception or a retirement party. And you wouldn't go there for a business lunch or to impress a client or a marriage prospect. There weren't any flowers on the tables or counters or in the booths, and no pretty pictures on any of the walls. You didn't come to Terry's for the decor. You came to Terry's to eat! And when he was busy, Terry hoped you would go as soon as you were finished. He never kicked anyone out, but he let you know when it was time to leave. Customers were standing in line and you had had your turn.

You went to Terry's for one purpose and one purpose only…..to get the best hamburgers you have ever tasted anywhere! I have been to lots of places since then and I have had lots of hamburgers, but I have never ever tasted a hamburger as good as Terry's. They were just the BEST! After I left town to live in other places, and came back to visit, one of the things I ALWAYS did was go to Terry's to treat myself to one of his hamburgers.

During my 18 years in Sheboygan, I must have eaten thousands of Terry's hamburgers. They were something you just couldn't get tired of and couldn't get anywhere else. This was a long time before Mr. Koch discovered he could mass-produce hamburgers, started McDonald's, and started to brag about how many he made. I will bet that Terry had already made a million hamburgers before Mr. Koch was even out of high school, and anyone who ever ate one of Terry's hamburgers has a hard time eating the ones that McDonald's puts out now.

Of course, Terry served other things too, like brats, hot dogs, and french fries. Most people drank a Coke with their hamburger, a few might have had coffee or milk and, if you had a little more money, Terry would reluctantly make you a malt. He didn't like to do that and he never pushed people to buy ice cream. He just had it there in case you wanted it.

But his specialty was HAMBURGERS, cooked over a charcoal fire, topped with a large pat of Wisconsin butter, on a hard German roll. If you asked for it, you could have Terry add onions and/or pickles, and you could add your own ketchup and mustard at the table or counter. He didn't want to fuss with that. I asked Terry once why he didn't like to make cheeseburgers. He said that it was because the cheese took away from the flavor of the choice meat he always used. When it came to making hamburgers, Terry was a perfectionist.

Back then, a hamburger was five cents. And, if your mother sent you over to get a bag of them for supper at home, you could get six hamburgers for a quarter. How is that for a bargain? I used to ride my bike over to get such an order very often. At our house, we all liked Terry's hamburgers.

Terry's restaurant was not much to look at and it was located in a funny place. The only sign to identify it was the huge word Terry's. It looked like one of those non-descript little local restaurants you see in those old Western movies, right out there in the middle of the desert, with sagebrush and sand blowing all around. Sheboygan was not a desert, but that junction was as close to being nowhere as you could get there. The building was made of a stucco material and was always painted a terrible shade of green. I don't think the windows were ever cleaned. The rain just washed them off now and then.

Terry's was very handy to get to for me, because it was located very close to where I lived when I was going to junior high school, in that funny little triangle at the end of 14th Street as it crossed Calumet Drive. If you came out of Terry's and turned left, you would be on the Drive. If you turned right, you would be back on 14th Street. Calumet Drive took you to the South part of town and 14th Street took you to the North part of town. Terry's just sat there in the middle of that triangle.

Terry must have located on that spot because the land was cheap. No one would have ever built a house there and I can't think of any business that would want to sit on that little piece of nothingness. The little parking lot, if you could call it that, couldn't hold more than a dozen cars at one time, if they all got tightly squeezed together. It was not designed to encourage people to linger. It was a terrible location to put a restaurant. I am sure that many people warned Terry when he started his business not to do it and that he would soon go belly up because no one would want to come there. He proved them all wrong. But, if Terry had not put out those great hamburgers, I am sure everyone who drove past there would just have kept right on going and Terry's would have ceased to be a thriving business. As it turned out, Terry's was in business for decades and the entire lifetimes of some of his loyal customers.

The inside of the Terry's was not any better looking than the outside. There was nothing to make it attractive in any way. Terry never spent money on decorations, he spent it on getting the best quality meat he could buy. It was always fresh. It never lasted long enough to get old.

As I remember it, and it never changed over the years, the restaurant was divided into two parts. On one side there was a long kitchen where the food was stored and prepared and the actual cooking was done. Right in the middle of that area was the huge charcoal pit where Terry fried his hamburgers and other meats. It was always full of red-hot coals. Someone once told me that Terry lit it only once, on the day he opened. According to this account, that fire had burned 24 hours a day after that. That would make sense. Why would he ever put it out? It was like those eternal fires we hear about in ancient legends. That would have been something for the Guinness Book of Records!

In front of that cooking area, there was a long, curling silver and black counter. It looked something like a snake. I think there were really two horseshoe-like parts to it. There were permanently mounted high stools all around it, maybe able to seat about two dozen people.

The other half of the room had booths, not very many....maybe no more than six. You could only comfortably seat four people in each booth, but could get six in if the people were skinny and you squeezed together. There weren't any tables and chairs. There wasn't much room for a lot of customers, but at least half of Terry's business was takeout. People were willing to stand and wait a long time for one of Terry's famous hamburgers.

On the end of the whole room, right as you came in the door, there were several large entertainment pieces. There was one of those big fancy jukeboxes that were so popular at the time. It had all of those new bright colored neon lights and you could look through a glass window and watch the records drop down and play. It was always full of the latest and best records of the most popular big bands and singers of the day. You could get a tune for a nickel and it seemed to be playing all the time.

Then there was a big pinball machine (or were there two?), the forerunner of the video machines the kids like to play now. Again, you could play one game for a nickel and, if and when you won, you got your winnings in cash. Some of the kids got very good at it and won a lot. It was a good way to pick up some extra spending money.

But again, you didn't come to Terry's to be entertained. You came to eat hamburgers. And let's be clear.....Terry's restaurant, even with those great hamburgers, would not have been Terry's without Terry himself. He was kind of a local celebrity. Some people came just to watch Terry and soak up the atmosphere, whether they were hungry or not.

Terry was the sole owner, manager, cook, and head waiter. Now and then, during busy times, he might hire some young teen to wait on customers, take orders, or do the dishes. But Terry did most everything himself. He was tall and slim. He never wore anything but a pair of pants and a sleeveless shirt without a tie. He always wore one of those funny paper hats like soldiers used to wear when they went to town.

Terry was always in a hurry, though he always looked calm and relaxed. But that was deceptive. He didn't bother to be polite or go out of his way to be pleasing or friendly. He was all business, all the time. He made hamburgers. That's how he made his living. If you tried to get too familiar with him, he let you know that he didn't have time for niceties or small talk, unless it was a very slow time, when he might sit down and have a cup of coffee and smoke a cigarette. Then you could talk to him. But he never had much to say, and he never sat down long. I don't think he ever slept or went anywhere. If he had a family, I don't know when he ever saw them. It seemed that anytime you were in Terry's, day or night, Terry would be there, in front of his big burner, in his long and dirty white apron and funny little white hat.

When he saw you, he would say, "what'll ya have?" You were expected to know what you wanted and order fast. He never wrote anything down. He took your order and remembered it. There wasn't much to remember. There wasn't any long menu with lots of choices like most restaurants have. What he had to offer was up on a big black board for everyone to see. What more did you need to know? Just step up and order!

There was always meat on the grill, and when you ordered, another piece of meat would go on. He always cooked each hamburger to perfection; not pink, not well done, just right. And the hamburgers were big, always sticking out of all sides of the bun. You got your money's worth every time.

If you chose to eat in a booth you would have to sit down and wait until Terry was ready to take your order. When your hamburger (or brat or hot dog) was done, he would put it on the bottom part of a German hard roll, look at you and ask or yell from where he was, "butter?" If the answer was "yes," he would put a big chunk of butter on the hamburger; if it was "no," he would put the cover on it. If you wanted onions or pickles you would have to tell him that when you ordered. Otherwise, all hamburgers came plain.

Then, in one motion and in a manner unique to him, he would wrap your hamburger, which was very hot and greasy from the butter running out of the sides, in a cheap white waxy paper, and give it to you and take your money. It had to be cash. If you ordered anything else, like french fries or a drink, he would quickly get that for you, too. If you wanted dessert, I think he had some pie or you could get a dish of ice cream. He didn't seem to like to serve it. He probably didn't make much money on desserts. He made it on hamburgers. Desserts were a waste of his time.

And, that was it. You had been served and he went on to the next person. What about plates? What about silverware? What for? You ate everything with your fingers, and there were always napkins. If you were really fussy about cleanliness, you could stop at one of the small restrooms to wash your hands on the way out.

Terry kept everything simple. That's the way he liked it and that's the way his customers liked it. I don't remembering him ever saying "thank you," but when you would leave he would say, "come again." Of course you did, again and again and again. He did not need to thank you, you needed to thank him.......for his great food! You never went away from Terry's disappointed, and you always came back again very soon.

My richest memories of going to Terry's are of those stops we made on our way home from those Saturday night gigs at the Big Apple. The Big Apple was a tavern/bar/night club just south of the edge of town. A few of us from our larger orchestra played for dancing every Saturday night for about two years. We each got $2 for the four-hour gig and supper. We each took $1 for ourselves and put the other buck in the band kitty. Part of each dollar we earned ended up in Terry's pocket. We always stopped off at his place and stayed for about an hour on our way home. After eating our fill of hamburgers and drinking a few Cokes and playing the slot machine and the jukebox, we only had about 50 or 60 cents left. But what the heck, it had been a great night. I always still had enough money in my pocket the next morning to treat my mom, dad and me to a bag full of Terry's hamburgers sometime during the coming week.

Terry's was there when I was born and it was still there one of the last times I was in Sheboygan. However, the last time I was there, the place looked run down, the food was terrible, the buns were not hard rolls, the hamburgers were tiny, and the prices were outrageous. The waitress who served us looked sleepy or bored to death. It was obvious that Terry was no longer there.

And now Terry's is gone!

Too bad. It was such a great place.

There is a new hamburger place down on 8th Street now that is very good. It is in a better location, cleaner and more attractive, has a larger menu, and serves good quality food. In many ways it is a better place than Terry's ever was, and the hamburgers are made the same way and are almost as good.

But it is not Terry's, because Terry is not there, and we learned over the years that it was Terry, himself, that made Terry's the neat place it was.

Those Wonderful Friday Nights

Even now, after all these years, when I think about what used to happen in Sheboygan on Friday nights when I was a kid, I still get a lump in my throat. It was a little chaotic, but a lot of fun. Indulge me for just a few moments as I describe it for you, and relive it one more time.

Almost everyone who lived in Sheboygan, and the small towns from miles around, came to Downtown Sheboygan on Friday night. That was the day the farmers came to town and offered fresh fruits and vegetables at very good prices at an open market on the north side of Pranges. And that was the only night the stores Downtown were open after 6 p.m. Merchants always said it was the biggest and best shopping day of the week. Some of the best sales were scheduled for Fridays.

Friday was the night that the teenagers came Downtown to look each other over (if there wasn't a game or dance), and the older people came to see their friends and have a cup of coffee or tea. It was also family night, the one day in the week when a lot kids got to come Downtown and buy some supplies or get treats.

It was always VERY crowded Downtown on Friday night, and everybody was telling everybody else to meet them at the same time, 9 p.m., when all the stores closed and the lights went out. When everyone finally found the person or persons they had promised to meet, and got to their car or bus, the traffic was horrible! Everyone was leaving at the same time. But somehow it all got untangled and moving and everybody always got to where they wanted to go. Actually, on Friday night, no one was in a hurry to get home anyhow. Everybody wanted to linger a little longer and do something before they finally headed for home. From that 9 o'clock closing time, until well after midnight, every restaurant, tavern, bar, ice cream parlor, hamburger joint, club, or dance place was full.

Friday was also the day and night for a fish fry, having some brats and beer, or some root beer or a black cow at the A&W stand on the hill.

Often people, especially those with kids, would eat before they headed Downtown to shop.

The A & W stand (where I worked for a time) did great business every Friday because it was on a busy street, one that many people had to take to get Downtown or get back home. The street was Pennsylvania Avenue, which came up from 8th Street, past the train depot, and then up a steep hill to 14th Street. Then you could go to the north or the south to get home. Our stand was right near the top of that hill. Though we had good business every day, we did our best business on those Friday nights. As the cars came up that hill, they flooded in, filled our lot, and the carhops were kept hoppingly busy for the next hour or so, taking the root beer orders out to the cars and picking up the empties and bringing them back. I was often washing the glasses on those nights and could hardly keep up. It was an exciting time for us and we made a lot of money in that hour. We were pretty tired when it was time to close at about 11:00.

Friday night was also a night for singing and dancing. And after that, there might be a some time left for a little romancing, either in the rumble seat of your car, on the beach, on some front porch swing, or just in your own home after the kids were put to bed (if you were married). In a unique Sheboygan way, it all worked out just fine. For most people, Friday night was the fun night of the week, a way of ending the work week and getting ready for the weekend. It was a time to let loose and to enjoy being with loved ones and friends....and just have fun!

Of course, there were things going on on Saturday night, too, like dinner out at the Country Club (for those who belonged), or a wedding, or going out to eat at a nice restaurant to celebrate a birthday or anniversary, or just a quiet romantic supper with your sweetheart. Many people liked going to a movie on Saturday night, so the theaters were usually full. There wasn't any TV or videos then, so if you wanted that kind of entertainment, you had to go out somewhere.

For other folks, especially the ones who had small kids still at home, Saturday night was the night for baths, listening to the radio, and getting ready for church on Sunday morning. Parents might tell or read a bedtime story to the little kids before turning the lights out and going to sleep. Most everyone, including the adults would be in bed early. And in a few hours, it was Sunday, known then as "the day of rest."

What started out on the corner by Pranges on Friday night ended in the sanctuary of some church on Sunday morning. For those so inclined and able, church was an activity for the entire family. Most people in Sheboygan went to church on Sunday. I don't know what the rest did. After church, there was usually a wonderful Sunday dinner. In the afternoon, the adults might read and nap and the kids would play around their houses and yards. Teenagers would get bored and couldn't wait for the afternoons to get over. At night, the whole family might gather around the radio and listen to those fun programs, like Jack Benny, Edgar Bergen and Charlie McCarthy, Fibber McGee and Mollie, and those other great radio stars. In summer, there might be a picnic in one of the parks, with a big game of some kind or a concert to end the day. That's how people in Sheboygan spent their weekends.

Working people who had to get up early Monday morning to go to work wanted to get to bed early on Sunday nights. If everything went well, most folks in Sheboygan went to bed on Sunday nights, rested, relaxed, and contented. And, in most cases, it had been an active, fun, and delightful weekend.

In only five days, they could do it again....it would be Friday night again!

Part 2

Parks, Playgrounds, Picnics, and Parades

The things I remember best about living in Sheboygan when I was a boy were the many beautiful parks, having fun on the playgrounds, going on picnics, and marching in parades.

Parks

Kiwanis Park—1937   Kiwanis Park—1953

PARK FACILITIES CHART

NAME AND LOCATION OF PARK

Name and Location of Park	Total Acreage	Date Acquired	River Acquired (Natural)	Amphitheater	Archery	Band Stand	Basketball	Bridle Trails	Comfort Station	Concession Stand	Cooking Grills	Football	Fountain or Springs	Flower Beds	Horseshoe Courts	Hiking Trails	Picnic Areas	Play Apparatus	Sand Box	Shelterhouse	Softball Fields	Softball (Lighted)	Baseball	Baseball (Lighted)	Skating	Stage (Portable)	Supervised Play	Swimming Beaches	Sled Slides	Toboggan Slide	Tennis Courts	Tennis (Lighted)	Track & Field	Wading Pool	Zoo	Winter Skating
COLE PARK 4th St. & Grant Ave.	2.50	1908	A				X		X		X			X X X																					X	
DELAND PARK Broughton Drive	43.80	1927 1936	A B				X X X X		X X 2 X X X X		2	1			X X X			2																	
END PARK 13th St. & Bell Ave.	3.47	1904	A				X	X		X X X								X										X							
EVERGREEN PARK Highway 42 & North City Limits	135.63	1918 1940	B	X		X X X X	X	X 9 X X X X		5			X		X	X X																			
FOUNTAIN PARK 8th St. & Erie Ave.	2.62	1836	C	X		X X	X X							X																					
GENERAL KING PARK 7th St. & Spring Ave.	6.50	1934	B			X X X	X	X X X							X X																			
KIWANIS PARK 17th St. & Ontario Ave.	26.00	1924	A B	X	X	X X X X		4 X X X X X 4	1		X X			X	2	X X	X																
MOOSE PARK 18th St. & Indiana Ave.	3.90	1930	D			X X X		2 X X X X X 2			X X	X	2					X																
NORTHEAST PARK 6th St. & Evergreen Parkway	12.00	1922	B		(Under Development)																														
SHERIDAN PARK 14th St. & New Jersey Ave.	2.62	1836	C	X		X X	X	X X X						X				X																
SHOOTING PARK Lakeshore Drive, South of Wilson	10.40	1912	B	X		X X		2 X X X X	2																									
ROOSEVELT PARK 12th St. & Mead Ave.	8.11	1930	B		X	X X X	X	2 X X X X X 3	1	1	1			X	2 2	X																	
VOLLRATH PARK 3rd St. & Park Ave.	18.13	1917	A B	X		X X X	X X	X X X		2			X X	X	4 2	X																	
SOUTHWEST PARK 24th St. & Union Ave.	8.75	1946	B		(Under Development)																														
TRIANGLES & BOULEVARDS N. 3rd, N. 7th, North Ave., Geele, S. 17th & Union Ave.	3.70		C																																
RIVER ISLANDS Penn Ave. & W. Water St.	4.00		C																																
TOTALS	289.13				1 2 3 3	1 10 6	11	2 2 7	3 21 11 11 11	6 3 10	1 3	13 8	2 5	4 1 16	6 1 5	1 3

NOTES: A—Donation; B—City Purchase; C—Original City Plat; D—Leased. Additional Rinks at Giant School, Longfellow School, Cooper Avenue, and Washington School. Additional Tennis Courts: 2 at Cooper Ave., 2 at Kuehno Court. Two Portable Stages available for use at locations indicated.

WHILE USING PARKS

Help preserve Park property! It belongs to you! Enjoy it! Do not destroy it!

1. Help keep your Parks clean—Trash cans are provided.

2. Build fires only in fire places provided, and make sure your fire is out before leaving.

3. Your help in reporting vandalism will stop any misuse and make your Parks a better place in which to relax.

A Million Parks

Sheboygan was a beautiful city, not just because it grew up next to a large fresh water lake, but because it was not overdeveloped like cities are now. When I lived in Sheboygan, there was still lots of open space and many things were left to grow naturally. It was full of trees, bushes, and flowers, and the grass was always green (except in winter, of course, when everything was white.) Not only did people take good care of their own yards, but they saw to it that there were a lot of public places to share and places to play. Those were also well kept and maintained. I have already told you about the lakes and the part they played in our lives. Now I will tell you about the parks and playgrounds that I enjoyed while I was growing up in Sheboygan.

If I told you that there were a million parks in Sheboygan, you would know I was exaggerating. But the truth is that there were more parks than we could count and they were all over town. We loved them and used them regularly. In summer, we spent half our waking hours in some park or on some playground….that is, if we weren't on the beach.

Sheboygan was full of parks, all kinds of them. There were very large ones scattered throughout the city and lots of smaller ones in the neighborhoods. (This did not include the many playgrounds, usually in back of our schools or in the many vacant lots or open spaces scattered all over town.) These were parks, owned and operated by the city and were maintained by the city or the recreation department.

All of these parks had some things in common; lots of green grass, tall trees, paths for walking, and benches to sit on. There were also lots of things for kids to play on. In the bigger parks, there were large fields for baseball, soccer, football, or just running around. One of them had a zoo. Most of the public parks had lots of picnic tables for people to use when they came to have family or organization picnics or just a simple meal. Some had fryers to fry on, and they all had toilet facilities and lots of containers for trash and cans. At that time, you didn't litter!

Anywhere! Some of the parks were close to Lake Michigan, with lots of sand to walk on and play in, and water to swim in.

The parks all had names so they could be easily identified, and they were "free and open to the public." If you had a very large group you might want to make a reservation in advance, which was easy. You could walk to most of them, or find them conveniently near a bus stop.

During the summer, the parks were usually filled with people who welcomed this opportunity for free entertainment, especially during the Depression. Sheboygan wouldn't have been the Sheboygan it was without its parks. Many of them are still there, in the same locations. As I tell you more about them, I will be thinking about four of my favorite parks in particular:

- Vollrath Park on the North Side
- Terry Andre Park on the South Side
- The little park near my Grandma's
- Fountain Park Downtown

Vollrath Park

The largest park on the North Side was Vollrath Park. It took its name from the Kohler family who lived in Kohler and owned the Kohler Company. They must have given some money to originate or maintain the park. It was a beautiful place and we went there often because it was only about three short blocks from where my Grandma Huebner lived. We could easily walk there from her house. My mother, my aunts, my two girl cousins and I went there often and sometimes would spend an entire day there. The men often joined us after work for supper. We might all stay until the mosquitoes got too bad.

The park had several parts to it. As you entered the park from the South, you would be in the picnic and recreation area, where the benches and tables and the athletic fields were. It was flat, covered with nice lush green grass or soft sand and dirt. There were lots of tall trees everywhere. A good share of the park was in the shade all day, which was nice on hot summer days. The park could accommodate lots of people at one time. Around meal times and on weekends, it was always crowded.

If you entered the park from the North Side, where the best parking places were, you would come directly into the zoo. It was not a big zoo and didn't have those big wild animals in it, like the ones that most big cities have. There weren't any elephants or camels, giraffes or pandas, or huge snakes. It did have some monkeys, and we would stand at their cage for a long time watching them. But if you wanted to see bigger animals, like ones from Africa, Asia, or South America, you would have to go see them somewhere else. Most of the animals and birds in our zoo were local (statewide), but we didn't care. There were lots of them and they were fun to watch. The zoo in Vollrath Park was one of the prettiest areas of the park, because there were little creeks running through it with little bridges going over them, and a few small waterfalls. It also had lots of shrubs and flowers. I didn't remember that it smelled bad like some zoos do. Maybe that was because everything was well kept.

In the middle of the park was the bowl, which was very large and oblong and looked like a huge grassy bathtub. It was always called "The Vollrath Bowl." It was in the park, but it was sort of a separate part of it. It was all covered with grass. There was a grass floor on the bottom, and large terraced banks on three sides.

On the east end of the bowl, near the zoo, there was a flat space where they could put up platforms for ceremonies, programs and concerts. People would bring their own folding chairs and blankets to sit on. Now and then, for very special occasions, like high school and college outdoor graduations, worship services, ethnic programs, or patriotic ceremonies, they would cover the grass floor with folding chairs. It was always a good idea to bring umbrellas, rain gear, and sweaters or jackets when you came to the bowl. Being so close to the lake, weather conditions could change fast.

On the far west side of the bowl, away from where the platforms would be erected, there were several sets of wide and long stone steps, the only stairways or paths into the bowl. The graduates would walk down those stairs during their processional. There were other times when there were processionals down those stairs, too, like for religious services and pageants.

Unfortunately, after waiting for four years for it to happen, our Central High School 1942 class graduation outdoor ceremony in the bowl had to be canceled because of a heavy rainstorm and we where the first high school graduating class to have our exercises in the new Armory down by the lake. We were very disappointed. By then, those outdoor graduations had become a fond tradition. And every class got only one chance to take part in that tradition. But, unfortunately, we didn't have control over the weather.

Near, but outside the park itself, there were two other attractions that we kids loved. On the east end of the park was the city Water Treatment Plant. The public was allowed to come inside and see how they purified the water we drank every day. I don't think there was a time that my cousins and I didn't go through the Water Treatment Plant when we were at the park. I don't know why. It wasn't all that exciting. But it was something to do when we got bored doing all of the other things.

Also on the east side, and for a long way up the shore, there was a nice beach. It was not the official North Side bathing beach and did not have paid lifeguards, but we spent a lot of time swimming there anyhow. There were always lots of parents around to watch the kids.

With all the wonderful space and fun activities, you can see why we went to Vollrath Park as often as we did. And we made lots of great memories there.

Terry Andre Park

On the other end of town, the South Side, there was the big Terry Andre Park (the name has been changed since then). It was a neat park, too, but very different from Vollrath Park. I think it was meant and designed to be. This large park bordered Lake Michigan on one side and went on for a long distance down its shore going south. West of the park there was open country or farmland. The city had not yet grown or built out that far. Going to Terry Andre Park was like going out of town, which made it even a more special place.

As you entered the park from the North, you passed through a heavily wooded area. There were paths that took you through those woods to a very large picnic area. There were some permanent buildings there, lots of picnic tables, old-fashioned park benches, and even a nice, large covered bandstand. Everything was painted a bright green. And there were open areas where games could be played, like baseball or soccer. That is where groups might hold competitive races of all kinds.

If you kept on going further south, you came to a totally different area, know only as "The Sand Dunes." People came from all over just to see them. The fine pure white sand stretched for as far as your eye could see, and it kept constantly shifting, making hills and valleys and all kinds of pretty and mysterious shapes. If you didn't know better, you might have thought you were in the Arabian Desert. People from the universities use to come to take pictures of them and measure them. Our Boy Scout troop liked to hike out there, play games like the "Capture the Flag," and sometimes camp out overnight. It was hard to find places to pitch a tent and there wasn't much wood for fires, but we seemed to manage somehow. I vividly recall one memorable experience I had out there with a friend that I will tell you about in another story.

It was in Terry Andre Park that the big Labor Day Picnics were always held every year. They were put on by the local Unions, and we never missed one. Everybody in the community was invited to come and many people did. It lasted all day and into the night.

Other large community organizations like churches, schools, businesses, and fraternal organizations, used the park for their picnics.

It was also sometimes used for another important and popular activity. It was a good place for young couples in love to "park" late at night. They usually preferred the sand dunes, but they had to be careful that they didn't get their car stuck in the sand, which was very easy to do. I am told that it was a much better place to go than the "Cabbage Patch." It was rumored that the police did not check the dunes as often.

During some summers, someone would put up a huge circus tent on the edge of Terry Andre Park and turn it into an outdoor roller skating rink. When a real circus came to town, it always set up on a large plot of unused land on the North Side. Carnivals liked that location better too. Maybe there were too many trees and two much sand at Terry Andre Park.

As a kid, I spent a lot of time and lots of happy Sundays out at Terry Andre Park.

The Little Park Near Grandma's House

In contrast to those bigger parks, there were also very small neighborhood parks all over town. They were usually built as play areas for small children, and some of them had nice shady spots and benches for mothers to sit and watch the children. Sometimes old men would come there too, just to chat with other old men or smoke their pipes and meditate.

One of these parks was right across the street from my Grandma's house on 3rd Street. It must have had a name but I don't remember what it was. It must also have been one of the larger neighborhood ones. The park itself was about a half-block square and had a path running through the middle of it so you could get back and forth between the two streets that bordered it. I remember that we always went through that park to get to the school where we used to ice skate in the winter. It saved us several blocks of walking.

At one side of the park, there was a nice playground for kids with a big high slide, swings, a teeter-totter, something that went around in circles, and a big sandbox. There might even have been a small wading pool. When my cousins and I got bored, hot, or didn't want to walk up to Vollrath Park, we would go over there to play. It was also handy for Grandma when she called us home for meals. We spent lots of happy and carefree hours there.

When I was growing up in Sheboygan, kids played outside a lot. We didn't have TV and video games to distract us. I don't remember any adults ever coming there to watch us. If we fell off something or got bumped or scratched, we just ran to Grandma's house and got patched up. If the bigger kids came and hogged the equipment, we may have cried a little, but they usually soon got bored and left. Most times, we smaller kids had the park pretty much to ourselves, and we were not the kind to bully or pick fights.

Another thing that was handy about that park was that it was only a block away from a small grocery store where we could get penny candy or maybe an Eskimo Pie or a Coke. That is, if we brought some money along, or if Grandma or one of our aunts or uncles decided to treat us.

We loved that little park. I hope it is still there for the little kids who might live in that neighborhood now to enjoy.

Fountain Park

The other park that played a big part in my life was Fountain Park. It was right on the edge of the main downtown area, about a half a block from the Sheboygan Theater. It was very different in every way from the big Vollrath and Terry Andre Parks and any of the small neighborhood parks.

Some people might not even have considered it a park because the things usually associated with parks didn't go on there. It was there for different reasons and had different purposes. It was more like the old-fashioned town squares that you would see in most every small rural town at the turn of the century, like the ones we used to see in New England, and all over the states of Wisconsin, Minnesota, and Iowa. They were like the ones you see in musicals and movies like "The Music Man" or "State Fair." Those delightful parks were great places for people to gather in, a kind of central spot where people come to meet and be a community.

Fountain Park might have been the first park that was ever developed in Sheboygan, but I don't know that for a fact. I can't tell you much about the history of the park, only some of the things that went on there when I was a boy. I know about that because I went there frequently.

The park was only one full block square, and was located between 8th and 9th Streets. Across the street, on the southwest corner, was the Sheboygan Hotel; on the southeast corner was the Rex Theater; and on the northeast corner was the old Sheboygan Clinic. To the north, there was a big Evangelical Brethren church (now a United Methodist Church). The rest of the streets around it were filled with small stores like photography shops, dentists, jewelers, a music store, and a place to buy papers and magazines. There were several very good restaurants nearby, and a very large funeral home. A popular gymnasium and health club was only a block away.

This small park (or square) served many purposes and met many community needs. It was always a very good place just to stop and rest, to walk through, or to stop for a drink of water. There were two wide paths that crossed each other in the middle of the park, making a big X. It kind of cut the park into four equal parts.

On the southeast corner of the park, there was a huge statue of a Civil War soldier. It was almost as tall as some of the high trees. Patriotic ceremonies were held there on holidays. I used to play with the Boy Scout Drum and Bugle Corps for those. The most important one was always held in the morning on Armistice Day (which was in November). I can remember that it was always cold and often raining. But lots of people came out to honor the dead and pay their respects to the heroes who had fought and died for their country. I think some workers were excused from work to be there. One of the highlights of that service was the placing of a great big wreath, right at the foot of that big statue. It was either for the unknown soldiers who had not been identified or all of the soldiers from Sheboygan who were killed in all of the wars. We played long drum rolls on muffled drums while that was being done. And then, of course, the color guard would shoot their rifles and a bugler would play taps.

On the corner closest to 9th Street, there was a great big band shell, used mostly for concerts, programs, plays, and musical shows. I went to many of those, even after I came back home to visit. I don't remember ever performing on that bandstand, so it probably was not there when I was a kid. There must have been an earlier one that the new and bigger one replaced. On the east side of the park, right in the middle of that stretch of sidewalk, was the infamous mineral water fountain. My dad loved that water and would often bring bottles of it home. I hated it and thought it tasted terrible. There was also fresh water there, too. On hot days, lots of people stopped to quench their thirst. I was one of them.

I don't think I ever visited Sheboygan without stopping at least once to walk through Fountain Park. It was part of my history and heritage, and I have many fond memories of it.

Many, Many More Parks

The parks I have told you about were my four favorite parks, but there were lots more. There was a large park down by the river and one out near where I went to school. The one by the river was built by the Sheboygan Kiwanis Club. It was called Kiwanis Park, of course. But it wasn't developed until I was older and about ready to graduate and leave town, so I never spent much time there. Later, when I came back to Sheboygan to visit, I would sometimes go to that park for some event. It was central, large, and easy to get to, so it was a popular place to hold activities of all kinds. I am sure there were a lot of brats, beans, and potato salad eaten there, and lots of beer consumed.

And then there was Roosevelt Park, just a block or two from the school that I attended. I spent many happy hours either ice skating or playing baseball there. I always thought that it was one of the prettiest parks in town. It was completely flat, covered several blocks, and had lots of area to play group games. I think it even was one of the first parks to install lights so those games could be played at night. And, as usual, it was full of trees, bushes, and flowers, and very green grass. Because it was so close to my home, I probably spent more time in Roosevelt Park than any other park in town. You might say it was my very, very favorite park. I am sure there were other large parks like Roosevelt in other parks of town, but I don't remember where they were and probably seldom went to them.

No, we didn't have millions of parks in Sheboygan, but we had lots of them. They were provided by the city for our pleasure and enjoyment. Part of the fun of living in Sheboygan was those parks. Whoever designed them, developed them, and created them deserves a medal.

Playgrounds

Playgrounds Everywhere

Like parks, there were lots of playgrounds in Sheboygan. They seemed to be everywhere but most of them, the bigger and important ones, usually were in back of the schools. Every school had to have its own playground. If it didn't have one, where would they have recess?

All of these playgrounds seemed to have been planned by the same guy. They were mainly large open fields, often on a piece of land larger than the school itself, with a lot of badly trampled grass. There were usually baseball diamonds on the four corners, with their pitcher and catcher mounds of sand or clay, the base lines running to the four bases, and great big high fences that served as backstops for stray balls. If they were really fancy, they might have green benches that the players could sit on while they were waiting to bat, and some even had green bleachers that people could come and sit on to watch the game. Not many of them had lights, so most activities went on during the day. The rest of the field was plain and open, for sports like soccer and football, or just general running around. Some of the larger playgrounds had tracks around them for those sports. The basketball courts and hoops were usually inside in the gym.

In the winter, on some of the playgrounds, the recreation men would make large rinks for ice skating. Hockey was not big in Sheboygan, so they didn't have to make two rinks like they might do now, and the sledding was done on the hills around town. When there was a rink, the men would also put up a temporary warming house.

The playgrounds that I spent the most time playing on were in back of the Longfellow School on 8th Street, the big one in back of the new grade and junior high school that was on Union Avenue, the smaller one in back of Jefferson Junior High and, of course, the big playground that was not attached to a school, but was in Roosevelt Park.

We had lots of playgrounds in Sheboygan, and they were all well used, not only during recess, but after school and on weekends, all year round.

Those Wonderful Vacant Lots

Vacant lots....those small parcels of undeveloped land that were found in most every neighborhood throughout the city. They came in all shapes, sizes, and were in all kinds of locations. They were set near the alleys that ran through the middle of every block. Sometimes they were on the corner lot, like the one on the corner near our house. No one wanted to build a house there and I suppose it would have been expensive to haul all that dirt away. So it was left vacant waiting for a buyer. Nobody ever bought this one while I lived there.

Some of these vacant lots were unattended and overgrown with weeds and brush. No one seemed to care for or about them. Though, in most neighborhoods, the yards were well tended and cared from, vacant lots were supposed to look like prairie land or jungles and not like well-groomed front yards.

No one seemed to know who owned them unless there was a "For Sale" sign on it with the name of the owner and his phone number. Those lots became "ours" by their location and right of occupation, unless the owner would put a "No Trespassing" sign on it. That warning was respected and strictly observed. If it was violated, the police enforced the owner's rights and you could get a ticket. I am glad there was not such a sign on the vacant lot in the back of our house.

There were seldom any fences around these lots either, and usually the owners allowed people in the neighborhoods, especially the kids, to play on them, as long as they didn't dig up and take the dirt or build fires on them.

And, at that time, they knew that no one was going to sue them if one of us fell down and got banged up a little. Our moms would just put a bandage on the scrape or wound, and send us back out to the lot to play.

The lot in back of our house on Swift Avenue was a good-sized lot, right across the alley between the first two houses on two sides of those streets. It wasn't very large and didn't take up too much space. But it sure was handy. It was mostly flat, but there was a slight incline or small hill at the end of it, facing the sidewalk and street on that side. In the winter, little kids could bring their sleds and slide down it, but it was not any challenge to us older kids. There were lots of other steeper, longer, and more exciting hills for us to slide on. And, there was a danger factor to consider. Those fast sleds that were used at that time could go out into the street and get hit by a passing car. If we saw little kids trying to slide there and no parents were around to watch them, we would shoo them away or send them home. The only time we older kids used that hill was to play a game of "King of the Hill," until we got even older and used the big hill on the corner of the other side of the street. The whole vacant lot there was a hill.

There wasn't any planted or green grass, as such, on these vacant lots but just a kind of a brown grass covering of some kind, always badly trampled, and then lots of either sand or bare ground in spots all over. There weren't any trees or flowers, but maybe a few bushes on the edges. It made a great natural playground. In early spring, some dandelions might have tried to grow there but were never very successful. They were soon trampled down and blew away to pester someone's lawn.

I suppose that all around town, kids were doing the same things we did on the vacant lots near their houses......having lots of fun playing on them!

They were all territorial. You seldom, if ever, saw any kids from other neighborhoods on your vacant lot. That probably prevented turf wars and gang fights like they have over territory in big cities. We didn't fight over our vacant lots, we were too busy playing on them.

Balls And Bats

If you never played sand lot ball when you were a kid, you might have missed one of the really great experiences of life, and probably some of the happiest moments in your childhood. Unfortunately, most kids don't do that anymore. It seems like now everything has to be organized and if you want to play any sport, you have to have special expensive equipment to play with, special fields or courts to play on, leaders and coaches to guide you, and fancy uniforms with somebody's business name on the back of them. Adults have taken sports away from kids, and that is too bad. It was better when we were doing it ourselves. Not as neat and orderly, perhaps, but a whole lot more free and fun! Here is the way we used our balls and bats in the "good old days."

As soon as we were old enough to hold a ball and throw it, we started to play catch. My cousin, Dick, and I played catch endlessly when we were little. We didn't use gloves for a long time and we used softballs. I doubt if I ever owned my own glove. Dick had a couple and I used one of his. At school, I used theirs. Later, we got a bat somewhere and began hitting the ball around, usually on some vacant lot. We didn't play a game. We just hit balls at guys out in the field. They did a lot of chasing, and the guy trying to hit the ball missed it a lot. We all took turns hitting and fielding and we learned how to do both pretty well. We didn't really worry about learning the fine points, we just had fun playing.

The next step was to find some other boys and a vacant lot or a field that was not being used, and get up a game of Scrub. That meant we didn't choose up sides or form teams. We just all took our turn pitching, hitting, running, catching, and throwing. Everybody got to do everything. That was neat!

At this stage, we didn't bother to keep score, and we didn't care about winning or even performing well. This was just to develop our individual skills and our muscles, and for the pure joy of it! We didn't have innings, we just played until we got tired and quit, until the older kids bumped us off to play their own games, or until it just got too dark to see the ball.

Sometimes we would do a simple variation of Scrub called Round Robin. In this game, there was only one batter at a time and no running of bases. The rest of the boys would get out in the field. The batter would hit the ball and the guys in the field would try to catch it. Whoever caught the ball would get to bat next. It was not as easy as it sounds. We got good at hitting and catching. Later, we had to work on throwing and running. We played a lot of Round Robin in that vacant lot I told about that was in back of our house.

When we got tired of Scrub or Round Robin, we would find some flat rocks, pieces of cardboard, or gunny sacks, and make bases. Then we would choose up sides and play a game and keep score. But there were no adults there to supervise us and no referees to settle conflicts. We just made up our own rules and fought it out when we had to. Most of the time, we got along very well. It was simple, but it was fun.

This is the way we learned how to play baseball in Sheboygan, and this was where and how the stars of yesteryear were born. The great players who later played on the Major League teams when I was a boy probably all started out playing catch, Scrub, Round Robin, and then sandlot ball. Now they do it differently, maybe better. But I wonder if they are still enjoying it as much.

I was never destined to be anything more than a fan. I stopped playing baseball when I started to show a serious interest in music and girls. Now, I watch either the Minnesota Twins or the Milwaukee Brewers and really like the games. I even like to see the games on TV. And as I watch them, I sometimes remember the many happy hours we spent just throwing and batting balls around, at Dick's house in the street or in my backyard. And I don't even need a beer and a brat or an ice cream bar to keep my enthusiasm up!

Marbles And Horseshoes

Whenever we didn't have to do something else or had nothing better to do, we would play marbles. Every boy at that time owned lots of marbles. I don't remember that any girls did. Marbles were cheap and we usually bought them at the five and dime stores by the bagfuls. In case you are of a different generation and never played marbles, you might not even know what I am talking about.

Marbles are small glass balls of many colors. There were big ones called "shooters," and there are small ones just called "marbles." Sometimes we called them "glassies." When I was a kid, we could easily carry lots of them around in our pockets, ready to go whenever we could get some other guys to play a game with us. Unlike stamps, baseball cards, and Lucky Bucks, marbles had utility. Not only could you collect them, but you could also play with them.

When we were in grade school, some of us were addicted to and obsessed with playing marbles. We played marbles any place and any time we had the chance. My friends and I got very good at it. As they say, "practice makes perfect."

Marbles were used in three games we all learned to play.

When we started playing marbles, we first played a simple game. We would stand in line a short distance from a garage door, a wall, a fence, a step, or a line drawn in the dirt. Then we would each throw a marble at that object. The one who got the closest to it would win and take all of the other marbles to keep.

Then, someone got the idea of doing it another way. He dug a hole in the ground, threw his marbles toward it and then pushed them in the hole with his index finger. He suggested we should take turns, pushing the marbles closer toward the hole each time it was our turn, until our marble would fall in. The first person to get his marble in the hole would win all of the rest. And then we would start over and play another game. That game kept us busy for a long time, until we started to watch some of the older boys play another more challenging game.

214

They would draw a very big circle, either in some hard dirt, clay, or even on a sidewalk. Each person playing would put a marble in the center to start. Then, taking turns, each boy would take a bigger marble (the shooter) and shoot it at the marbles inside the circle, trying to knock them out. It took a lot of skill and some time to learn how to hold that shooter just right between your index finger and push it out with the right force with your thumb. You also had to have a good aim. We called it "kissing" when the marbles were hit and they rolled out of the circle. You could keep shooting marbles until you missed and then you had to put another marble in the middle of the circle. At some times, there were a lot of marbles collected there. You, of course, could keep all the marbles you kissed out and the game continued (sometimes for a long time), until all of the marbles had been knocked out of the circle.

That game was the most fun because it took much more skill. Once we started playing it, we gave up playing the other games. This game got so popular that there were a few professional players who traveled all over the country putting on shows and competing in tournaments.

I got good at it, but not that good! But playing with my friends, I often won, and I hardly ever had to replenish my supply of marbles. I just used the marbles I was winning over and over again.

Some of our games were played in our schoolyard or in our own backyards, but the place we liked best was that vacant lot in back of our house. And it served a social as well as a recreational purpose.

During the Depression, it was sometimes difficult to find steady jobs, workers were temporarily laid off when sales were down, and some men could only find manual labor day jobs and work only a few days a week. They frequently found themselves unemployed for long periods, and had a lot of idle time on their hands. There wasn't any TV or videos to watch and they got tired of doing chores or pursuing hobbies around the house.

So some of them began to spend a lot of time hanging around the corner taverns, where they played cards, gambled and drank a lot. That got them into trouble with their mothers, girl friends, and wives, and took money out of their already strained paychecks. They decided they better find something better to do.

One of the guys down the block in our neighborhood spotted that vacant lot one day and got an idea. He got permission from the owner of the lot to make some horseshoe courts on it. He talked some of his out-of work friends to help him. We little kids got bumped and had to find other places to play our ball games and marbles. We did, but we soon got fascinated with and wanted to play horseshoes like the big boys played. We began to come to watch them more than we played marbles.

The guys went to work in earnest and made several professional quality horseshoe pits. They were beautifully constructed and regularly maintained. They really fussed over them, wanting them to be perfect.

They first got some good quality lumber and made the required sized square frames. They filled those with a fine quality clay that they hauled in from some place. In the center of these pits at each end of the courts, they put regulation-sized metal pegs and then trimmed all the grass about the pits and the long lanes leading up to them. They sort of looked like the dirt bowling alleys that were also popular at the time.

When they got going, no one could stop them. They went on to build some benches to sit on and put up a big scoreboard. They had everything that the playgrounds had on their athletic fields, except bleachers. Those courts were really fancy. Then they bought regulation size and style horseshoes for each pit and built small cabinets to store and lock them up in when they were not in use. These horseshoes were the kinds that had those hooks on the ends. They claimed it made it easier to throw more ringers. That was true....it was!

They started out by just practicing by themselves. When they got good enough, they began to play scrub games with each other. Then they formed teams. Before long, they were holding tournaments with the guys from other neighborhoods and awarding prizes. The whole neighborhood would come out to watch them and the Sheboygan Press began reporting the scores. Our neighborhood became very popular and people came from all over town to watch our guys pitch.

They were into horseshoes in a very serious way and they began to spend most of their days and nights at the horseshoe courts they had created. They got obsessed with playing horseshoes and kind of secretly hoped they wouldn't get jobs that would take them away from their passion, taking night shifts at the factories so they could play during the day. There weren't any lights so they couldn't play at night. They might have just as well been working and making a little money.

We were awed by how good they got. We longed to play, too. But they kept telling us that "we had to grow up first" because the horseshoes were heavy and one had to be strong to pitch them. They told us that they didn't want us to come over and use the courts by ourselves. They didn't want to get them messed up.

But they finally agreed that we could use one of the courts, if we would be careful and let them teach us how to play properly and how to take care of the courts and pits. One of them even found some smaller and lighter horseshoes for us to use. Some of us took them up on their offer and became quite good at pitching horseshoes ourselves, but we never got good enough to complete with the older guys. When they had their games and tournaments we just went and watched.

We still played marbles for many years, maybe into junior high or even high school, until we got interested and caught up in other or more challenging games and excitements. Of course, I no longer play marbles, but whenever I see a horseshoe pit I can't resist throwing a few and if someone else is around, I try to challenge that person to a game. I am pleased to say, that if and when that happens, I still usually win. And I must admit that I have pitched a lot of ringers in my time. Lots of leaners, too! That still counts two points.

There is a P.S. to this story....

Over the years, I have tried to find marbles to buy, just to keep and display for memory sake, but I seldom could find any. One day, many years ago, I found a few nice ones at some garage or rummage sale, but I couldn't talk my girls into playing with them and eventually threw them away. I was also successful, for a short time, in getting them to play horseshoes with me, but they gave up on that very soon, too. I left those behind on one of our moves.

Then, one day, I was in a small variety store in some small town in Minnesota that had lots of old fashioned things. I saw this small bag of marbles and got all excited. They were pretty glassies and were in excellent condition. The set even had two big shooters. I had to buy them and bring them home.

But I didn't know what to do with them, until I found a pretty small cut glass bowl and put them in it. Since then, they have always been right up there on the top of my big desk. Now, every time I look at them, they remind me of all of the fun times we had as kids on that vacant lot in back of my house on Swift Avenue.

And I think how neat it might be to be a boy again.

Our Very Favorite Lake

In Sheboygan, we didn't have a sea and we were very far from any ocean, with Wisconsin being in the center of the country. But we had something just as good, actually better. We had Lake Michigan, and as they say now, "it doesn't get much better than that." The big lake dominated one side of the city and took up the whole east side of town. It still does. The white sand beach went on for miles and miles, going all the way up to Green Bay to the north and down as far as Chicago to the south. We were lake people, and the presence of the lake significantly influenced how we lived, our economy, our social life, and our character. I have fond memories about that lake, but the most vivid ones are about swimming in it.

I must admit that there were days at Lake Michigan when the water was too cold to swim in. On those days, we kids played in the sand, collected stones in buckets, or ran up and down the beach instead of diving into the water. But, when the weather was nice and the water was as warm as it was ever going to be, you couldn't keep us out of the lake, even if we would turn blue and have to frequently come shivering out of the water to sit in the sun and warm up for a bit. Mother always had a hard time getting us to leave the water when we finally had to pack up and go home.

Lake Michigan water at that time was as clear, pure and blue as lake water is ever going to get anywhere. But, when the St. Lawrence Waterway opened up for shipping, our lake got fouled up for a time and lots of the fish died. There was even a short period of time when no one was allowed to swim in it. But by that time, I had left Sheboygan. It did not affect me, but it did affect my kids when I brought them to visit their grandma.

When we lived on Swift Avenue, we spent a good share of our young lives at the beach. Mom would take me there anytime I wanted to go, and she would unusually invite any neighborhood kids who wanted to join us to come along. She was like the Pied Piper, up in front with her little charges tailing along behind her. I am sure that when the other mothers looked out from their front porches and watched us tramping by, they said, "There goes Mabel again, taking the kids to the beach." Some of them confessed that they were glad they didn't have to go and sit out in the hot sun all day.

One of the benefits of living on the South Side and on Swift Avenue was that it was so close to the beach. The part of the beach where we most frequently went was only about six blocks away - past the butcher shop and the grocery store, across 8th Street, over that vacant lot with the high bluff at the end of it, down that bluff, over the outer road running along the lake, down the long flight of steps, and onto that wide beach. My mother loved to walk, so it was no big chore for her. We kids were so excited, we always urged her to run. If she had, she could have easily beat us.

Sometimes the pavement and the sand would get so hot that they would burn our feet if they were bare, so mom always made us wear sandals or tennis shoes until we got on the beach and into the water. Once we got used to the sand, she would let us go barefoot and the sand felt wonderful running through our toes. The sand was very clean so it was easy to wash or brush off before we started back for home. It also made neat sand castles when mixed with the proper amount of water. Then it turned a rich brown and got firm and stuck together. We didn't know it then, but we were being sand sculpturers. I thought about those days when I was at the Minnesota State Fair one day and saw the spectacular sand sculpture show they put on that year. I decided that it was more fun to make them than to see them on display.

We were down at the beach, sometimes several days a week when the weather was nice, and we would be there for hours and hours and hours, from early in the morning until late in the afternoon. Mother always timed it just right to give us the maximum amount of swim and play time. If you are a parent, you know that there is nothing better you could use to entertain small kids for long periods of time than lots of water and sand. We never complained that we were bored when we were at Lake Michigan, only when we were told we had to pack up and leave.

Mom always let us stay at the beach as long as she possibly could. But the time would finally come when she had to announce that we had to get out of the water, dry off and get dressed, and head back. Like kids everywhere, we grumbled, complained, and pleaded, "Just one more dive," or "Just five more minutes." But she was pretty firm. There was one important deadline she would never miss. She had to get home to make supper for our family. Dad had to be to work at the plant by 6:00. In German households in Sheboygan, meals were always at the same time and always on time.

Now and then, it would get too cold and Mom would decide it was time to go home early. Then there were times when we got so cold that we would be the ones who would ask to go home. Sometimes, she would see the storm clouds gathering and worry about thunder and lightning and decide it was time to pack up and head out fast in order to beat the storm. She would have made a great weatherman (woman). She was hardly ever wrong. As soon as we got in the door, the thunder would roar, the lightning would streak across the sky and rain would come down in sheets. We always marveled at mom's sense of timing.

But usually, like all kids, we would complain and beg her for a little more time. In those situations, Mom would use bribery. She would say, "If we start for home right now, there will still be time to have a piece of that good fresh rye bread with peanut butter or jelly on it and a glass of Kool-Aid without spoiling our supper. "

That would do it every time. Mom would have made a great child psychologist. But she was a homemaker and mother who gave away lots and lots of bread, peanut butter, jelly, and Kool-Aid to any kid who was in her care or happened to be around when she was handing it out.

My mother was really something!

Going To The Beach
With My Mother

In the last story, when I was telling you about Lake Michigan, I also told you some things about my mother.....but not enough. I would like to tell you a little more, like what SHE did when we were on the beach having such a good time. So what was Mom doing all those hours?

First of all, my mom loved being at the beach as much as we did. She didn't mind sitting out in the hot sun and she always brought along a blanket to put down over the hot sand to sit on. I don't remember there being any shade trees on that beach, and the few scrubby bushes on the edge in the back were not high enough to give off any shadows. I often wondered why my mom never seemed to get sunburned. If you wanted to go to that beach, you had one of two choices - get in the cold water or sit out in the hot sun. Mom chose the sun! We kids chose the water, at least most of the time, leaving my mother to sit alone.

It didn't surprise anyone who knew her that mom would go to the beach as often as she could. Mom just loved to be outside doing anything, whether it was in her own yard or garden, on some porch, at a picnic in a park, or watching some kids play on a playground. One of the reasons my mom liked to take us to the beach was that it was outside. Another was that she liked to be with kids. I often thought that my mother, even in her later years, was a kid at heart.

Mom liked to watch kids and observe the things they did, whether it was me or just any kid who happened by. Maybe she was trying to make up for the things she couldn't do when she was a kid herself, which must have been many, since she was raised by a very strict stepmother who was not a very lively or fun person. I think the main reason Mom took us to the beach so often was to watch us have some of the fun she was never allowed to have. She also came to our games, concerts, programs, or any other activity we were in. She was our best fan!

My mother was not just a good parent, she was also a good companion and a good sport, ready to play with us or cheer us on. She was fun to be with!

Mother loved to go to the beach because WE loved to go to the beach. She just seemed to like to be there with us. Though she seldom went into the water, except with the very little kids, she would sit out on the beach all day and watch us kids swim and play. At times, she would get down and play with the kids in the sand and teach them how to make things. She was a born teacher and would have made a good one, had she had the chance. But, best of all, she would always bring treats along for when we would get hungry or thirsty. She was always bringing little "surprises." She knew what kids liked and knew how to please them. The kids in my neighborhood loved my mom.

Mother also knew how to entertain herself. I don't think she was ever bored in her life. She could be very active when that was necessary, but she could also be very quiet when there was nothing she had to do. Because my dad worked all night and slept most of the day, Mom had to learn early in her married life how to entertain herself. She was very social, but she didn't mind being alone. Maybe that's where I got it from….I am like that, too!

Mother loved to read and would come home from the library about every other week with stacks of books under her arms. As a kid, I never paid attention to what she was reading, just how many books she had around. She would bring some of those books to the beach, being very careful not to get them wet, dirty, or full of sand. I don't think she ever owned a book, except the Bible, until later in her life when family and friends started giving her devotional books or books of poetry as gifts. She didn't have to buy books. Sheboygan had excellent libraries. Mom was always good at finding things that didn't cost anything.

Wherever Mom went, she usually took a book along, in case she found some free time. My mom and my dad should have gone to college. They both had active intellects and curious and fertile minds. They were just born a generation too soon. They both might have been excellent teachers.

Now and then some other mother would go with us to keep Mother company at the beach, but most often it was just her and us kids. She would spread her blanket out on the sand, not far from the water, and watch us like a hawk. She wouldn't bother us, unless we did something that was a violation of her rules, like getting out too far in the water, splashing or trying to dunk other kids, or throwing sand or stones. Then she would scold us. She was always kind and fair, but she could be very firm when she had to be.

She was also there to patch us up if we got hurt, and to comfort us if we got water up our nose. And she would not let us stay out in the hot sun for too long. Even then, she was conscious of the harmful affects of too much bright sun. Mom would also have made a good nurse. But she wasn't any of the things she could have been. She was what she was and was happy to be - a housewife, a mother, and a lover of children. She did those jobs very well. She did that last one best on the beach.

These fun activities went on day after day all summer long. It was a wholesome, easy, and cheap way for parents to entertain their kids. My mother took full advantage of this wonderful opportunity.

Other Lakes And
Places To Swim

I may have given the false impression that the beach near our house, was the only place we went to swim. That was not true. There were lots of other good places in and around Sheboygan where we went to swim (and sometimes fish) as well, when we had someone to take us. To get to some of the best lakes around Sheboygan required a car. They were too far away to walk or ride bikes to.

However, one of our favorite places to swim was close enough that we could ride our bikes to it. When I tell you about it, you will be surprised. You may wonder, why on earth, with that great Lake Michigan a few blocks away from our houses and lots of very good fresh water lakes nearby, we would even be interested in going to a dirty old river to swim in. We weren't supposed to and were warned never to go there. But we did! Just like Tom Sawyer and Huckleberry Finn did in those great books by Mark Twain. It was a kind of adventure into the past. This "ol' swimmin' hole" was right out of fiction.

It was a peculiar spot, not a pretty one, probably crawling with nasty bugs and tons of mosquitoes, on this small river about halfway between the west end of Sheboygan and the outskirts of Kohler (about two miles either way). We never bothered to find out where this river came from or went to. It didn't seem to have a name. The water in this river was a mucky, dirty, muddy brown, and the bottom, if you could get down and touch it, was also a slimy, mushy mess, with no solid bottom or stones. You didn't stand in this water, you had to swim in it or tread water. We just liked to jump in it or endlessly swim from one side to the other. It didn't take much to amuse us. I don't think it even had one of those long ropes tied to a tree like you always see in the movies.

The river was narrow, so even poor swimmers could easily swim across it. It was usually very quiet, almost still, unless the wind whipped up some waves now and then. But mostly, it seemed to stand perfectly still and not move at all. It might have been said to be stagnant and even putrid. It always had a bad smell.

Some people, when they warned us about the dangers of swimming in rivers, would talk about "undertows." We knew about them in lakes, but never felt them in this river. So we were convinced that the adults only told us that to scare us. I never heard of anyone drowning in this river. But lots of people drowned in the lakes that were supposed to be such safe places to swim. So much for adult wisdom and integrity.

Maybe part of the charm of this place was that it was hidden and forbidden, and only older boys came there (girls were not dumb enough to come to such an unattractive and smelly place). Another attraction was that you didn't have to wear a swimming suit to swim in the river. You could wear some old shorts, your underpants, or nothing. Nobody cared and no one could see you. There were trees and bushes hiding this whole area. I mean it was private. That may have been its main allure.

Some of the boys didn't come there to swim. They came to smoke cigarettes, take a few sips from some liquor bottles they got their hands on, or tell dirty jokes and stories. If they ever brought any girls there, the girls would have never come back a second time. It was a ridiculously unpleasant place to go, much less to swim.

But, for some stupid reason, me and my buddies liked to go there and actually came to swim. Maybe it was the privacy, maybe it was the secrecy, maybe it was the thrill of the potential danger and doing something we weren't supposed to be doing. Maybe it was just getting away from our mothers, the girls, the lifeguards, and the well-groomed and supervised beaches or a change.

One summer, when we were getting up into the junior high years, probably when we got to the boredom of late July and early August, a couple of us guys from our neighborhood hopped on our bikes most every day and went out there. It was fun at first, but the novelty quickly wore off as we discovered for ourselves what a really lousy place it was to swim and stopped going. I think we got tired of sneaking in the house and getting into the shower before our mothers could see us to wash that smelly ucky yucky mucky stuff off our bodies. Or it might just be that we got tired of pulling those nasty bloodsuckers off of our feet. Anyhow, the thrill soon wore off and we went back to the public beaches for the last few weeks of summer, where we could get a few last glimpses of the girls in their bathing suits, still lying in the sun and developing nicely.

As we got older and no longer wanted to go to the beach with our mothers, we started to go to several spots on Lake Michigan by ourselves. It was like having our own private beach, like the ones that people had when they bought a cottage on one of those smaller lakes. On these unsupervised stretches of beach, only a few swimmers came at any one time. But soon we outgrew those spots, too, as we discovered girls and no longer wanted to hang around with guys all the time.

When we got out of grade school, we boys started to go to the two public beaches in Sheboygan. The girls had been going to these for a long time and they were always crowded. They had lifeguards, rafts, diving boards, play equipment, and refreshment stands. Being watched by lifeguards had its advantages, but, unlike our mothers, they did not bring us free Kool-Aid, cookies, and candy bars. We had to buy those ourselves.

But we came to love those public beaches. And we often came to them, not to swim, but for special celebrations. Just about everybody in town came to the North Side beach on the Fourth of July. They came to swim in the afternoon, to hear the band concert in the early evening, and to see the fireworks over the water at night. When my own kids were little, we used to go to see my mother often. She lived close to the North Side Beach and we would go down to the waterfront for the activities. The big stone breakwaters were there and we used to like to watch the people fish off them. We also liked to walk way out to the end of them to look at the lighthouses.

Another place we liked to swim was the beach near Vollrath Park. When we went to picnics there, we would take our bathing suits along and swim at that beach. But, mostly, if we kids went to a public beach, it was to the one on the South Side. That one was very near the harbor where the boats came in and where the C. Reiss Coal Company was. Parents liked all of the Lake Michigan beaches because they were close, shallow, and safe.

I don't remember if there were indoor pools at the schools at that time, but I know there was one at the YMCA. It was used more often for giving swimming lessons than for recreational purposes. I probably learned how to swim there, and at Boy Scout Camp.

And last but not least, there were those nice smaller lakes around Sheboygan. They did have a few advantages over Lake Michigan, if you could get to them. The temperature of the water in those lakes was always much warmer, so you could stay in the water longer without getting frozen. And there were piers and rafts to jump off of and sometimes even a diving board. Some lakes had slides and merry-go-round things in the water to play on. At some lakes, you could rent a boat, usually by the hour, to go fishing or just to ride around the lake. At that time, the rates were considered expensive. I don't remember that we ever did that.

They always had refreshment stands that sold more than pop, ice cream, and candy bars. You could get a whole meal, if you wanted one. Adults could get brats and beer while they were buying a hot dog and pop for the kids. On a few of these lakes, there was a ballroom for the night crowd.

We didn't go to these lakes very often. The only times we could go was on one of those rare holiday days when Dad got a whole day off with no commitments and nothing that needed to be done at home, or on a Sunday afternoon. One of the pictures on the cover of this book was taken on one of those lakes on one of those days. They were always a special treat.

On those rare occasions, my mom would pack a big picnic lunch with sandwiches, maybe some potato salad or coleslaw, carrot sticks and celery, potato chips, cookies, pie, or cake, and a very large container of Kool-Aid. She might treat us to some ice cream after we had a chance to swim. If, by chance, my dad had just had a payday and we stayed long enough, he might buy our supper, which meant a brat, hamburger or hot dog, to go with the German potato salad that Mom had made special and brought along, and pop (the adults always had beer), and a big double dip ice cream cone. That might cost over a quarter a person.

These trips to the small lakes were very special for three reasons....

First, we got to drive there in a car, which meant we got to ride through the countryside and could see the farms with their cows, horses, and chickens, things we didn't get to see often......at least, not alive.

Second, we got to float on inner tubes, something we weren't allowed to do in Lake Michigan.

And third, and the most important of all, I got to be with my dad for a WHOLE DAY! We even got to swim together. What could be better than that?

Learning How To Swim

By this time, you might be wondering how we learned how to swim and who taught us in Sheboygan. Having lots of lakes nearby can be a wonderful thing, but what good are they to a kid who doesn't know how to swim in them? That kid can only play in the sand and splash water with his/her feet for so long before getting bored. The time comes to get out there into the water. As kids get older, they all have the desire to get out into the deeper water and swim, maybe even dive. In Lake Michigan, in most places, you could only go out beyond the sandbar if you could swim in water over your head. Until then you could only walk, jump, splash around, and fall in the water.

I learned early in life that SOMEONE HAD TO TEACH ME HOW TO SWIM! My mother or father couldn't do it, and it is something that is hard to learn all by yourself. Fortunately there were a lot of other adults in Sheboygan who could.

At some of the beaches the lifeguards were trained to give beginning swimming lessons. But I don't think I learned from them because I didn't start swimming at the beaches where the lifeguards were. Now and then some adult would come to our beach to give us kids a few tips on how to handle ourselves in the water, but that is far different from getting formal swimming lessons like my two grandchildren got during the summer in Litchfield at the school pool. When I was a kid, I thought I was a good swimmer, but I wasn't. All I was doing was playing in the water. I needed a swimming teacher to show me how to do it right.

I think most of my formal instruction came through the Boy Scouts, either down at the pool at the YMCA or at summer camps. That would not have happened until I got up into the grades and was old enough to at least join the Cub Scouts. Later, I earned merit badges in Swimming and Water Safety, and was working on the last merit badge I needed for Life Saving. The Boy Scouts prided themselves with having one of the best swimming and water safety instruction programs around, and I think the very best instruction we got was at camp each summer.

If you went to summer camp at that time, I don't think you could NOT learn how to swim. They wouldn't let you. You had to learn how to swim or else they wouldn't let you swim! Or they wouldn't let you swim where you wanted to, which was out beyond the ropes and the piers, where you could jump or dive off the raft way out beyond the ropes that marked off the beginner's area. You also had to be an accomplished swimmer before you could take a boat out for rowing or sailing. Those things were considered to be privileges, and you had to earn them.

On the first day of each camping period, EVERYONE was tested to see what swimming group you belonged in. There were four levels: Beginners, Intermediates, Swimmers, and Lifesavers/Instructors. What you were allowed to do on the waterfront and how far out in the water you could go was determined by this test. But you could move up as fast as you wanted and were able to. Many of us did that and went at least from Beginner to Intermediate in a week, and maybe even to Swimmers in two. I was one of those fast learners because I was eager and determined to become a good swimmer as soon as possible. I also wanted to be able to get out to the raft and into the boats.

After everyone had taken the test and was classified, every swimming period was divided in half. The first half was for instruction for everybody, whatever level you were in. As you progressed, you could move out farther and farther into the deeper water, until eventually you were beyond the ropes. The last half of each swimming period was for recreational swimming. That was just for fun, without any direction from the adults. Much as I liked to swim for fun, I could do all of that kind of swimming in Lake Michigan anytime I wanted to. I would rather have had instruction for the full time when I got to camp. I was in a hurry to learn and become an excellent swimmer.

All of the pools and waterfronts were run very strictly and according to the best water safety rules (a prelude to how it was going to be in the summer camps I was later to direct myself). Everything was done "by the book," and the Waterfront Director or Water Instructor (at that time all or most of them were men) was completely and fully in charge. When his whistle blew, we stopped dead in our tracks, shut our mouths, and listened to whatever instruction he had to give us. Those swimming instructors in Sheboygan were really good! Usually they were kind, patient, and excellent teachers, but they were also firm and didn't put up with any monkey business or fooling around in the water. One of the first things we were taught at camp was that swimming was serious business and to respect the water. We had a lot of fun on the waterfront, but no horseplay was allowed that might compromise safety. Water safety was always a primary concern and in all of my days at scout camp there was never an accident on the waterfront that I can remember and, thankfully, never a drowning. This experience was to come in handy later in life. To this day, I respect the water and follow the best rules of water safety, not only for myself but also for my own children and grandchildren.

Because I had excellent instruction and direction by the time I got into junior high, not only was I in the top swimming group and had all of privileges good swimmers were allowed on the waterfront, but I was often put to work teaching some of the Beginners and even the Intermediates. That made me feel important and grown up.

One year I came to camp with one objective and one objective only in my mind - to pass my Water Safety merit badge for my Eagle award (which I did the second day), and to train for and pass my Life Saving merit badge, which was the last merit badge I needed for Eagle. That is the highest rank the Boy Scouts award. And I was under a great deal of pressure to accomplish this. I knew this would be the last year I would be coming to camp. It was then or never!

The problem was that for some administrative reason there was only one person on our Scout Council who was qualified to give that training, do the testing, and grant the certification, and because of the nature of what had to be done, this could only be done at summer camp in the lake. To this day I do not understand why this could not have been done in the pool at the YMCA. But rules are rules, even if sometimes they don't make much sense or turn out to be unfair. At that time, you didn't question rules, you followed them.

So, the great expectation that I had when I came to camp that week, turned out to be one of the deepest and most bitter experiences and disappointments of my young life. It was announced on the first day of camp that the person who was to test and qualify us was not coming to camp that year. I don't think they said why, but there probably was some good reason. But I was crushed and it took me a long time to get over this severe blow, not only my disappointment but my anger. It was a terrible way to end my Scouting experience. It was not a happy ending, to say the least. I had already earned my Life award and was only that one merit badge away from Eagle, but the committee responsible for awards wouldn't make any exceptions. They held strictly to the rules. So

I never got to be an Eagle Scout, something every scout looks forward to, works hard for, and sets his heart on from the day he first joins a troop. Just thinking about it again now still makes me mad!

It wasn't fair! It wasn't my fault! It was nothing I did or didn't do! And I don't think I have ever completely gotten over it. I felt cheated and angry when I realized that I wouldn't get another chance. I was about to graduate, I had started to take paying jobs in the summer, and for many reasons, I wouldn't be able to go to summer camp again. That part of my life had come to an end. In response, I did a foolish thing (young kids often do foolish things, only to be sorry for them later). I quit the Troop I was in and joined the Sea Scouts, which was a part of the Scouting program, but it was not quite the same and did not give out Eagle awards. And that was it. No more awards, no more troop, no more swimming lessons or certifications. And, I never looked back.

As I got older, and cooled off, I began to realize two things - I had done a very foolish thing by quitting the troop (I could have found a way to go back to camp one more time to get certified and get my Eagle award before I moved on), and that the experiences I had and the instruction and training I had been given was not a total loss.

I had learned how to be a very good swimmer, which was more important than getting an award. And, when I got to be a Sea Scout, I got to take some of the prettiest girls in school to the dances at the Yacht Club.

When I think about it that way, I am not really mad anymore!

Ice Skating

As I am writing this, the Winter Olympics in Italy have just started. One of the main events will be speed skating. Many of the men and women who are on the United States team train in Wisconsin. That is logical. Where would you find a better place and a better tradition than in places like my hometown?

Watching these great Olympic skaters whiz around the track reminds me of how much I loved to skate when I was a boy. We all skated in Sheboygan, boys and girls alike. Soon after we learned how to walk, we learned how to skate. It was sort of one of those genetic things. Or was it our heritage? Or was it just that we had lots of ice and ice skating rinks in Sheboygan in winter? I did a lot of roller skating, too, on the sidewalks around town and at the roller rinks, but ice skating was probably my very favorite sport.

I was a good skater and I did a lot of skating. If you couldn't find me at school or at home during the winter months, you would probably find me at the skating rink, usually at the one that was closest to my house at Roosevelt Park. We had great rinks at that time - large, well designed, and well groomed. There were rinks all over town. There was one in back of the school near my Grandma's house on the North Side where I used to go skating with my cousin, Luverne, and my aunt, Nellie Mae. We always went there on Christmas afternoon.

But our skates did not match the quality of the rinks, at least not at first. My first pair of ice skates were pretty primitive. They were just like the first roller skates, except they had blades instead of wheels. You would fasten them onto your heavy shoes or boots with a skate key, like you did your roller skates. Those shoe skates were always coming off, which was a nuisance, and sometimes dangerous if they came loose or off when you were going at top speed going around a fast turn. Every time I see one of those Olympic skaters take a spill, I cringe, remembering the many I took in my lifetime. But, fortunately, though I got skinned up a little now and then and sometimes spilled a little blood, the bulky clothing we wore was great protection, and I never broke a bone, though I had lots of friends who broke their arms trying to break those falls. We were all glad when they started making shoe skates. They were a little warmer, and they stayed on your feet.

There were two kinds of those newer ice skates - the "figure skates" with the short runners, and the "speed skates" with the long runners. When I was a boy, I preferred the speed skates. When I got to be an adult, I liked the figure or hockey skates better. Those are the ones I bought my own girls when I first taught them how to skate. They were not interested in speed or racing. They were happy to just stay on their feet and not fall down too often.

In Sheboygan when I was growing up, we didn't play hockey and we didn't get into any fancy figure skating either. We were into speed skating because we wanted to race. The only time we went slow was when we were skating or skate dancing with a girl. Most of the time, we wanted to burn up the ice and go as fast as we could.

We didn't have any fancy clothing or gear like skaters have now and we didn't have Nike or Addidas symbols all over us. We just wore the warmest clothing we had; woolen coats or jackets, a couple of pairs of wool socks inside our boots, woolen hats and scarves, and maybe some earmuffs (I don't remember when they were invented but they were great). And, of course, mittens (not gloves). We often stayed out in sub-zero weather for long periods of time and needed to keep as warm as possible. We didn't have any shin, knee, or elbow pads or any helmets. It is a wonder we didn't get hurt more often than we did.

I almost always skated at Roosevelt Park because it was handy. It was within easy walking distance from my house on Swift Avenue. By cutting through some alleys and yards, I was soon crossing Union Avenue. That's where our school was. Then it was one long block past the playground and another long block beyond it to the park. The park was large and was designed with spaces for all kinds of active team games. In summer, we played baseball and rode our bikes there. In winter, we went to skate. The recreation department hired men to keep the ice perfect, flooding it every night after skating so it would be frozen, slick, and smooth for the next day. They also tended the stove in the warming house, sold refreshments, and kept order. They were very strict. If you refused to behave, you were sent home.

Other things we liked about this rink were some of the first outdoor flood lights and the music. They had large speakers both inside the warming house and outside facing the rink. Just like the jukeboxes, they played the latest and most popular dance music of the day. It was fun to grab a girl and either skate around the rink holding her hand or with your arm around her waist. For those who liked to dance and were good at it, we would dance on our skates in the middle of the rink and show off. The Olympic dancers are too fancy. We just danced the same steps we did on the dance floor. We were not there to win any prizes, and we were not trying to impress anyone, except the girl we were skating with.

The rink was always open (unless the weather was much too cold or the ice was too rough) after school every day and all evening until 9:00 p.m. About 8:45 the man in the warming house would make the lights flicker, which was the warning that we needed to come off the ice to take off our skates and go home. That time always seemed to come too soon.

Then, if we were lucky, some girl might be willing to let us walk her home. On weekends, the rink was open all day Saturday and Sunday. And I think older kids and adults could stay an hour or two later on Saturday nights.

Maybe we were so healthy then, and so slim and trim, because we did so much walking, bike riding, running, and skating.

Several times during the winter, there would be weekend races on our rink, which was one of the bigger and better rinks in town. They were big events and very exciting. Kids from all over the area came to compete. Their parents and friends would come to watch them, standing in back of the guard ropes, yelling and urging their favorites on. You had to be an excellent skater even to dare to enter these events, and the best of the best to win one of the top prizes. Even if you didn't win anything, it was fun to compete and to say that you raced. There were events for all ages, up to and including adults. The guys and gals in Sheboygan were really great skaters.

When I got a little older, I did complete in those races a couple of times. I don't remember if I ever won any prizes, and I know I was never good enough to get to any of the regional, state, or national events, though some kids from Sheboygan occasionally did. And, of course, there are always some Wisconsinites in the Olympics. But I was a good skater and held my own in Sheboygan, which was all I cared about. I skated for the thrill, not the glory.

It is surprising that after graduation from high school, I don't ever remember skating again until I had my own family and took my children out to our local rinks in Minnesota and taught them how to skate. Maybe that is because during the three years I was in the Army, I always was stationed in warm weather places where they had never heard of ice skates or rinks. When my kids were old enough to skate, I had to buy a new pair of hockey skates so I could skate with them. I don't know what happened to those skates. They probably got put in one of our garage sales when we moved. Too bad. They served me well and I spent many happy hours on them.

Maybe I should buy a pair of skates one of these years and try again. I don't think I am too old to still skate well and it would be great exercise. But I guess I wouldn't sign up for races anymore!

Sliding Down That Great Big Hill

If we were not at the rink skating, we were probably at one of the big hills sliding, that is, after we outgrew the less risky things that all little kids who live up North like to do in winter, things like running and jumping in the snow, begging our parents or some older kid to pull us on our sled down the street or alley, throwing snowballs at each other, and making snowmen and forts.

If there was not a big hill at the end of some field near your house or a park nearby, the neighbors who lived on a hill would kindly allow the authorities to block off a street or two in front of their houses and make them into an icy, slippery, fast track for sledding, either with our large Flexible Flyer sleds or those long toboggans. There was one of those hills only two blocks from my house. To walk there all I had to do was go up one block to the Lutheran Church, turn right, and go down another block and there it was. On top of the hill there were those long yellow and black barriers and there were bright streetlights at the top and bottom of the hill. At the end of the run, there were other barriers that the police must have put up. For most of the winter, the nice people who lived on the hill and the street below used their alleys to get their cars in and out and didn't use the street in front of their houses so we could use it for sledding. It must have been a major inconvenience, but they seemed glad to do it. People in Sheboygan were good to kids.

The hill itself was long and steep, taking up a whole city block. There were houses on one side of the street and a large vacant lot on the other. My friend, Joe Bifano, and his family lived on the corner house right next to it. The big hill at the end of that vacant lot was much too steep for sliding, so sliding in the street worked best. Another straight and level street below that hill was also blocked off as a safety measure. Once you got to the bottom of that hill going full tilt, there had to be some space to break and slow down before you could come to a full stop. So, in all, the slide was two blocks long. It was kept icy and slippery and was ideal for fast rides.

I suppose it could have been dangerous, but we were well trained on what precautions to take, like not bunching up and giving other riders plenty of room, hanging on tight, and how to fall off, if and when we tipped. Now and then someone would get banged up a little, but I don't remember anyone ever getting seriously injured. There must have been adults around to watch and help us.

Each of us would bring our own long Flexible Flyer sleds. Usually we got those as presents at Christmas. They were made of a shiny, light wood with red and gold trimmings and bright red runners. Skis were not allowed and it was too early for those round plastic dishes or ski boards that the kids use now. We tried cardboard pieces but they didn't work, because we were sliding on ice, not snow. All of those things would have been hard to control on the ice on that hill. We stuck to our sleds and toboggans.

Of course, the most thrilling rides were on those long toboggans. When they were loaded with kids and ready to come down, they would ring a loud bell to warn everyone else to get out of the way. All of the other sleds would stop going down the hill or hurry to finish their runs and get off to the side. Those toboggans were the kings of that hill and had the right of way. I don't remember how many kids we could get on them, but it was a lot, like maybe 12 or 15.

One of the kids, usually the smallest, was put way up in front and called "the headlight." Often that was me. It wasn't until I grew up that I realized that was the most dangerous place to be! The biggest kid was usually assigned to the back and he was expected to steer.

Now and then, but not often, a toboggan would overturn and spill everyone off. We would just tumble off and continue to slide on our sides or butts down the hill, pick ourselves up, and walk back up the hill to do it again. The toboggan would just slide down the hill by itself until it stopped. Then someone would pull it back up the hill and get it ready for the next run.

We used to slide down other hills, too, which had more snow than ice, and we used our sleds in other ways and to pull and transport things. But for pure fun and lots of thrills, nothing could compare with those slides down that street.

Would I do it now? Don't be silly, of course not!

Do you think I want to get killed?

Picnics

Let's Pack A Lunch
And Have A Picnic

Picnics in Sheboygan were not always planned. Sometimes they just happened. People in Sheboygan loved picnics! And so did I. Maybe they liked picnics so much because of the long winters. When summer finally came, people tried to do things outside as often as they could. You didn't need to do much to organize a picnic. If there was not a park near your house, you could have a picnic in your own backyard. All you needed to do was prepare some food and find a shady spot. The mosquitoes and flies might get you, but you soon got used to those. You could have your outdoor meal for yourself, with your spouse and kids, with some of your relatives who lived nearby, or just invite some neighbors on your block to bring some food and come over and join you.

In those days, women liked to have those kinds of picnics because it meant they didn't have to put in any time over a hot stove that day. All they had to do was make some cold sandwiches, or, if the men were at home, they always did the frying of the meat, outside, of course. Store-bought cookies and ice cream could take the place of cake or pie. And the kids didn't have to eat the cold vegetables if they didn't like them. It was a winner for everyone.

Some picnics were more elaborate and took more planning, like the ones we had with our relatives several times a week at Vollrath Park near Grandma Huebner's house. Some picnics were for lunch and some were at night for supper. When the men were working, and it got too hot and uncomfortable in the house (these were the days before air conditioning or even those big fans we have now), the women and kids would gather under a big shade tree and eat outside. Or they might just gather on someone's front porch. When they did that they would call it a "picnic lunch." If the outdoor meal was at night it was a "picnic supper." I don't ever remember having a "picnic breakfast." But why not?

At those backyard picnics, you didn't have to entertain. Everyone would entertain themselves. The kids would eat fast and then scamper off to play in the yard, in the street or the alley, or run off to play with their friends in a park close by. The adults would sit and talk for hours on end. Conversation was one of the main pastimes at that time. Some people called it gossip. It was a good way to share the news and get important information around. Maybe the best part of those picnics was that there wasn't much of anything to clean up. Most everything that was left, which was very little (people didn't waste much then), ended up in the garbage and trash can at the end of your lot.

Picnics were a great institution. They were cheap and easy and a good way to socialize, which is probably one of the reasons why there were so many picnics in Sheboygan in the summer. My mom liked picnics, so we were always having them in our backyard. But if my dad was to get in on them and get to work on time, we had to have our supper picnics early. He had to be to the plant at 6:00 p.m. sharp. He was never late! When he was able to be at a picnic, he always fried the meat, then would eat quickly and take off for work.

Take my word for it….if you didn't like picnics you had better leave Sheboygan and live somewhere else.

German Potato Salad And
That Yummy Chocolate Cake

I suppose most women in Sheboygan could make German Potato Salad if they wanted to, and lots of kinds of chocolate cake. The women in Sheboygan were excellent cooks and bakers, especially the German women in my mother's family. I could make long lists of the wonderful and delicious things I used to eat in Sheboygan. But for now, I just want to tell about two things that I used to eat often in Sheboygan when I was a boy.

No one made German Potato Salad as good as my mother made it. It was one of her specialties. And no one in Sheboygan could make that special kind of chocolate cake as good as my Aunt Myrtle made it. Just thinking and writing about those two things now makes my mouth water.

Because people lived so close together at that time and got together so often, we had a good opportunity to eat whatever special dishes the women prepared for the meals that we ate together. The women were identified with the dishes they made best. When they got on the phone and planned these gatherings, I could hear the person whose house we were going to and was planning the meal saying, "Mabel, why don't you make some of your German Potato Salad for us" and "Myrtle, please bring some of your cake." Everyone coming would agree to that.

I don't know how my mother made the German Potato Salad, and it doesn't matter. I just liked the way it tasted. I still do, when one of my daughters makes it, using their grandma's recipe. The things that I remember about it, the things that distinguished it from the other potatoes we regularly ate, was that it tasted very different.

I am told it starts with a pot full of thinly sliced potatoes. Then some sliced onions are added. I can remember mother frying the bacon and breaking it into small bits and putting them in next. Then she would add some flour, salt, and sugar, and maybe some celery seed and a little pepper. She would keep putting her finger in it, licking her finger to taste it as it cooked. It must have been the vinegar she added last that gave it its unique, lightly sour flavor. Not too much and not too little. Always just right. Then it was all cooked in some kind of light brown cream sauce until it was ready to serve. It took a long time to make and she used to say it "stunk up the whole house." I must admit it did have a strong and distinctive aroma. It could be eaten hot or cold, which made it wonderful for picnics, where you didn't always get a chance to heat things up. There was no in-between about German potato salad. You either liked it or you didn't. Most of our present family members liked it when my wife made it, but some didn't. For them, we would have baked beans.

Aunt Myrtle's yummy chocolate cake was probably not much different from the other dark German chocolate cakes that were so popular at the time. They were light and fluffy and moist and all had a rich chocolate flavor. But that is not why we all relished Aunt Myrtle's cake so much. It was her frosting that separated her cakes from all of the others.

Again, I have no idea how she made it, only that it looked and tasted GREAT! This frosting, which she never put on any of her other cakes, was a kind of yellow/tan color and had a rich caramel flavor. It was always spread on real thick and had a lot of chopped nuts sprinkled on top. That's why we kids liked it so much. It was very sweet. And she always cut the cake into great big pieces, which is another thing we liked. I have never tasted anything exactly like it then or since. Everybody loved it and she brought it often to parties for our dessert.

After we got married, my wife got the German Potato salad recipe from my mother and made it often, usually for our brat fries or picnics. She passed the recipe on to several of our daughters and her granddaughter. Now they know how to make it. It is always good, but I secretly think (I would never say so to them) that my mother's is just a wee bit better.

Sunday School Picnics
And Ice Cream Socials

For some people in Sheboygan, their church was the center of their lives. Not only did they look to the church for forgiveness of their sins, absolution, salvation, and a way to heaven, but they also looked to their church to provide many of their other personal, family, and social needs. One of those needs was to celebrate and have fun, and two of the things that the churches sponsored were Sunday School picnics and Ice Cream Socials. They happened every summer and they were always delightful. The picnics were private, but the whole community was invited to come to the ice cream socials.

Every church in town had some kind of Sunday School picnic. They were usually scheduled for the first Saturday or Sunday in June, after classes at the schools ended and just before summer vacations began. They were timed to catch families before they went off to their cabins on the lake or left on their summer vacation trips, or before the kids from the country had to start working on their family farms. They were held rain or shine, outdoors under tents, or at the church, if necessary. Thankfully, most years it was a sunny day!

These picnics were generally held at the closest playground or park near the church. Usually the activity would start with a parade (but not like the big parades I liked to march in with the Boy Scout Drum and Bugle Corps). There weren't any bands or floats. We just all marched from the church to the picnic spot. Sometimes we would carry flags and banners and blow whistles or make sounds with homemade noisemakers, to let the neighbors know we were on our way.

When we got to our site, there would be a nice lunch with the kind of food that we kids liked to eat. There was always lots of pop and ice cream. After a short formal program, during which some awards and prizes were given for perfect attendance, learning Bible verses or hymns, or for contests of some kind, we were all graduated and moved on to our next classes for the fall.

The rest of the time was spent playing games. There were lots of prizes, and before the afternoon was over, everyone got something to take home, like little crosses, pins, cards with Bible verses or pictures on them, or even new Bibles.

The picnics did not last very long, but they were lots of fun, and we felt very important because it was all planned for us.

The Ice Cream Socials were held throughout the summer, mostly during July and August. They always took place in the afternoon and early evening, before it got dark and before most of the mosquitoes came out.

And they were not just for us kids. They were very popular with kids and adults alike. Anyone could come. We liked them because of all the good stuff to eat. And we never got tired of ice cream.

Sometimes what were called Ice Cream Socials were more like carnivals or the public picnics I will later describe. But the ones I am telling about here are the simple ones that were held in the back or to the side of the church, or in the church basement, if the weather turned bad.

The purpose of these Ice Cream Socials was not really to make money (if they did make some, it was always sent to missions.) The purpose for these summer events was to eat and to socialize. And it was a dessert lover's heaven! Not only was there lots of ice cream, but there were all kinds of pies, cookies, bars, and cakes. Some of the adults drank coffee. We kids drank Kool-Aid of various colors and flavors. Big scoops of ice cream of different flavors were served in dishes with all kinds of delicious toppings, like those great banana splits we used to get in the ice cream parlors. Everyone paid one price and you could eat all you wanted.

There wasn't any entertainment or program. We just came and ate lots of ice cream and goodies and then went home. We looked forward to these events with great anticipation.

They were called Ice Cream Socials, because that is exactly what they were....a time to socialize with our friends and eat more ice cream than we could afford to buy if we went to the ice cream shops or parlors.

Public Picnics

With all of the backyard picnics, family picnics, church picnics, and organization picnics (like the Firemen's picnic) going on in and around Sheboygan all the time, you would think that the people of Sheboygan would get picnicked out and would not need any more than the ones they were already going to. But that was not the case. People in Sheboygan loved picnics and never seemed to get enough of them. It might have had something to do with that nice, fresh cool air blowing off of the lake on really hot days.

So, in addition to the picnics mentioned above, there were also lots of others - ones I will call Public picnics - going on besides. By this I mean, picnics that anyone could come to; you, your family, your relatives, friends who might be visiting you, or tourists who just happened to be in town. You didn't need to buy tickets in advance or make a reservation. You could just drop in and stay as long as you liked.

There were some very good reasons why people in Sheboygan liked picnics so much. To put it simply, they only had three months out of the year to enjoy them. During the rest of the months, the weather was always iffy. Also, this was Depression times. People did not have a lot of money to spend on entertainment. Picnics were a cheap and convenient way to do a lot of things at the same time and place, like eat, socialize, and have lots of fun. And, you could take your whole family.

Just think of it! Public picnics provided what might be called non-stop, multi-entertainment for kids of all ages. For the price of a brat, a beer, and an ice cream cone (which was about a quarter) we could spend all day and never get bored for a minute.

In the big parks, we could hike or walk on the beach or swim. We could play a few games of horseshoes or get up a game of baseball or volleyball. We could hear some of the best bands, musicians, and singers in town, and watch some of the best dancers perform. These were performances we would have to buy tickets for and pay a lot of money for if we went to a concert, or a club, or a ballroom to see and hear them.

At some of the picnics, people who liked to gamble, could play some dice games or throw some balls and darts at things to try to win prizes. Lots of people liked to play Bingo, so at most public picnics, there would be a very large Bingo tent. My aunt and uncle used to win a lot of stuff at those Bingo games. My parents were never very lucky and didn't play those games often. Those who did not gamble could spend that money on ice cream and candy. If folks did not want to do any of those things, they could just sit, relax in the shade, and enjoy some good conversation.

But best of all, there were always lots of things to keep children amused, busy, active, and out of trouble. Public picnics were excellent baby-sitters. You could let the kids loose and not have to watch them too closely. If they got temporarily lost, someone would bring them back. It was a good deal all around, one of those "something for everybody" affairs - good, wholesome family entertainment.

Of course, for those who sponsored these public picnics, it was a good way to make a lot of money in a hurry. Often times, we didn't even know who was sponsoring the picnic. But no one seemed to care. We came for what we got out of it, and we always assumed that the money we spent would go to some good cause. Public picnics were a win-win situation!

So, on most days, during the summer months in Sheboygan, if you went out to Terry André Park or Vollrath Park (and later to Kiwanis Park), there would be some kind of public picnic going on that you could take part in and enjoy. The weather was usually perfect and those picnics were hardly ever canceled. If it started to rain, there were always covered shelters and tents to duck under until the rain stopped and the sun came out again.

We knew that there would always be some kind of picnic somewhere. All we would have to do is put a quarter in our pocket and go. We would have a nickel for a hamburger, a nickel for a bottle of pop, and a nickel for an ice cream cone. Unless we stayed longer than we planned and spent some more money on things to eat, or were tempted to play two games of Bingo, we would come home with a dime in our pocket, which we could use to go to a movie in a day or two.

It was a great way to spend our time in the summer!

Helping Uncle Gilbert
At The Labor Day Picnic

Uncle Gilbert was not only a movie projectionist by trade, but he was also the Secretary of the local Stagehands Union. His full-time job was showing movies at the Sheboygan and Rex theaters, but he often made extra money working as a stagehand for live shows and concerts at other places. He usually ran the sound equipment and worked the lights. He probably also got paid something for his Secretary job at the Union.

Everyone in town who made a living in entertainment knew and liked Uncle Gilbert. Like the old ward bosses in the big cities, he had a great deal of say about who got the Union jobs. But everybody said he was always fair, and that he saw to it that everybody got a turn. He was also respected by the employers who hired the Union workers. He sent them good workers and worked out fair contracts. He collected the dues, kept the minutes of meetings and good records, and saw that everything at the Union office was administered in an honest and businesslike manner. He was really an excellent administrator.

Because he was an Officer of his Union and a great organizer, he was also always put in charge of the big Labor Day Picnic for all of the local Unions in Sheboygan. It was held every year out at Terry Andre Park on Labor Day. The Unions took over the whole park for that day and night.

Labor Day was always on the first Monday of September and it marked the transition from summer to fall, just like it does now. Though fall did not become official until later in the month, for all practical purposes, fall schedules and activities began the day after Labor Day. On Labor Day, all summer vacations came to an end, and on Tuesday, all of the kids went back to school and everyone went back to work. Like the Fourth of July, Labor Day was one of the most important holidays of the year in Sheboygan. The Fourth of July was the day to be patriotic; Labor Day was a day to rest from one's labors and play.

Life in Sheboygan had a nice rhythm to it. So, at that time in Sheboygan, most people did not go away for the weekend. They stayed home, or came back home on Sunday, to get ready to go back to work on Tuesday. That left one more day to play and have fun, and what better way to play and to end the summer than to have one more big super duper picnic. Most of them joined the Union members as they celebrated out at Terry Andre Park. It was probably the biggest and best public picnic of the summer. It had all of the features of the other public picnics but much, much more. The park was always filled to overflowing with people of all ages, and the activities every year were always the same.

First there was a parade out to the park, headed by a band made up of professional players from the Musician's Union. The band was followed by a contingent of some kind from each Union, proudly flying their local's flag. Later, the musicians played a concert and provided music throughout the day. At night, one of the local Swing bands and a Polka band played for a free dance. As I got older, my mom and dad stayed for part of that so I could hear the music.

During the day, there were programs, speeches, and activities of all kinds. Each Union had some kind of a booth with handouts about their Union and what they did. They might also sponsor some kind of activity or game. There was always plenty to eat and lots of beer to drink. People consumed a lot of both. The one thing that might have been different at this picnic was that there were more booths of all kinds and more games to play. Union members had to come out to the park very early in the morning to set them up and get them running.

The picnic was not only fun, but the year's biggest fundraiser for the Unions. Uncle Gilbert found all kinds of ways to help the picnickers part with their money. The first thing you did when you got to the park was buy tickets. The only cash that changed hands at this picnic was between you and the ticket sellers. No one used or handled cash. That way every cent that was spent could be strictly accounted for. All of the money raised was later divided fairly and equitably between all of the Unions that took part. Uncle Gilbert saw to that.

By this time in the summer, we kids were kind of tired and bored with picnics and parades, but my cousin Dick and I liked to go to this picnic to help Uncle Gilbert. We went with him early in the morning and stayed all day. My parents and my Aunt Myrtle came later, but we seldom saw them. We were too busy!

Uncle Gilbert put us to work running some of the games that were so popular at picnics at the time. But he was always very careful where he assigned us. We might take tickets in the booths we worked in because we didn't have to make change or handle any money. He would never let us work in the booths where there were "games of chance" (where gambling was involved). We had to work in the other games, where some skill was involved in order to win, or the games for little kids where everyone who played won a prize. Sometimes there was a thin line in what constituted gambling and what did not, but Uncle Gilbert figured that out to see that we did not bend any rules or break any laws. Gambling might have been legal then, but not for minors. Uncle Gilbert loved to gamble himself, but he was very careful to observe the law.

For a time, we would work the Fish Pond. We liked to do this. This was only for little kids. Dick and I would take turns. One of us would stand outside, take the tickets, and help the little kids put on the hooks and handle the poles. The other would work inside and put the prizes on the hooks. Every kid got a nice prize. Then we would change places.

Then we might work for a time at the booths where players would throw balls, darts, hoops, or pennies, nickels, and dimes at something in order to get some prize (that was the only game where money was used.) All of these games did require skill, sometimes lots of it, to win, and none of the games were rigged, as they sometimes were at the carnivals. Some of the prizes were big and some were valuable. We were not allowed to be in the booths where dice games were played, or at the Wheel of Fortune, or in the Bingo tent. Only adults were allowed to work in those booths where any hint of gambling was involved.

We worked all day, we worked hard, and we loved it. We did have some time off to eat, watch the entertainment, or play some games ourselves, but most of the time we were in the booths. And what did we get for our efforts? Not Union wages, but all of the free tickets we wanted and could use, all of the ice cream we could eat, and all of the root beer we could drink. We also got hamburgers when we got hungry. But most of all, we worked for the satisfaction of knowing that we were helping Uncle Gilbert, who always did so much for us. He appreciated our returning the favor.

We wouldn't have missed the Labor Day picnic for anything. Then, when the picnic was over, we were ready to go back to school for another year. It was always a fitting end to a perfect summer.

Parades

The Boy Scout Drum
And Bugle Corps

My whole life changed the day I joined the Boy Scout Drum and Bugle Corps. That was the day I fell in love with DRUMS and lost interest in playing the violin. Any red-blooded Sheboygan boy would have done the same, unless he decided to seriously get into sports instead. I must have been in the fourth or fifth grade when I joined the corps. The Sheboygan Boy Scout Drum and Bugle Corps was sponsored by the American Legion Post and was led by a magnificent man by the name of Art.

I have saved some of my best stories, about the corps, for the last part of this book because for that period of my life it was the most important organization I belonged to and how I spent most of my time, practicing or performing with the corps. I am devoting a whole section to the corps and Parades. That's what the corps did, march in parades.

The corps was so important to my musical development because of what I learned from the leaders and teachers of the corps. I became a good drummer because of the lessons they gave me, things I have never forgotten and found very useful all of my life, as a professional musician and entertainer, like how to keep good time, swing a band, and be flashy when necessary. It was in the corps that I paid my dues and earned my stripes.

In order to join the Sheboygan Boy Scout Drum and Bugle Corps, you had to belong to a Boy Scout Troop in town. There weren't any auditions and we didn't even have to know how to play an instrument. Once we were accepted, our leaders taught us everything we needed to know about playing the drums or bugles, and, all of the equipment was furnished and the lessons were FREE. You could buy your own drumsticks, if you wanted to, so you could practice on your drum pad at home and use your own sticks when you played in other bands. I always had my own sticks, except when I played the Scotch or bass drums. Then I used the beaters the Corps provided. We were also given neat uniforms to wear, but we needed to keep them clean and repaired. Our mothers were good at doing that. All drummers started out on the snare drum and all brass players started out on a bugle. Later, we were assigned the instruments we were to play in the corps. I ended up usually playing one of those neat Scotch drums, which were small and narrow bass drums. They were lightweight and easy to carry when they were strapped on your shoulders.

We met for practice once a week in a large garage in back of the Legion clubhouse, and our equipment (there was a lot of it) was stored there. I am not going to say much about how the corps was organized, how we practiced, or the disciplines we had to observe. It was all very military, a good preparation for later being soldiers or sailors. And Art honed us into a fine musical group and had very high standards. Instead, the following stories will be about our performances, which were mostly marching in parades. Unlike bands and orchestras, that is what drum and bugle corps were organized and designed to do. We were a PARADE organization, and when there was an important parade anywhere in Wisconsin, we were in it.

But first, let me tell you a little more about our leader, Art, who not only had ample ability, abundant energy, and great enthusiasm.....but a magic touch.

Crazy Art And
His Magic Touch

I am sure that if it hadn't been for Art, there would never have been a Boy Scout Drum and Bugle Corps in Sheboygan. He was its founder, its inspiration, and its driving force. I don't think that any of us knew or would remember his last name. And, contrary to Sheboygan custom, he did not want us to call him Mister. Everyone called him Art. When he wasn't listening, we kids used to sometimes call him "Crazy Art." Of course, he was far from crazy…..he was brilliant. Art was there when I joined the corps and he was still there when I had to quit the corps to go off to fight the war.

Art was some guy! A rare gem! I don't think they make guys like Art anymore. I guess we called him Crazy Art because he did lots of unconventional things that other guys would never have dared to even try. He was full of energy and had a great imagination. He always wanted to try new things, liked to play practical jokes and stunts on his friends, and liked to experiment. We were known all over the state for the unusual turns we made when we came to corners when marching in a parade. No other corps did it the same way we did. It was Art's invention.

Art was very disciplined, very dedicated, and a stickler for being on time and following the rules. And he was a great role model for young kids like us. He never smoked, drank, or swore in front of his boys in the corps. He was known for his high standards and ethical behavior. He was a responsible adult and he expected us to behave. If he had any bad habits (which he probably did), he expressed them on his own time and in private or when he was with his peers inside the Legion Club House. We never saw that side of him, if there was one.

Art was honest, always fair, and patient and understanding with the mistakes we frequently made. But he had his limits, and he didn't put up with any crap from anybody. Anyone who got out of line, didn't behave, wouldn't shape up, or caused too many problems, was out! Period! You

257

might get a second chance, if you were not a habitual troublemaker, but never a third. We could fool around and have fun when we weren't playing, but you better not mess around with the music or get out of line when we were marching. We were a class outfit, and Art expected us to act that way.

Art was always neatly dressed, even at practices, and his shoes were always shined. He had the bearing and posture of a soldier and sometimes the vets or other soldiers would salute him along our parade routes, thinking he was an officer. He firmly returned their salutes, but when he turned around, he would have a big grin on his face.

Art was one of the most important role models for my musical life. When I became a bandleader myself, I applied all of the things I had learned about being a leader from Art. My guys didn't salute me, but they respected me and followed my direction. I was strict, but not stern. I was patient, but constantly striving to be as perfect as possible. I was friendly, but didn't take any crap from my musicians or our employers either. I wanted to be a crazy leader just like Art.

Art was in his 40's and probably had a wife and kids of his own. He was not very tall, but he was slim and what used to be called wiry. He always walked and marched very straight, with his head up high and his chest out, and focused on whatever it was he was doing. He knew how to concentrate and not get distracted. He didn't wave his hands around or show off like some directors do. But he always had a whistle around his neck and would blow it regularly to give us our signals. He always walked right up in front and to the right side of the first row of drums. At those times, he never smiled. It was as if his face was set in stone. He was all business then and would not allow any fooling around. He was always there, in his place, in control of everything that was going on. There was never any doubt who was in charge. I don't remember Art ever missing a rehearsal or performance. I think he would have had to be in the hospital and dying if he ever did.

But, when we were not practicing or performing, he was lively and jolly, stirring things up, and getting the action going. When we were traveling, he mixed with the boys, and some of the best tricks that were played on us were done by Art himself. When we bit on one of his pranks, he would be the first to laugh. He got a kick out of being silly and having fun. The public never saw that side of him, but we did. And it made us love him even more.

I don't remember seeing him play any of the instruments (he had other guys teaching us), and I don't know if he ever had any formal music training. He may not even have been a veteran or a member of the Legion. I don't think he got paid anything for being our director.

I think Art was so successful as a leader because he really liked kids. In many ways, he was still kind of a kid himself. He always put us at ease, made us feel important, and was quick to praise us when we did a good job. Unlike other adult leaders I have known, he never insulted us, humiliated us in front of our friends, yelled at us when we made a simple mistake, or made us feel bad. He was a guy who could really build you up and make you feel good about yourself. Today it would be called "building up our self-esteem."

Art was a born leader. He knew what he wanted, and he got it. We not only knew he was in charge, but we respected, admired, and were very fond of him. We would have done anything for him. If he had told us to march into a lake or jump off a cliff, we would have done it. But, he was not that crazy. I have played for and under a lot of very good directors in my life in music, but there were not many who could work the kind of magic that Art could with us kids.

Everyone said it, and I think it was true, that we might have been the best Boy Scout Drum and Bugle Corps in Wisconsin at the time. We were proud to be Art's boys, and proud to be playing in his corps. That was our Art; our leader, our teacher, our mentor, our role model, and our adult friend. For me, there was never to be another quite like him, at least not in my life and experience.

As you read the stories to follow, even if I don't use his name again, you will know he was always there, blowing his whistle or waving his hand, as he, like the Pied Piper of Hamlin, led us children down the street.

The Firemen Had Their Day

Every Sunday during the summer, and sometimes on Saturdays, the volunteer fire departments in the small towns around Sheboygan would have big public picnics. Towns and townships like Haven, Oostberg, Plymouth, Sheboygan Falls, Elkhart Lake, Herman, Greenbush, Lima, Holland, and Gibbensville, to name a few. The corps played them all! It was the way the departments raised most of their money to support their organizations. These "Firemen's Picnics" were very popular and people would come from miles around to attend them, often staying for the entire day and into the night. We used to see some of the same people week after week as they traveled around to attend these events.

The activities would usually start around noon time, after the local people got out of church, with a big parade down Main Street. At these events there was always a big parade. I used to think that sometimes there would be more marchers in the parade then the whole population of the town.

The parades would start at some school and end at some park, where the picnic would be held. There were always lots of bands and drum and bugle corps in those parades, and we were usually one of them. It was generally agreed that we were one of the largest and best drum corps in that area of Wisconsin, so we were in demand. Art used to tell us that when the firemen decided on whom they would invite to be in their parade, we would almost always be the first on the list. We were also always given the choice spot in the parade route, usually right in the middle. When we came down the street with our honor guard up front and our flags flying in the breeze, stretching out from curb to curb and almost 100 strong, the crowds started to clap for us as soon as they could hear us, even before they could see us. We always played loud and marched with great spirit. We put on quite a show. When we passed the judge's stand our drummers would twirl their sticks in the air and our buglers would lift their horns up and down and wave them from side to side. If there were prizes, we always won, usually first place. The schedule and activities at those picnics were almost always the same, and we knew the routine by heart.

Depending on how far we had to travel, we would meet at the Legion and get on our buses, in time to get to the town by at least an hour before the parade was to begin, which was usually on or around 12:30 or 1:00. Art always told us to "have a good breakfast" before we came, because we wouldn't be eating again until after the parade, which sometimes lasted for hours. Like all kids, we were always hungry. He only had to tell us this once. The new kids caught on quickly.

The marching bands and drum and bugle corps like ours were there to furnish the music. Then there would be organizations, in their uniforms, marching behind us, like members of the local American Legion and Veterans of Foreign Wars, police and firemen, sometimes Women's Auxiliary groups, boy or girl scout troops, etc. There were lots of horses and wagons, old cars, tractors, and trucks. Anyone who wanted to march in the parade was welcome to do so. Sometimes the kids in town were encouraged to decorate their bikes and coaster wagons or make floats. And, of course, the firemen would be right up there in front, in their natty uniforms, riding their clean and polished trucks, blowing their horns, sounding their sirens and ringing their bells. The trucks were always bright red with lots of gold. These parades stretched for blocks and sometimes miles. Everyone at that time loved parades. They stood or sat on the curbs, lining the whole parade route, yelling, whistling, or clapping as the units went by.

Now and then it would rain, but seldom were the parades canceled because of the weather. No one seemed to mind getting wet. But no one liked it when it began to thunder and lightning. Sometimes parades were delayed until those kinds of storms let up or passed by. Usually, the sun was soon shining brightly again and it would be a hot day. We never liked it when it was too wet or too humid, because it affected the bugles and knocked our drums out of tune. And we were always ready to take off our sweaters and shed our ties as soon as we got to the end.

After the parade was over, we would always get lots of free tickets to get our lunch. There were, of course, lots of friers making brats. And there was lots of beer consumed. Many of us kids didn't like brats, but we loved hamburgers and hot dogs and ate our fill. We drank root beer, pop or many, many glasses full of lemonade. And, of course, we ate ice cream all day long. We never went away hungry or thirsty from a firemen's picnic. We were lucky if we didn't get a bellyache...but sometimes we did.

At most of these events there were "games of chance," like the ones they had at carnivals. A lot of free tickets were wasted on those, but sometimes we might win a small prize to take home. I don't remember if they had carnival rides at them, but there were always playgrounds in those parks. As we got older, we ignored those....we didn't need them. There were always more interesting things to do, like the non-stop entertainment. Local musicians and bands would play, mostly old time music or marches and show tunes, and there would be singers and dancers and sometimes a magician, clowns, or acrobats from the local gymnastics groups that were so popular at the time. There were also organized or pickup ball games, and sometimes races with prizes. Sometimes, if there were a large field nearby, the visiting bands or corps would put on exhibitions. People liked those and we liked to do them. It gave us a chance to show our stuff, and was good practice, particularly if it was a year when we went to the State Fair.

The older boys did a lot of girl watching and flirting. The local girls usually flirted back. Sometimes couples could get set up for the dance sets in the evening. Art always let us stay into the early evening, so we could get in on at least the start of the evening dance. They always had a dance band or a polka band, or both. Some of the dancing was done outside, some inside. I guess it depended upon the weather and the anticipated mosquito count.

As we got older and learned how to dance, we would eagerly get on the dance floor and dance as many sets as we could with the local girls before we had get to our bus to leave. But we never stayed until the end of the dance.

As it began to get dark, depending on how far we had to drive, we would have to board our buses again and head for home; tired, hot, hungry again, and ready to take a nap once we got to our seats.

Our Boy Scout Drum and Bugle Corps played in lots of big parades, and for some very important events, but for pure fun and enjoyment, nothing could beat the great picnics in the those small towns.

The Somber, Solemn Ceremonies
To Honor The Dead

I think our Boy Scout Drum and Bugle Corps was first organized to perform at the somber and solemn ceremonies that the American Legion and other veteran groups sponsored several times during the year. They were usually memorial services to remember, honor, and pay tribute to the men who had given their lives for their country in one of the many wars our country fought in. The two biggest ceremonies were held on Armistice Day (in November) and Memorial Day (in May). The Fourth of July was not really the same, but it was a patriotic holiday and the veteran groups were out in force to celebrate that, too. And then there were other times that we marched or played for events where the Legion Post was involved.

The Armistice Day program was always held in front of the big statue of the civil war soldier at the entrance to Fountain Park. I can remember it was always a cold, rainy, and miserable day, and we always had to stand through the whole thing. We did get excused from school for the morning to do it, but it was not one of the events that we looked forward to with great joy or anticipation.

Memorial Day was better, because it was in the spring and the weather was usually grand. We would march from the Legion Club all the way out to the cemetery, which was a very long way, and then stay for the entire program before marching back. The ceremony always took place in a section that was reserved for veterans, with graves marked by plain white stones and white crosses. On that day there were always flowers or wreaths on every marker.

The programs at these ceremonies were all pretty much the same and we didn't do very much in them, except to march the color guards and veterans to the sites. There would sometimes be another band, or a singer or musical group, to sing the songs or lead the crowd in the singing of 'The Star Spangled Banner" or "America the Beautiful." There was always a flag ceremony of some kind, the bringing and laying of wreaths, speeches, and then a closing. As the Rifle Company would come forward, one of our drummers would play a long roll on a muffled drum, and, after the company would shoot, one of our buglers would play taps. And then we would march back to the Legion by ourselves.

I must admit that these ceremonies were impressive and I learned a lot about the meaning of patriotism from them, especially about the painful costs of war and the sacrifices that young men make who have to fight them. But I had a hard time getting too emotionally involved, partly because I was too young and wars had not yet directly affected me personally.

We were lucky. Most of the men in our families did not have to go to war. I think some of the grandfathers might have been in the military (I know one was in the Spanish-American War), but none of them had gotten killed. My Uncle Carl was a member of the National Guard for a time, but I don't think he was ever called up. There was a story about my dad's father being an ambulance driver in one of the wars, but that was never verified or authenticated. My dad never served in the military and neither had any of my uncles. They were all too young for World War I and too old for World War II. Some had families or were involved in necessary defense work and were exempt. By World War II, it was my generation's turn.

So, we didn't have anyone to memorialize. The people that they talked about in those ceremonies were not people I knew.

Later, at the beginning of World II, I remember that we would get called to march the draftees down to the train station where they left to go to their first assignments. We did that about once a month. Then later, after we had graduated from high school, it was our turn to get marched to the station. It seemed kind of odd to be played to rather than to play for.

And then we were gone. Some of us never returned from the war, and of those who did, I was one of those who never came back to Sheboygan to live.

So, that was how my career as a drummer in the Boy Scout Drum and Bugle Corps, sponsored by the American Legion Post in Sheboygan, ended. I was on my way to play with military bands, where I played lots of ceremonies of all kinds in many different places. But now, instead of playing only for fun and enjoyment, it was my duty and my job.

Those Wild Legion Conventions

There used to be a phrase that said it all and described it well, "Get off the streets, hide the girls, and get out of the way, the Legionaries are coming to town." The veteran groups still have their conventions, but I doubt if they are anything like the ones they used to have when I was a boy. At least I hope not. They were wild then. They are much more tame now. That may be a good thing if you are a civilian of this generation, but may be something that you sorely miss if you are a vet and did or still belong to one of the veteran organizations that came into being after World War I. If you are one of these, you might be looking forward to this year's convention, knowing that it will not be quite the same as it was in the "good old days" but still might be worth going to.

There were two kinds of veteran conventions when I was a kid: the State Conventions, which happened every summer, and the National Conventions, which took place every few years. Of course, the national ones were the big ones and only came to your state now and then. Vets from all over the world would come to those. They were noted for their mayhem and their great parades. The one I went to did have a great parade, but it also had lots of mayhem, something I was not quite prepared for.

Because we were sponsored by the Legion Post, our Boy Scout Drum and Bugle Corps always went to the State Conventions wherever they were held around the state. I enjoyed those. I only remember going to one National Convention, the one that was held in Milwaukee. These are some of the things I still recall about that particular convention. There were a few pluses, but many more minuses connected to that experience.

Everyone in Milwaukee knew months, maybe years, in advance that the Legion was coming to town and when. The natives there couldn't say that they hadn't been warned. It didn't help! How could any city get ready for such a storm?

On the opening day, the vets, dressed up in the uniforms of the outfits they served in, came to assault the town (at least the downtown section), capture it, and take it over for several days or up to a week. If you didn't know it was a convention you would think someone had started another war when you weren't looking. The townspeople who were smart had fled to their cabins on the lakes nearby, scheduled their vacations for that time, or just got out and stayed with relatives or friends until it was over. They might have sneaked back to see the parade, if they were brave or foolish enough, and knew how to get out fast if things really got out of hand. You didn't want to mess with the vets when they came to reunite with their old buddies, swap war stories, drink a lot, and raise hell. The conventions those days were really something….a blast if you were a Legionnaire, and downright dangerous if you were not.

We kids learned a lot by just being there, but they were mostly things our parents tried to warn us about, shielded us from, or prevented us from doing; things like smoking, drinking, using profanity, fighting, breaking things, and molesting girls. The Legionaries did all those things at their conventions, big time! I saw them with my own eyes. It was like one of those disaster movies they make so many of now. It is an understatement to say it was an amazing eye-opening experience for this young kid. I led a very sheltered life. How innocent we were when we left to go to the convention that day.

I remember we left early for Milwaukee that day on the Interurban. They must have put on extra cars for us because we were such a big group. We kids always liked to ride on the Interurban, so that part was fun. Those trains were better than buses because we were not as confined and could roam around while they were moving. We were only to be there for the day. We were going there to be in the biggest parade we were ever going to be in and we were very excited. We had practiced long and hard for this major event.

But no one had prepared us for what was about to happen. We were in for some disappointments as big as the parade we would be in.

I don't remember what, where or how often we got something to eat, but it must have been the junk food of the day. I don't remember how we got from the train station to our staging area along the parade route on Wisconsin Avenue. It was all very confusing and we had to stick close together so we wouldn't get lost. Actually, we saw very little of the convention itself or the parade. We got off the train, went to our spot, marched in the parade, and then got back on the train and came home. As it turned out the experience was not at all what we expected it to be. But it was an eye opener. I must say that. We sure got an education about how "the other half lives." The other half being people who did not live in Sheboygan and act as good as we did.

The first disappointment came when we found out that we were not going to be allowed to wander out of the parade route area that had been assigned to us. We were stuck there, in about a three-block area, for many hours waiting to get in line. Unless we went out to the street (Wisconsin Avenue) to watch the parade as it went by, it got pretty boring. Later, we found out that the parade was very long, covered several miles and had hundreds of different units in it, each unit with several bands, marching groups, horses, vehicles, and floats. It was said that if you wanted to see the entire parade from beginning to end, you would have to sit or stand in one spot and watch it go by for up to six or seven hours. (When I got to be adult I did that at the Legion Convention in Minneapolis once.)

Our corps was given a unit number and we were told that we had to gather with all the others who were in that unit on an off street, in order, and ready to march out onto Wisconsin Avenue when it was our turn and we were given the signal. We had to wait there until the unit before us had passed by and then we had to line up in formation, ready to move up to take our place in the parade. It was hot and it was boring. I think we waited in that small area for about four hours. No kid can wait for anything for four hours. Some of us did sneak up to see some of the parade, but soon got bored with that, too. You can see only so many bands, flags, and floats before they all begin to look alike. I think we were about in the middle of the parade, so once we got out into the parade, we must have marched a couple of miles and it probably took us an hour or so to get from our spot to the end of the parade route. So, we spent hours there, with nothing for us to do but wait and watch what was going on around us, which was mostly some of the shocking things that the Legionaries did. Most of them were too drunk to watch the parade. They just hung out on the side streets doing their mischief.

What a contrast! The Legionaries that we knew in Sheboygan were all nice guys. Some of them were the brothers and fathers of our friends, and we only saw them when they were on their best behavior, at the club, at our schools, out shopping, or at church. Some were our teachers and a few were doctors, lawyers, bankers, or ministers. Later, when we got older and became adults, we used to see some of them at the taverns, bars, and dance halls and they were not always behaving as well. But they never did anything like we saw in our staging area that day in Milwaukee. The Legionaries we were watching that day certainly could not have come from Sheboygan. No wonder the locals cleared the streets, hid their girls, or just left town.

Every few blocks, we would notice something we had never seen before, except in the train yards back home. They were big boxcars, known then as the "forty or eight" (forty men or eight horses) that were used to transport troops across Europe in World War I. But when the vets opened up the big sliding doors, there weren't any soldiers or horses in them. They were filled with big kegs of beer and cases full of bottles of whiskey. I don't know if prohibition was still on at the time. If it was, these heroes were breaking the law. Either way, they were obviously drinking a lot. I had seen men get a little drunk before, but I had never seen men suddenly fall over on the ground and pass out. We saw lots of them do that that day. At first, we thought they must be sick but, when so many of them did that, we learned the truth. Fortunately, they didn't lay there long. Their buddies soon picked them up and whisked them away. We began to realize that many of the veterans we saw at the convention were drunk most of the time they were there. We didn't like that at all, and we wondered if these were the heroes we heard so much about at those other ceremonies, the courageous and brave men who went off to fight and die for their country and save the world for Democracy. Or did all the good guys die?

And another thing we saw offended us almost as much. Everywhere we walked there were cigarette butts or cigar stubs. The guys would smoke them and toss them on the ground until the sidewalks, roads, and grassy spots were covered with butts. They were messy smokers. What we saw there on the streets of Milwaukee came back to me when I was in the Army and had to "police the area" and pick up cigarette butts other people had carelessly tossed on the ground. I always resented and hated that. If people wanted to smoke, they could certainly clean up their own messes. It was obvious that the Legionaries in Milwaukee did not clean up theirs.

Then, the language the veterans used was very shocking to us; words and phrases that we never heard in our homes or places where we gathered. It was more than swearing. It was downright filthy language. And when we heard some of the jokes they were telling, we were embarrassed and got red in the face. Another blow to hero worship.

But we really got disgusted when we saw how some of the vets treated the women and young girls who had come downtown to see the parade, These drunken vets would rush up to a girl, try to put their arms around them, and hug and kiss them. They may have done even more abusive things that we could not see. Surprisingly, some of the girls did not seem to mind. They squealed and giggled and did not try to get away. But there were a few who did not appreciate that kind of attention, and would give a guy a slap in the face or give him a good hard kick in a sensitive place. The vets also tried to get the women to drink and get them drunk. We didn't like that at all, but we could not do anything about it. These guys were all much bigger and stronger and more powerful than we are. And they had learned how to fight. We were only little kids.

There were some fistfights in the area where we were waiting, usually between guys who had had too much to drink. And now and then there was a little rumble, usually between a bunch of soldiers who took on a bunch of sailors. There were regular MPs and SPs to take care of such things. Those fights soon were stopped and civilians were usually not involved.

Finally, our turn came to get in the parade. We lined up in straight lines in ready to go. When Art blew his whistle, we stepped out smartly into the street to march. As usual, we spread out from curb to curb and took up about a city block. We looked sharp in our uniforms and we played loud and strong. We twirled our sticks and threw them into the air and the bugles shone brightly in the sun. As usual, we got loud applause from the crowd as we passed by. If they gave out prizes, we probably got one, and I am sure that would have been put in the trophy case at the Legion with the other ones we had won in other parades.

As I think back now, I have lots of confused and mixed feelings about that convention. There is no doubt in my mind that going to the national convention of anything is a big deal. Not many boys our ages got to do that. And we were treated well and our performance was excellent.

We should have been pleased and proud of our performance. We probably played better that day than we had on any other gig that summer.

But, it wasn't as much fun as we expected it to be, not like the Firemen's picnics we had already played and the State Fair that we were still looking forward to. And the experience wasn't as impressive and inspirational as those Memorial Services we played for back home. I guess it was the veterans we saw there that spoiled it for us. We were not only disappointed, but disillusioned. They did not act like the heroes we had heard so much about, and they were not as noble and good as we wanted them to be.

I never forgot what I saw there, and when we went off to war I hoped that we would come back better men then the ones we had observed at the Milwaukee convention. I also hoped that when we got back home, joined some veteran organization, and went to our own conventions, that we wouldn't do the things we had seen vets do that day that caused us to lose the respect we once had for anyone who wore a uniform and went off to fight a war on our behalf.

I never went to a Legion convention again.

And I don't think I cared.

One Legion Convention in a lifetime is more than enough.

The Marvelous
Wisconsin State Fair

We looked forward to this trip all summer long….maybe all year long.

It came near the end of summer and may have been the last time we marched that season. It may have turned out to be one our best performances. Appearing at the State Fair was a big deal because only the best bands and drum and bugle corps in Wisconsin were invited to perform on the fair's annual "band day." It was to be a full day of activity.

Each band or corps would do a 20-minute exhibition in the field at the main Grandstand, and then also march in the afternoon parade through the whole fair grounds. The rest of the time we would be able to see the fair.

We worked up some special routines just for the fair and practiced hard for many weeks to get them right. Art pushed us hard because he wanted us do everything perfectly. It was very exciting and I can still remember that day very well. It might have been the highlight of my time with the corps.

The weather was perfect. It was hot, but there was not a cloud in the sky, which meant it was not going to rain, the one thing that always spoiled exhibitions and parades. But there was just enough of a breeze to keep things cool, and to make the flags flutter nicely. We met at the Legion very early in the morning on a Friday. There were over 100 of us going on the trip, counting the boys and our adult chaperones. And, of course, we had a lot of equipment to pack and carry along. We had spent many hours during the week polishing and shining our equipment, making repairs, and practicing. All of us were asked to have our mothers wash and press our uniforms. We wanted to look sharp because this was a big deal….playing for thousands of people! We were used to playing to the big crowds that came to parades, but going to the Wisconsin State Fair was different. This was the big time, the big leagues….the

271

big show! Only the best of the best got to play at the fair. For some of us, it would be a once in a lifetime experience. Every time we went to the fair, we never knew if we would ever do this again. And, as it turned out, I never did.

When the boys were assembled and the roll was taken, not a boy was missing. We were all there ahead of time. One could feel the excitement in the air. It was necessary to take several buses to hold us all. They were not as fancy as the buses are now, with plush seats, toilets right on the bus, with TV sets and radios, but they were comfortable. We didn't have school buses then so riding any bus was a treat. Because there hadn't been time to eat breakfast before we came, we were fed on the bus with some very good sweet rolls and donuts, and juice or milk. It didn't take long for all of the food to disappear.

I always liked to ride buses and trains. I sat in the window seat so I could see everything that passed by. There was some horsing around, but Art always kept that to a minimum and never let it get out of hand. He demanded good discipline and following the rules.

The State Fairgrounds was on the west side of Milwaukee, so the buses didn't have to go through much of the city. But I wished they had. I didn't get to Milwaukee too often so I wanted to see as much of it as I could. Because we left early and the traffic was light, it didn't take long to get there. Milwaukee is only about 50 miles from Sheboygan.

When we got into the fairgrounds, we were directed to special parking lots reserved for band buses. The whole event was well planned. All we had to do was follow instructions and do what we were told. We were used to that. Art always had everything organized and everything ran according to his plan and his schedule.

Because we got there early, there was lots of time before we had to perform. Art planned it that way. He wanted to make it a grand day for us. We were given meal tickets so we could buy our lunches at one of the eating places near the Grandstand and additional tickets to use for rides and games. We were instructed about where and what time to meet for the afternoon performance and the parade.

Our performance in the Grandstand was scheduled for 2:00, so Art wanted us assembled by 1:00. Then, the parade we would march in would kick off at 4:30, so Art wanted us assembled by 3:30. Art had no patience with latecomers. If you weren't there on time, you didn't play. That seldom every happened, because guys who broke the rules didn't last long in the corps and they would not be on this trip. Then

Art turned us loose. We were pleased that he trusted us. It's real easy to get lost at a state fair.

We had several hours of free time to enjoy the attractions at the fair. Our free tickets were not going to be sufficient so, fortunately, Art had warned us to bring some of our own spending money. The free tickets did not last long. Neither did our money. There was just too much to do.

The younger boys immediately rushed off to the roller coaster, probably the most popular ride on the fairgrounds, and some of them quickly spent all of their tickets there. The Wisconsin State Fair roller coaster was an antique and a legend. It was probably the oldest, most rickety, and ugliest ride in any fair in the country. I always wondered if it was safe. But there had never been an accident or any injuries, so it must have been. It just went on and on. And the people who rode it continued to be thrilled, including us.

Some of the older boys were more interested in roaming around the fairgrounds looking for girls from towns all over the state. They thought that they were hot stuff in their neat uniforms. So did the girls. Some of them connected and made plans to meet later after we were done with our performances. I was not interested in girls.....not yet. So I headed for the other things that the fair had to offer. During the day, I didn't go on lots of rides and stayed away from the gaming booths. I took one ride on the roller coaster and then headed straight for the animal barns. I liked to see the livestock; the cows and sheep, the rabbits and some of the birds. I spent a lot of time in the horse barn.

Like any growing boy, I also liked to eat. I quickly found the dairy building and had several treats there. First, I had some of that new strawberry-flavored milk (all you could drink for one price). Later in the day, I came back and had a banana split. During the course of the day, I also had a pronto pup, corn on the cob, some root beer, and a nice big peach. I could always get hamburgers at Terry's or one of my mom's great and healthy meals when I got back home. Then, as it is now, the stuff you eat at the fair is junk food....fried and greasy, and sweet and messy.

On my way back to the Grandstand, I saw the Arcade and stopped to play a few of the games. There were a lot of machines that only cost a penny. But I couldn't linger long. Before I knew it, it was time to get back to the assembly place. I did some other things later, after we finished the parade. But by 7:00, we had to be ready to board the bus and head on back home.

I am pleased to report that we did our show at the Grandstand perfectly and got a huge standing ovation from the crowd. We also won a first prize for our performance. Because we had made such a good showing, we were placed at the head of the parade, the first musical outfit right in back of the policemen on their motorcycles. As usual, we spread out from curb to curb and took up about a whole city block as we did our stuff and showed off as much as possible. Again, we were loudly applauded. Man, were we ever proud! The corps couldn't have done better. I don't think anyone made a single mistake. All of our lines were straight, we made our special and unique turns perfectly, the drums never missed a beat and the bugles sounded like the trumpeters with the military bands in Washington, D.C. Those extra practice sessions paid off.

Art was pleased and proud of what his boys had done. And he told us so. That is all we needed to make us feel very good and very special. We were all sure that ours was the best outfit at the fair that day. Everybody said so, and we believed them.

But by evening, we were bushed. It had been a very long and demanding day. All of that marching and walking around in the nice fresh air and the excitement had done us in. When we got back to our buses, we were ready to crash. At the gathering spot many of the boys were sitting or lying on the ground. Our uniforms were rumpled and our shoes were full of dust. Our ties had been pulled off and our caps were in our pockets or tucked in our belts. We no longer looked sharp, but it didn't matter. We no longer had to impress anyone.

A few of the older boys were over on the side under a clump of trees with some girls. When the buses started off, the boys waved at them out of the bus windows and the girls started to cry. They knew that would never see the boys again. If there had been any budding romances that day, they quickly came to an end as our bus went off into the night. By the time we left the fair grounds, it was dark and I was in no mood to do any more sightseeing. I just dozed off and slept all the way home.

It had been some day. I knew that I would be ready and eager to do it again, if we got invited to come another year. I don't think we ever did.

But my experience at the State Fair that year created memories that would last me a lifetime!

The Fourth Of July
In Sheboygan

It was the Fourth of July yesterday, but you would never have known it, unless someone told you. It is much too quiet. I got up early, as I always have done on the Fourth of July, but I did not hear a single BANG, BOOM, WHAM, OR SHHZZWOSH! There was only one flag flying on our apartment house (we have a small flag decal on our patio door), and I didn't smell anyone cooking brats, hamburgers or hot dogs, all day.

The banks and public buildings were closed, there wasn't any mail, and most businesses were shut down. But I was able to fill my car with gas, the Walgreens store on the corner was open all day, and my wife and I were able to buy a few groceries she needed at the nearby supermarket. The buses were running on a holiday schedule, and I am told that the shopping centers were open for business until 6:00. They even had some special holiday sales.

It was the Fourth of July on the calendar but, for all practical purposes, it felt like any other day in Minneapolis, except for those who left from work early on July 3 and headed for the lakes and resorts up north, something many people do every weekend they can all summer long. There wasn't any parade downtown in the morning, but some of the parks had activities throughout the day. There was a band concert and fireworks later in the evening at a park near where we live. We went to that and enjoyed it. But our Fourth of July yesterday was nothing like the grand festivities we had in Sheboygan when I was a kid.

WHAT HAS HAPPENED TO OUR BELOVED HOLIDAY?

Is patriotism and love of country a thing of the past? Are the things I enjoyed so much when I was a kid dead and gone forever? I don't want to think so, but it almost seems so.

Except maybe for Christmas, the Fourth of July was the most important day of the year when I was growing up in Sheboygan. It was colorful and noisy, and we kids loved it! Our blood ran red, white, and blue that day and we rushed from event to event, until our excitement was ready to explode like the fireworks that were shot into the air over Lake Michigan to end the day. We were proud to be Americans, and we wanted the world to know it. Believe me, we knew how to celebrate back then.

Back when I was a kid, this is how we celebrated the Fourth of July.

The kids were up bright and early. Before breakfast, our neighborhood sounded like a war zone. Every kid, at least the boys, saved up their money for months to buy as many fireworks as possible, which they would then proceed to shoot up in about a half hour. At that time, not only was it legal to buy and use fireworks, but you could buy anything from ladyfingers to three-inch crackers. You could also buy rockets, bombs, and sparklers. One year, my uncle, who owned a nursery and sold fireworks, brought us a whole pile of the ones he had not sold and shot them all off on the curb in front of our house. It was spectacular and very exciting. He could have burned down the neighborhood!

When we were little, we usually started out with those tiny ladyfingers. You could hold them between your fingers until they blew out and up without getting hurt. Then we graduated to those red inch-long firecrackers, then the red two-inchers. Before long, we weren't satisfied with anything but the green three-inchers. The firecrackers got lit with a punk, and the bigger they were, the quicker we got them out of our fingers. The safest way to use the big ones was to put them into or onto something and then run away as fast as we could before they went off with a big BANG! As we got older, we got more daring (or foolish?) and would put the biggest firecrackers we could buy in a crack in a fence or under a can or a wooden box. They made a loud BOOM and whatever they were near or under was blown to pieces. Now and then, some kid would lose a finger or a hand, or get badly burned if he did not get away fast enough. That was lamented, but to be expected. It was the risk you had to take. When one messed around with explosives, there were bound to be some casualties. This was dangerous sport, no doubt about it.

Our mothers hated fireworks. Our fathers cheered us on and sometimes got a supply for themselves. I was always lucky, or maybe I was more careful. I never got hurt. But fireworks were sure a whole lot of fun. And sometimes even now, I wish I could shoot some off and not just twirl a few sparklers out on the deck.

Along with those early morning noises were those tantalizing early morning smells. It seemed that all the fathers in town started up their fires early on the Fourth of July. The smell of burning charcoal permeated the air. It was the one morning of the year that lots of people had brats and beer for breakfast. And this went on all day long. It is no wonder that Sheboygan came to be known as the "bratwurst capitol of the world." Somehow eating brats and drinking beer got caught up and confused with patriotism.

It wasn't long after breakfast that everyone headed downtown for the big parade. Besides the American Legion and Shrine convention parades, the Fourth of July parade was perhaps the best, longest, and most exciting parade of the year. And it was strictly American, in mood and theme. After I joined the Boy Scout Drum and Bugle Corps, I always marched in the Fourth of July parade. It was always long, starting at the Central High School and ending at Vollrath Park. The military were out in their full dress uniforms, there were hundreds of flags flying, and many of the bands and marching units were dressed in red, white, and blue. All of the floats had patriotic themes. You had to get downtown early to get a good seat on some curb. If you were an adult, you probable stood in back of your kids. If you were marching and the day was hot, you knew that that route was an especially challenging one and covered many miles. You could count on having sore feet and a few blisters. But it was exciting, so we never complained about the physical discomforts.

Though there were some activities in other parks, the best ones took place in Vollrath Park. People would come early and claim a picnic spot (if you were there early enough and got lucky, you might get a park picnic table and fryer), and then go to the bowl to watch the races, the ethnic dances and demonstrations, and listen to the music, which went on non-stop most of the day. In between those activities, some of us went swimming in Lake Michigan, took another tour of the Water Treatment Plant, played on the swings or had a pick-up ball game. And we ate lots and lots of brats and drank lots and lots of beer (the kids had root beer). No one seemed to be hungry anymore when supper time came around. By that time, many people had already headed for the North Side beach to get a good space for the evening activities.

There was always a good band concert by the Sheboygan Community Band before the sun went down. The mosquitoes came out in droves at about the same time the band concert was over. People would put up their portable chairs or lay out their blankets for the fireworks display. The fireworks were always shot off from a barge out in the harbor of the lake. They were always spectacular and noisy, and lasted for a long time. It was a fitting end to a very stimulating and exciting day.

And then.....there was a mass exit as everyone left, all at the same time, to find their way home. It was undoubtedly the biggest mass traffic jam of the year. But we left satisfied and fulfilled. It had been another glorious Fourth.

The object of the Fourth of July was not to rest, but to show that you loved your country so much that you were willing to wear yourself out for it. We got home filled with gratitude that we were lucky enough to be Americans, and proud that we had just demonstrated it again in the right, proper, and most wonderful way.

Of all the people on this earth, we Americans know how to show our loyalty and dedication to our country, as we loudly proclaim every Fourth of July that the United States of America is the best damn country in the world. And nowhere in this country was that done better than the way we used to do it in Sheboygan!

Was It Worth Doing
For An Eskimo Pie?

When I was a kid there was only one thing better than getting a double dip ice cream cone, and that was getting any kind of an ice cream product FREE!

All of them were worth five cents, but it seemed to taste so much better when you didn't have to pay for it. Take, for instance, those Eskimo Pies we used to get when we marched in parades.

For some reason, when we came to the end of the parade route, someone would come up and give us all an Eskimo Pie. That seemed to be our payment for all our efforts. I don't know why they did that or who paid for them, but it was a nice gesture, a most welcome gift, and we appreciated it and accepted it gladly. Next to a glass of water, there was nothing better they could have given us. It was a neat treat.

But you might ask, was it worth it to march those many miles, get all hot and sweaty, and often get blisters on your hands and feet, just to get a free Eskimo Pie that you could have bought for yourself for only a nickel?

What a silly question!
OF COURSE IT WAS!

A Special Memory:
Camping Out With A Friend

As I wind down the stories in this book, I've saved a special one for last. It is a story about a very important and formative experience that happened to me in one of those Sheboygan parks I have told you about.

It is both a happy story and a sad one, because it was to be the last time my very best friend, Wesley Jerving, and I were to be together before we both went off to join the Army and become a part of World War II. We didn't know if we would come back alive or ever see each other again.

That's why that weekend at Terry Andre Park was so important. It turned out to be one of those final precious times that we would never forget.

The date was early in September of 1942.

As a way of saying good-bye, Wesley and I decided to spend a weekend together camping. Because we had had so many good times out at the dunes when we were growing up, we decided to go out to Terry André Park, right on the edge of the sand dunes, where the ground is still hard enough to stake a tent, and there are still lots of trees for both shade and firewood.

Summer had ended and I had just come back from playing at a summer resort with my band at Crystal Lake. I was going to go to Milwaukee to enlist in the Navy. Wesley had already enlisted, or had been drafted, and was due to leave the day after we returned from our weekend together. As it turned out, I did not get into the Navy and stayed in Milwaukee playing band jobs and working until my number came up. By that time, Wesley was long gone. I don't remember where he served. We were both gone for about three years.

We borrowed an old pup tent from somebody, gathered our camping equipment together, bought enough supplies for the two days and two nights, and went off, just the two of us. It was early autumn so the days were still warm and the nights were cool. We took ample bedding and a lantern. We didn't take any books, magazines, or radios. We were not there to entertain ourselves or goof around; we were there to be with each other and to talk. That's about all we did. We just talked and talked, well into the night. First, we tried remembering all of the things we had done together so far in our lives. There was a lot to talk about and to review.

We had gone to school together, from kindergarten right up to graduation from high school, often being in the same classes and having the same teachers. We had played games together, skated and sledded together, rode our bikes together, and did lots of swimming together. We even had done a few things we shouldn't have done, together. Not many, but some. All of our young lives, we lived only a few blocks from each other. We had lots in common.

We went to the same churches and were in the same Boy Scout Troop. We went to the same camps and on the same outings and trips.

It was only as we got older that we began to get involved in different things. Wesley was always on the varsity athletic teams; I was a member of the bands and choruses. It wasn't until much later, when we got into high school, that we got interested in girls. We did go on some double dates to movies, to dances, and to teen activities. We sometimes even dated the same girls. We didn't go steady with any of them. And we both were still single when we went off to service. He got married before I did. He also had his children before I did.

When guys get talking like that, I am sure they remember different things than the girls do, some things that would not seem to be all that exciting or important.

We both remembered our first job together. For several years, every Thursday after school, we delivered those grocery handbills for the local grocery store across the street from the school. Like the mailmen, we did it in all kinds of weather, some of it pretty miserable. For both of us, it was our first steady paid job.

As they used to say in Sheboygan, Wesley and I "went through thick and thin together." If I had been able to have a brother, I would have wanted Wesley to be mine. But, as it turned out, we were closer than brothers, and we were more than just friends. We were buddies. At that time, I suppose that Wesley was the most important person in my life. I knew I was going to miss him terribly and I am sure he felt the same way about me. This would be the first time that our lives would not be closely intertwined.

So we quietly spent those two days and nights together, walking up and down the beach, running in the sand, throwing flat stones out into the lake and watching them skip across the water. We made our fires and cooked our food, and after all of the supplies were put away for the night, we would put some more wood on the fire, and sit there, looking up at the stars, and talking. Just talking. We had lots to talk about.

We reviewed and relived our lives up to that point. And were we wondering what the future would hold for us and whether we would ever see each other again. Our thoughts were not that orderly and many of them were not expressed. We tried not to be too sentimental and we tried to remember the good times and the happy moments. We told jokes and laughed a lot. And then we would be quiet and not say anything at all. We didn't want to say any of those silly things to each other that we were told girls might say when they knew they had to part.

And we certainly weren't going to cry, or hug, or stuff like that. Boys didn't do thinks like that then. But we felt it deep down in the gut.

This was it. Things would never be the same again. Suddenly, we had grown up and now we had to go our separate ways and live our separate lives. And for me, that was not going to happen in Sheboygan.

And so it went, hour after hour for those two days, until we got talked out. We had said everything we wanted to say and remembered everything we wanted to remember.

When the time was up, we just packed up our things, walked back to town, socked each other on the arm, and said something like, "be seein' ya." It was over. We both knew we were never going to do this or anything like it again. And we were right....we didn't.

I did not see Wesley often after that, only for a brief time at a church service or a class reunion, or when we bumped into each other on the street when I was visiting Sheboygan. We both survived the war, but unlike Wesley, I did not come back to Sheboygan to live and work. We never got to have any long talks again, and he died before me, so we didn't get to grow old together.

But, even now, every time I think about Terry Andre Park or go out to see it (which is very rarely), I think about Wesley, like I am doing right now.

I hope there is an after-life, and that in that after-life there is a place like Terry Andre Park; a place by a big lake with lots and lots of that fine, pure white sand.

And it would be nice if Wesley and I were there.

Maybe we could borrow a tent from someone, and make a fire and talk some more. Then, we can look down on the earth, see Sheboygan, and remember how good it was that weekend when we had to say good-bye.

All Good Things Must
Come To An End

This will be the last book I will write about my boyhood in Sheboygan and it will probably be the last book I will ever publish. It is not because I am getting old (which I am) or getting tired of writing (which I am not), but because I have said everything I wanted to say. I have enjoyed writing but it is probably time to hang it up and quit while I am ahead.

When I first started to write these Sheboygan stories many years ago, I had a simple goal. I wanted to be remembered. That's why I called the first book, "Remember My Name in Sheboygan." I wanted the generations that followed me to remember me and to remember what a wonderful place Sheboygan was to live in and be brought up in.

My writing had nothing to do with fame or fortune (I have been lucky to break even) and very little to do with ego (though it was a whole lot of fun). It was all about *Legacy*, the desire to leave something behind for the next generations. That's why I wrote my book "The Things I Learned Along the Way." I was born to be a reporter and teacher, and writing books was the best way I could think of to communicate what I wanted to say.

I got carried away writing Sheboygan stories and ended up with enough of them for two more books. But now that I have finished this second one, I think it is time to stop lingering in the past, to get on with my life and enjoy what is ahead in my future. Like all good things, my recollections and memories of Sheboygan must sometime come to an end.

Now is as good a time as any. I don't live in Sheboygan anymore. I don't belong to Sheboygan anymore. And I don't have any plans to go back to Sheboygan again. Now my home, I hope for the rest of my life, will be Plymouth, Minnesota. If there is a to be a book about this final period of my life, one of my kids or grandkids will have to write it.

If I wrote another book, it would not be a book about Sheboygan. It would be about what happened to me after I left Sheboygan. It might be about our band gig at Lauer's at Crystal Lake after we graduated from high school or the times I spent in Milwaukee, playing band gigs and going to Milwaukee State Teacher's College. I would tell you about things that happened in Madison when I went there to finish my degree in Journalism. I have already written some stories in my other books about the three years I spent in the Army, and how I lived in Boston for another three years while I was going to Seminary. I have told my readers about my careers in radio and television, as a teacher, in music, and in the ministry. I have written about our family, my wife, my five children, and my grandchildren. If you want to know about these things, you will have to go to Barnes and Noble or Amazon and buy and read my other books. I hope you do.

I could write a book about Minnesota. I have lived here more than half of my life. It is also a very good place to live and work and bring up children, just like Sheboygan was. Or I could write a book about my retirement. It is almost 20 years since I stopped preaching and launched new careers in music, teaching, and writing. But why would I do that?

If all of my seven books were put together side by side, that could add up to a full-blown autobiography, something I never intended to write when I accidentally became an author at the age of 75.

I never intended to reveal as much about myself as I did. All I wanted was to be remembered now and then by people who knew me and loved me for a time. I have no desire to reveal any more.

If my readers liked and enjoyed my books, I am pleased and satisfied. I accomplished what I set out to do. I have finished my work. I don't need to do anything more, except to live in peace and enjoy every moment of every day that the Lord will still give me.

Thanks for reading my book. And have a good life!

And, of course, if you are ever in Sheboygan, and happen to mention my name, please be sure you spell Glenn with two n's.

About The Author

Glenn Martin was born in Sheboygan, Wisconsin in 1924, where he lived for the first 18 years of his life. After graduation from high school and three years of service in the U.S. Army in World War II, he returned to Wisconsin to attend the Milwaukee State Teacher's College and the University of Wisconsin, where he graduated in 1949 with a degree in Journalism.

For several years, he worked in Minneapolis, Minnesota as a writer, director and producer of radio and television shows for a local advertising agency, and as a freelance actor and musician.

In 1951, he decided to attend the Boston University School of Theology, where he earned a graduate degree in 1954. In that same year, he was ordained a minister in the United Methodist Church. He served in the Minnesota Annual Conference for that denomination for 35 years, doing many kinds of ministry throughout Minnesota.

During his years in the ministry, Glenn was known for his preaching, teaching, and administrative skills, serving as the pastor of local churches, urban missioner, Radio-TV Consultant for the church, Christian Educator, camp director, and Lab School instructor. He was known for his writing; including articles for local newspapers and church publications, radio, television, and dramatic scripts, short stories, and educational curriculum for church schools, confirmation training, and camps. He was also in demand for Bible studies, small discussion groups, leadership training, and retreats.

After retirement in 1987, he continued to do freelance writing, speaking and teaching in senior programs. Several of his short stories and articles have been printed in national church magazines and he has published seven books.

Glenn and his first wife, Margaret, were married for 57 years until her death in 2007. He now lives with his second wife, Jeanne, in a senior residence in Plymouth, Minnesota. They are active in musical, church, and small study groups, and enjoy reading, movies, and watching sports events. Between them, they have and enjoy seven children, and many grandchildren and great-grandchildren.